HARD
RIGHT

HARD RIGHT
The Rise of
JESSE HELMS

Ernest B. Furgurson

W · W · Norton & Company · New York · London

Copyright © 1986 by Ernest B. Furgurson
All rights reserved.
Published simultaneously in Canada by Penguin Books Canada Ltd, 2801 John Street,
Markham, Ontario L3R 1B4
Printed in the United States of America.
The text of this book is composed in Times Roman, with display type set in Novarese.
Composition and manufacturing by The Haddon Craftsmen, Inc.
Book design by B. L. Klein.

First Edition

Library of Congress Cataloging-in-Publication Data
Furgurson, Ernest B., 1929–
    Hard right: the rise of Jesse Helms
    1. Helms, Jesse. 2. Legislators—United States—Biography. 3. United States. Congress.
Senate—Biography. 4. Conservatism—United States—History—20th century. 5. United
States—Politics and government—1981–. I. Title.
E840.8.H44F87 1986 328.73'092'4 86–2366

ISBN 0-393-02325-7

W. W. Norton & Company, Inc., 500 Fifth Avenue, New York, N. Y. 10110
W. W. Norton & Company Ltd., 37 Great Russell Street, London WC1B 3NU

1 2 3 4 5 6 7 8 9 0

Contents

Preface   7

1   True Believers   *13*

2   The Man and the Movement   *21*

3   "Mr. Jesse" and Son   *30*

4   Baptism   *41*

5   Climbing onto the Platform   *56*

6   Horatio at the Bridge   *69*

7   Coattails I   *92*

8   Nobody's Republican   *103*

9   Senator No   *121*

10   Riding High   *132*

11   The Generalissimo and the Troglodytes   *152*

12   Coattails II   *165*

13   The Long Spiritual Struggle   *188*

14   Jesse and "Fred"   *207*

15   The Red, White, and Blue Bible   *233*

16   The Media Conspiracy   *252*

17   The Truth Next Time   *270*

Acknowledgments   *285*

Bibliography   *289*

Index   *295*

Preface

Politicians, especially demagogues, especially southern demagogues, have fascinated me since I was a boy living under the genteel dictatorship of old Harry Byrd's machine in Virginia. We did not have demagogues in our cavalier commonwealth. They were for other, politically rowdier states farther south, like Alabama, Georgia, and Louisiana. I envied those places their George Wallaces, Gene Talmadges and Huey Longs. I was excited by the very names of Theodore G. Bilbo, "Cotton" Ed Smith, "Kissin' " Jim Folsom, Leander Perez, Orval Faubus, Lester Maddox.

Of course Hitler and Mussolini were demagogues, too, as was Joe McCarthy. Dick Nixon was a presence in my journalistic life for a generation. But the ones I locked onto were those from my own South, men with whom I could identify, or whose prejudices I could understand.

Jesse Helms, when he came to the Senate, was somehow different from all them. Yet to me, when I learned about how he came up, he was most fascinating of all. That was because I could see so much of my own background in his. He is older than I am, but both of us were brought up as Baptists in modest, straight-arrow, teetotaling families. Both of us gravitated to high school newspapering, got a job on the local weekly, started college in little hometown Baptist schools because that was what we could afford. Both of us stuck a toe into the radio business at an early age. Both of us got into writing opinion columns, in one form or another. But we peddled very different opinions. Of course he never heard of me back then, and I had never heard of him. But I knew a lot of southern boys who started off like him, and one of them was me. Yet look at us now: Why did he turn out the way he did, instead of like me—and vice versa?

How, why, did a gangly, bespectacled boy who described himself as "the cow's tail" in his high school class become the herd bull of a major American political movement—a maker of presidents and breaker of senators, able to deploy many millions of dollars for or against those who pleased or annoyed him? How did an unbookish youngster who never finished college become such a force in American foreign affairs that he ambushes the nominees and harasses the cabinet secretaries of his own favorite president? What motivates him to head some of the meanest—and most effective—political campaigns in U.S. history? What made him that way?

I wanted to know, and as his importance grew, I realized the country needed to know.

In looking for answers, I have come to see that he is a unique personality, stylistically far different from classic southern demagogues. A book about him is not so much a complex character study as a narrative of a developing political will, one that has broadened but not swerved over the years.

In putting it together I have had generous help from politicians, clergymen, scholars, newspapermen, and others in North Carolina, and senators, newspapermen, bureaucrats, and political managers in Washington—every one of whom has a strong opinion, pro or con, about Jesse Helms. This is strictly an unauthorized project; I have had modest cooperation from Helms and his associates.

I did not find nor did I expect evidence that Helms has enriched or even entertained himself on the largely untraceable proceeds of his massive fund-raising machinery. Early in my research, one who has known him for more than forty-five years told me, "I'd trust Jesse with every cent I ever owned. But damned if I'll trust him with my country." Whether there are other kinds of scandal in his career is a matter for the reader to judge. To help that judgment, I have done something Helms once made clear he hoped no one would ever do. When his friend Tom Ellis was being questioned in a Senate Committee, Helms said, "I doubt that any of us would relish having everything we have ever written or said examined with a fine-tooth comb." Within the constraints of time and government classification, that is just what I have done with Helms's long, prolix record—combed it, synthesized and analyzed it.

After introducing him, I have followed him from boyhood through most of his Senate career before digressing into chapters about areas where his influence is greatest or his controversy hottest.

They include foreign policy, race, religion, and media. Finally, I have projected him into the country's political future, to congressional and presidential elections yet to come, and to legislative and constitutional battles over the way we live our very lives. His greatest impact is yet to be felt.

In writing and revising this book, I have responded gratefully to advice from my friend Thomas N. Bethell and my wife Cassie Furgurson. Many of those who gave me substantive help are mentioned in the Notes following the text.

Ernest B. Furgurson
Washington, D.C.
May 15, 1986

HARD RIGHT

Chapter 1

True Believers

Jesse Helms is among friends. Straitlaced, business-suited preachers and their wives fill the ballroom of Washington's biggest hotel. They have come for the annual convention of the National Religious Broadcasters. They have halted to hear Helms between seminars on direct mail techniques, satellite services, federal regulations, and sales strategies. They are mostly white, with only a few black faces among them. I take a seat in the back row near a big, seamy-faced man in a plaid lumberjack shirt. His name tag says he is from a small town in Florida. As I take out my notebook, he tells me forcefully what he thinks of "the media." He is not forgiving of our biases and mistakes. As for those unidentified Washington sources on whom we lean so often, who like to disclose the inner workings of government to us—they are "nothing but a bunch of worms."

He has more to say, but hushes when Helms appears from stage right, holding his text under his arm. The broadcasters are eager to hear him. Already they have listened to some of the most talented radio and television evangelists in the land, and witnessed a friendly debate between Jerry Falwell and Ted Kennedy. But now they are primed to hear their main man in Washington, the one brave enough to tell even Ronald Reagan when he is wandering off the holy trail.

Their hero is lanky and slightly stooped. His neck leans forward, as if he is bending to listen to confidential truths. His chin recedes and his cheeks puff out a bit, and he is made popeyed by his trade-mark spectacles. Once one of his advisers suggested changing their style, to something more modish, better on TV. For years, wiser advice prevailed; he kept his horn-rims, thus extending the life of the adjective "owlish," over-used by those describing him. He also preserved the old-fashioned, country-boy, intentionally square image so trusted by his followers.

Waiting for the program to start, Helms leaves the platform briefly to have his picture taken with his friend Falwell. A few admirers come up to shake his hand, and he reaches down and grins affably. As the speakers gather, a choir of thirty costumed black children from Uganda sings native songs and familiar spirituals. Helms moves from the stage to a seat down front so he can see and hear them better. The crowd applauds him at each move.

When the choir is finished, it is Helms's turn to speak. The master of ceremonies who introduces him is a broad-shouldered, suntanned, golden-voiced, matinee-idol type who reminds me of Ronald Reagan's California minister, the Rev. Donn Moomaw of Bel Air Presbyterian Church. Standing beside him, the senator seems pale and wimpish.

But the applause that sweeps the room is not for a pale personality. Everybody seems to join in, except for a few reporters and cameramen and two black ministers conspicuous for both their color and their silence. Helms adjusts the microphone. He leans forward.

He jokes about Ted Kennedy's appearance with Falwell the previous afternoon. "If I'd known the new fashion was odd couples," he says, "I'd have brought Dan Rather."

They laugh. They know all about Helms and Rather. Helms has been attacking CBS for years, and this year has been fronting a noisy campaign for conservative control of the network. They are with him. Half-smiling, he gestures toward the black children who have sung before him. "Would you agree that Africa was a little bit closer to your heart just now?" he asks, and there is a light applause. The crowd seems uncertain how the question ties in with his political stance toward black Africa, where he has been supportive of white control in Rhodesia and South Africa.

No matter, it is a friendly token, and he sticks with the mood, moving on to talk about love. He speaks softly. His voice is nasal, but he can scoop it low at the same time. It has a rural twang.

He tells a story. Long ago, he says, there was a Japanese village where by tradition, old widows were taken up a nearby mountain and left to die in peace. Once as a son escorted his mother up the hillside, he noticed her dropping markers along the trail. The son asked why. She told him, "Because I love you, and I want you to be able to find your way home tonight." He was so touched he changed his mind and took her back home. There she lived happily ever after, while he started a campaign to change the custom of disposing of widows that way.

"Which proves," says Helms, "that love is the greatest builder the world has ever known." He ties ancient Japan to modern America by complimenting his audience "for marking a trail by broadcasting love . . . by showing millions the way back to the faith of their fathers." Applause rises.

As I watch, the little bulge in his cheek combined with his accent almost convinces me he has a wad of tobacco in there. Helms's style is as if he were sitting out in front of a crossroads general store telling tall tales on a Saturday morning, about to squirt a stream of juice into the dust. It is that kind of intimate.

But his style was not perfected in the Carolina countryside. It came out of broadcast studios in the capital city of a big, complex state, where shopping malls are wiping out crossroads stores. It was polished in thousands of broadcasts that began over a quarter-century before he came to national attention. His natural medium is not the country store. It is the microphone, of which he is master.

The audience hangs on his words. He has moved through the softer preliminaries. His tone hardens as he approaches the heart of his sermon. "I travel around," he says, "and I feel the American people are ready . . . The battle has begun, but it is nowhere near won." They know what battle it is. They are in it beside him. It is essential, he says, to realize the astonishing achievements of a man named Ronald Reagan. The man carried forty-nine states last time. What does this prove? That "Americans are God-fearing, conservative people despite what you hear in the secular liberal major news media."

That is the first stop on a tour of all the menaces to the things Helms holds dear—threats to The Family, the unifying theme that brings together politicians, preachers, and entrepreneurs of the New Right.

The Family, he says, is the future. But how is it faring in America today? Divorce, illegal births, child abuse are rampant. The only high schools not overrun with drugs are private Christian academies. Pornography is a social cancer. Helms says the columnist Jack Anderson once sent him a tape of a pornographic show he came across in a motel someplace out west. "I couldn't stomach it more than a few seconds," says the grandfather of five, "and I wish I hadn't seen that." VD rates are up, there's the militant homosexual movement, "and worst of all, abortion—the human holocaust with no parallel in history." He reads statistics on how many abortions are performed where. In many cities there are more abortions than live births, and "Washington, D.C. is one of them."

The broadcasters applaud this reminder that they are deep in enemy territory. In Washington they are surrounded not merely by the federal government, but by the 70 percent-black city that symbolizes street crime, welfare, abortion, all the social evils Helms preaches against. He turns to *Roe v. Wade,* the Supreme Court decision that legalized abortion. "Now the chickens are coming home to roost," he declares. He plugs the film, *The Silent Scream,* which purports to show the agony of a fetus being aborted. "I hope it will be shown over and over on every Christian station in America." He reports that he has introduced a new bill, "the Unborn Children's Civil Rights Act—with enough grass-roots support, it might get through." Few listening reflect on the fact that in his long career, he has never supported a civil rights bill for those already born.

The embattled family also will benefit from his legislative efforts for school prayer and against cable-TV pornography, Helms says. Not only that, but he hopes to move yet again to "stop the insanity called forced busing." He will do all he can to pass tuition tax credits for parents to send their children to private schools, and a balanced-budget amendment to end the federal deficit. All those, clearly, are family issues—"this should be the Year of The Family."

His concerns for the embattled family at home lead him smoothly to the plight of those embattled abroad. "Freedom around the world is under siege." Just think, he urges, of the millions denied freedom by the "ruthless, godless, brutal, atheistic force of communism."

Communism seems to remind him of Dan Rather, for almost incidentally, he brings up "Fairness in Media," the organization he and his colleagues in Raleigh have just announced. Its stated aim is to enlist enough conservatives to buy CBS stock to take over control of the network and, as he says, to become Rather's bosses. Contrary to public impression, his group does not want to convert the network into a propaganda mill for the conservative cause, he says. It just wants at least one network to give the other side of the news, "and let people make up their own minds." Fairness and objectivity are the goal, he says. Nobody could disagree with that.

Now he focuses in on communism, and his voice tightens as he comes to his time-tested peroration.

"I carry in my pocket," he says, "a little reminder of what communism really is . . . a letter from a grieving grandmother." He tells how Ronald Reagan called him in August of 1983 to ask him to go to South Korea to represent the president on the thirtieth anniversary of the two nations' defense agreement. He told the president he didn't want to. But reluctantly, because it was his friend Reagan, he agreed to go. He made a reservation out of New York. But then he got another call, "from that great Christian leader and football coach Tom Landry, offering to hold a fund-raising dinner for me in Texas. Tom said, 'Maybe we could raise a dollar and a quarter for you,' " Helms remembers, and gets a wave of chuckles. "So I changed planes, and arrived in Alaska twenty minutes after the plane from New York that I would have been on."

Waiting at Anchorage, he met "a handsome young family," with two little girls whose mother read them a book of Bible stories. He made friends, sat down and played with them a silly game he plays with his grandchildren, about an oil delivery truck. He holds out his arm and shows how the truck delivers here and here, up and down each finger, "and then you tell them to put their hand up to their nose to see if they can smell the oil"—he is illustrating all this, step by step—"and then you go 'Honk, honk,' pushing their little hands against their nose." Of course that draws a laugh, too.

"And then," the senator says dramatically, "Flight 007 was called."

At mention of the flight number, the laughter stops.

"They hugged me, and threw me kisses, and departed." Here his voice is sad with determination. One word at a time, he says, "Don't ask me to say communism is just another philosophy."

He opens the letter, from the grandmother of the two little girls. She wrote to him because he was among the last to see her grandchildren alive. She said she was cleaning out the family cottage on a lake in upstate New York, and came across toys belonging to little Noelle and Stacey. And then she had to stop—to write and ask, "Why? Why?"

Helms says, "I carry that letter to remind me when things get tough, or when someone says we don't have to worry about Central America, the Middle East, or Africa . . . I keep it to bring me back to reality."

He pauses again. There is utter silence. Then he says, "I'm here to salute you for doing so much to make a permanent reality of America. Thanks, and God bless you."

There is something special about the applause that thanks him back. It is not the cheering, foot-stomping response that some in the audience can raise among their own flocks. True, he has carefully touched each of their concerns, except perhaps some technical matters about depreciating videotape equipment, or difficulties with the IRS. But these are not vulnerable, easily frenzied worshipers. These are themselves merchants, not buyers of emotion. They are bright-eyed, serious. But as they stand and clap they are showing their respect for a fellow professional, as well as thanking him for being the uncompromising keeper of the true faith, there in the stronghold of secular liberalism.

Thinking about that speech, I realized that the peak of its professional expertise was Helms's transmission of his feelings about the departed girls. There were little swallows, as if to hold back emotion, and pauses, as if to control it just barely. There was calm anger, which made the perfectly controlled voice shake, then drop near a whisper. It was all sincerity.

Yet Helms already had related that story dozens of times, beginning when he returned from Korea, when about 175 campaign supporters had greeted him at the Raleigh-Durham airport, some with signs condemning "inexcusable Soviet barbarism."

Helms told newsmen that "I have never seen two more lovable little children. They were just beautiful"—and even then he told of the "silly little game" he had played with them.

His voice, those many months before, was "choked with emotion," one reporter noted. "It's very hard for me to think of what happened to them," Helms said. "I've been on a roller coaster of emotions since then . . . I can handle it when an adult dies, but when you think these two little girls were deliberately killed . . . Their grandparents must be going through hell."

It turned out that Noelle and Stacey's last name was Grenfell, and they were traveling with their father and mother, Neil and Carol. Neil was returning to his job as marketing director for Eastman Kodak in Seoul when Flight 007 was shot down. All were lost.

Almost exactly a month later, thousands of copies of a computerized letter went out from Helms senatorial campaign headquarters.

They included a photograph of the Grenfell family, reproduced from their Christmas card the previous year. It was heart-tugging: the model couple, kneeling with the two blonde daughters, who wore Korean costumes and wide, innocent smiles.

In great detail, the letter told of Helms's time with the little girls at Anchorage. It recalled how "the three-year-old was sitting on her mother's lap; the five-year-old was perched on the arm of the chair. The mother was reading a story . . ." When the mother put down the book, "I moved over and introduced myself," the letter said.

It told about playing the silly game with the imaginary oil truck, and about saying goodbye to the family. It said then, "It was difficult to express the shock and horror and anger that I felt, and still feel, about the Soviet Union's wanton, deliberate, premeditated, callous and cruel destruction of 269 innocent people—including those two lovable little girls."

The tragedy of the little girls and the other KAL 007 victims "belongs to all of us," the letter said, because "it should bring a renewed understanding of communist brutality."

Then it got to the point. If the reader agreed that it was time to rebuild U.S. defenses, it said, then "I need your help—if I am to continue my work in the Senate . . . Can you help once more with a specially significant contribution? Without your help, our work cannot continue."

It was signed, "Jesse Helms." It included a return envelope for donations.

Reporters in Rochester, N.Y., where the Grenfells lived, found out that neither the senator nor his staff had asked permission to use the Grenfells' photograph in campaign fund-raising. They also found that some recipients of the letter were angry. One Rochester man, who said he had sent money to Helms in the past, was outraged. It would have been fine for Helms to ask donations for the Grenfells' survivors, he complained, but instead Helms seemed to say, " 'If you give me money it won't happen again.' How the hell does he know?"

Helms may have lost that contributor in Rochester, but that letter was part of the most financially successful Senate campaign in history. Helms's fund-raising letters—their philosophy and content, the organization that produces them, the income they produce—are the stuff of political legend. His techniques have been copied on a minor scale by ambitious politicians in both parties. His legend fascinates those who have watched him since he rose out of the little mill town of Monroe, North Carolina, to push himself and his stern politics on the people of the state and then the nation.

Watching him, studying his roots, his rise, his impact on politics, senatorial traditions, foreign policy, and the very way Americans live, one question keeps recurring. It is illustrated perfectly by the tale of the girls aboard Flight 007, and the fund-raising letter that went out using their names:

Is Jesse Helms true believer—or cynic?

Chapter 2

The Man
and the Movement

On the wall of his outer office, there is a blown-up, framed clipping from a small-town North Carolina newspaper, the *Dunn Daily Record*. The big letters say, "The Truth at Last! . . . Senator Helms Won, the News Media Lost." I was peering across the room to read the small type detailing this triumph when Helms came smiling in from the hall, hurrying back from the Capitol.

He does not seem as tall when I stand beside him as when he is speaking behind a lectern, or leaning over one of his colleagues during debate in the Senate. He is round-shouldered. He walks ploddingly. Approaching his sixty-fourth birthday, his body seemed older than his voice. As we walked down the corridor to his private office, we talked about our family names, both with roots in North Carolina. He made a point of saying that although both his mother and father were Helmses, originally they were of altogether different lineage.

He slipped off his suit jacket, which always carries on its lapel a pin with the U.S. and Masonic flags side by side. He wore a red tie depicting the Cape Hatteras lighthouse. He offered me a Lucky Strike, did not seem offended when I declined, then lit one for himself. He pointed toward a couch and took a chair facing me. Behind him was a wall full of political cartoons, most of them unflattering, caricaturing his big eyeglasses and his political adventures. He said he liked them all, pro and con, and I am sure he does. Whatever their message, they constitute recognition, and one of the ways in which he is normal is that he likes all that—the trappings of power, reminders of how far he has come:

Editorial cartoons and Page 1 headlines. Suite 403 of the Dirksen Senate Office Building. Chairmanship of the Senate Agriculture Committee. Leadership of the angry political phenomenon known as the New Right. Proprietorship of the most formidable fund-raising and propaganda conglomerate ever assembled around an elected official. Political muscle enough to bully other senators, challengers, diplomats, cabinet officers, foreign governments, even his own party and president.

Jesse Helms is a long way from his boyhood as a policeman's son in a Carolina county seat. He has the potential to make or break— even conceivably to become—the Republican Party's next presidential candidate. Yet personally and culturally he is still somewhere back along U.S. 1, between Monroe and Raleigh, North Carolina.

As one astute Carolinian sees it, Helms is a conscious mid-cult figure. His clothes, off the rack at Nowell's, a conservative, old-line Raleigh haberdashery, are like those of a small-town banker. His face and haircut match his suits: nothing there to offend the subliminal sensitivities of the people who work in filling stations and tobacco warehouses, who go to fundamentalist churches on the edge of Piedmont textile towns. His favorite movies are *Patton* and *The Sound of Music,* his favorite TV show "Murder, She Wrote." Most of his reading is Senate reports and right-wing journalism, but among novelists he has fond memories of Taylor Caldwell.

One-on-one, his manners are a Claghornian exaggeration of southern courtesy. On the surface, he is wholly unthreatening. He remained so as we talked of old times, of his upbringing, of the schoolteachers and principals who inspired him, of the stern, uneducated parents who were "two of the finest people ever to walk this earth." Were they teetotalers? This brought a laugh. "You bet," he said. "People used to say my folks not only hated liquor, they hated the man that grew the corn that made the liquor."

He ground out his Lucky and lit another. Our talk turned to more serious things, like racial justice, school prayer, and media bias. His manner changed. He spread his arms as he told how Sam Ervin himself had advised him how to go about keeping the Supreme Court away from school prayer without amending the Constitution. He flicked his wrist like a drummer striking a cymbal when he related how his old nemesis, the *Raleigh News & Observer,* had refused to print a letter from a Notre Dame law professor upholding his viewpoint. His voice rose as he explained how those Republican senators who once badmouthed him had apologized to him afterward, and their apologies never got reported.

Just then a persistent buzzer sounded and a woman's voice said there would be a vote on the Senate floor in fifteen minutes. Helms was telling me about his black campaign press secretary when we started together down the hall to the elevator. There a young blonde woman stood beside us. He introduced me to her elaborately; I assumed she was one of his aides, or at least the daughter of an old friend. Then he introduced himself, and asked where she worked. She was interning in Paul Simon's office. Simon, of course, is a liberal Democrat from Illinois. Oh, said Helms. That's good. You'll learn a lot. He reached to push me ahead of him through the door, then off the elevator, then onto the little subway car that runs from Senate office building to Capitol.

As we sat down, Senators Jake Garn and Tom Eagleton approached, and he beckoned them to squeeze in beside us. Three years before, Helms and his protégé John East had a serious run-in with Eagleton over a tobacco bill, and East dropped an insult to Eagleton that left lasting scars. But on the subway, all was affability, in both directions. So it continued as Helms spoke and waved to elevator operators, tourists, and Capitol policemen on his way to the Senate floor. He went in, quickly voted, and came out again. He motioned me ahead of him through the revolving doors to the east front of the Capitol. We stood at the top of the broad steps, talking in the afternoon sun, watching a motorcade of limousines bringing a visiting statesman to confer with legislators. Eventually when Helms pulled out his schedule card and saw his next appointment approaching, we reached to shake again. Only then did I notice how small and soft his hands are for a man his size.

As I angled down the Capitol steps, I thought about the obvious contradictions between this man's personal cordiality and his political rigidity, between the great show of comradeship among senators in the subway and what they say about each other privately. What they have said to me specifically about Jesse Helms is often bitter.

One Democrat, a studious and patient man, sat looking out his office window and talked about working with Helms—or against him —for the past decade. Helms "simply has no respect for the processes of the institution," he began. "He'll do anything to gain his way. The processes here are based on two hundred years of ways to resolve differences . . . But he comes in with an end run to try to do by statute what should be done by constitutional amendment, if it's done at all. If he succeeded, there would be no constitutional system left. He has no compunction about what he'll do . . . He does things that are technically allowed, but in spirit they abuse the rules."

Helms, this senator said, "plays a highly political game, not an institutional game, with these interlocking political committees of his. He works not so much within the Senate as outside. Often the whole purpose of his programming a vote is politics, so then he can use it with a press release or by mailing off thousands of letters by pushing a button on a computer . . . You have to perceive that anything you say or do will be used against you in a political, often a distorted way.

"Toward him, most members don't apply the old fight-today, friends-tomorrow tradition. He's coming out of an element in American society that believes its view is right and there is no other reasonable viewpoint. Yet the consequences of his being a pariah here don't matter as much as they used to. The leadership can't discipline a senator as it once did. In the old days, you couldn't get a vote if the leadership didn't want to have one. Now it's gone the other way . . . People are coming to realize the only way to deal with him is not to afford him the usual courtesies, to recognize that he's fighting trench warfare and they have to fight it the same. He and his people drag you down in the gutter to fight them . . . It's wreaking havoc on the institution."

Not only Democrats feel that way. One dedicated Republican Senator, not a friend of Helms, said, "It's frustrating, often impossible to get serious and urgent business done. You might be working on a foreign aid bill or a change in the debt limit and all of a sudden you find you're voting on school prayer or abortion. Helms is no respecter of the institution. He uses the Senate for his own ends, his own causes, and they are not the same as the goals of the country."

The outspoken Barry Goldwater, the man who wrote *The Conscience of a Conservative* and made it socially respectable to be a Republican in the South, told reporters Helms "has not helped the conservative cause one bit . . . A liberal like Ted Kennedy would not have used tactics of the sort Helms has used in pushing for his New Right agenda." About the same time, Goldwater predicted that "as Jesse gets older, he'll understand you get what the people want . . . Right now, the majority doesn't want this at all."

Repeatedly, as they speak of Helms, other senators and political veterans refer back to the way things used to be, the old days, the institution and its traditions. Helms puzzles them when they look for a political mold into which he fits, another historic figure with whom he compares. In the Senate, Helms's own early heroes were Richard B. Russell, the courtly Georgian who led the southern block through the years of the civil rights revolution, and Robert A. Taft, "Mr. Republican." But while Russell was a dedicated segregationist, he was a man with whom an agreement could be made, who in fact lived by the traditions of the Senate. Taft was a stickler for the rules. Some mention Huey Long and the Talmadges: old Governor Gene Talmadge had Georgia's wool-hat (i.e., red-neck) vote sewed up, and in Carolina today the once solidly Democratic tractor-cap vote is called collectively "Jessecrats." Others bring up Orval Faubus, Lester Maddox, James O. Eastland, and Helms's good friend Strom Thurmond of South Carolina. But all of them were essentially regional politicians, though Thurmond ran for president in 1948 on the States' Rights ticket and Eastland affected federal law by chairing the Senate Judiciary Committee. Thurmond began as a New Deal Democrat, became a Dixiecrat, then a Goldwater Republican. But after he saw the effect of the Voting Rights Act of 1965, he gradually changed until he courted the black vote in South Carolina.

Helms's impact, his constituency are national, not merely regional. Politicians with whom he is best compared must have that kind of sweep. I see two. One is an erstwhile segregationist, George C. Wallace of Alabama. But the other has no southern roots, no connection with the long civil rights struggle at all. He is Joseph R. McCarthy of Wisconsin.

Helms was an admirer of Wallace when he was still a Carolina TV commentator and Wallace was standing in schoolhouse doors, then running for president. His editorials on the Tobacco Network out of Raleigh in the sixties could have been used whole as Wallace campaign speeches if they were colloquialized a bit for the crowds. They appealed to the same elemental prejudices.

But there are major differences. Wallace, with all his feistiness, was a warmer, more understandable human being—even, after his near-assassination, a figure of sympathy. Both men got the stock-car vote, but Wallace could go out and mingle with the sweaty beer-drinkers and their women in short-shorts in the infield. Despite his excursion into third-party politics, Wallace down deep was and is a Democrat, upper and lower case. Like Huey Long's, his economic instincts are for the little man. Because of that, when Wallace, like Thurmond, altered course on racial matters late in his career, he cut heavily into the black vote in Alabama.

Helms, despite his up-front affability, does not project warmth. He welcomes red-neck votes, but he would be ill at ease hobnobbing with beer-drinking, loud-cussing good old boys. He was never happy in the national Democratic Party, and when he left it he left for good. He spent years in his early career as paid spokesman for the banking industry, and always has backed business against labor, power against powerlessness. And unlike Thurmond and Wallace, he has never adjusted his policies to acknowledge the change in the racial makeup of the voter lists. He still gets elected by so arousing white voters that it matters not how heavily the black vote goes against him. Black men, white men, politicians, preachers, academics, journalists have volunteered to me their belief that he is a racist. He himself insists that those who know him know he is not.

There are remarkable similarities between Joe McCarthy's reign during Dwight Eisenhower's administration and the way Helms rides high during Ronald Reagan's. McCarthy's contribution to American history was an affliction that took his name—McCarthyism. He alleged that Communists riddled the government. They were there, a few of them, and he magnified the fear of communism until it caused near-paralysis in government and academy. Helms, too, seems obsessed by communism. Abroad, he supports the South African government and Latin American dictators because he sees communism as the inevitable alternative. At home, he has attacked the civil rights movement and many other social and economic changes as part of a communist scheme to do in America.

McCarthy held Harry Truman's and Eisenhower's foreign policy and diplomatic appointments hostage to his personal standards of anti-communism. Helms has exerted the same kind of pressure on Reagan's State Department. Richard Rovere wrote in his *Senator Joe McCarthy* that "when McCarthy had a mind to, he constituted himself an agency for the conduct of foreign relations." So does Helms. McCarthy had a cabal of allies within the government, within the FBI and other investigative agencies, often reporting to him things they had not yet reported to their superiors. Helms has a network of such friends, in and outside the government.

McCarthy, too, strained the rules of the Senate for his own crusade. "The truth is that everyone in the Senate, or just about everyone, was scared stiff" of McCarthy, Rovere wrote soon after the senator's death. McCarthy inspired red-baiting campaigns to defeat a series of senators who stood up to him. That is what Helms's colleagues are worrying about today when they complain that he pushes a button on a computer to use their Senate votes against them. Helms, like McCarthy, operates best in opposition; he is uncomfortable cast in support of even a president for whose election he fought so hard. Both men attracted a constituency of the socially and culturally aggrieved, which may have begun with a hard core of wild-eyed extremists but grew to meld blue-collar populists, educated ideologues, religious fundamentalists, big-money Texans, and newly graduated opportunists in a truly national upsurge.

McCarthy provoked fierce reaction from those to whom, in Rovere's words, "whatever is illiberal, repressive, reactionary, obscurantist, anti-intellectual, totalitarian or merely swinish will for some time to come be McCarthyism." So does Helms, although the word "Helmsism" does not roll off the tongue so smoothly. To their followers, however, both men symbolize militant patriotism. Fulton Lewis, Jr., a favorite radio commentator of Helms's when he was breaking into that business, said, "To many Americans, McCarthyism is Americanism." Helms's devotees feel the same way.

But about there, the likeness thins out, and the differences show how far beyond McCarthyism the Helms phenomenon is pointed. McCarthy, too, was an ex-Democrat, and never bothered much with orthodox Republican policies. He came across communism almost by accident, saw its potential, and saddled up. He was not a man with a plan. From postwar Europe, some correspondents reported that the Germans enjoyed contemplating McCarthy in America because it relieved their sense of guilt about their Führer. Both Hitler and McCarthy were screamers, inciters of mobs, who exploited fear of communism. But Hitler had dreams of a thousand-year Reich, and as Rovere wrote, "McCarthy had no program for tomorrow morning."

Helms does. He far outreaches McCarthy. In breadth if not coherence, his dream reaches beyond that of any politician now practicing in America. Anti-communism is only a part of it. It covers foreign policy, economics, education, justice, morality, and religion. Its priorities were laid out by Helms in an obscure foreign policy journal a decade ago. In it, he praised family life, property ownership, spiritual orientation, and anti-communism as fundamental American values—and condoned the suspension of what he called "secondary" rights, specifically democratic process and free press, if necessary to assure those higher values. Helms himself does not lay out elaborate plans and support them with lengthy documentation. He does not dwell on detail; he employs others for that. What he envisions is often summed up in the simple phrase, "a Christian America," which suggests heaven on earth to his followers but something very different to others, especially non-Christians. In Carolina, his denigrators sometimes describe him in a phrase: "Mean for Jesus."

But Helms's is not an ad hoc crusade, carried in his hip pocket like Joe McCarthy's. McCarthy had zealous followers, as does Helms. But Helms has more than that: organization—political action committees, foundations, corporations run on behalf of his crusade by men who combine political imagination with technical expertise. The payroll of his machine in North Carolina alone far exceeds that of the official Republican and Democratic parties combined. Altogether, his groups already have raised and deployed at least $50 million, and their computers and mailing machines never rest. Their financial muscle grows with each election cycle.

But those are only the organizations with his own stamp, put together by his own aides. They are at the core of something vastly more extensive, the coalition of often interlocking social-issue groups and fund-raising enterprises known as the New Right. Helms is its godfather. He was instrumental in forming many of its best-known operations, like the National Conservative Political Action Committee (NCPAC) and the Conservative Caucus. His name, his recorded voice have been freely given assets to countless groups and solicitation drives, the difference between their success and failure. Ronald Reagan himself owes his political survival in 1976, and thus his eventual presidency, to Jesse Helms's determined political support when others thought he was through. All of these pay tribute to Helms; only Reagan, because he now has a country to run, seems occasionally to be an ingrate.

The Baptist layman Helms is just as conspicuous in the politico-religious alliance. It is made up not only of TV personalities like Jerry Falwell and Pat Robertson, but of thousands of obscure fundamentalist preachers across the country, who have abandoned a long habit of non-involvement in politics to become experts in voter registration and precinct organization. Helms's allies are infiltrating the national leadership of the Southern Baptist Convention, which with nearly fifteen million members is the largest Protestant denomination in the country. This campaign alone carries immense nationwide political potential. With the other components of this coalition, the newly aroused religious right may become a decisive influence on American politics for years ahead.

Many of those organizations flaunt the word "conservative" in their title. Helms uses it to describe everything he does. Candidates within both parties rush to claim that label and deny it to their rivals. But some of their organizers and fund-raisers, who do not have to run for office, are more frank about what they want to do. They may use the word "conservative" on their letterheads, but they scoff at it. They say publicly that they are not out merely to conserve what is good about America. They are for change, radical change. Theirs is not a conservative coalition, but a radical movement—they emphasize *movement,* with all that implies about going somewhere together. Their priorities, their special issues may vary, but they move together in the same direction. They are pushing America hard right, and Jesse Helms is leading them.

Chapter 3

"Mr. Jesse" and Son

On that busy subway train between the Capitol and the Senate office buildings, a young staff professional took a seat one morning, alone with her thoughts. A tall, courtly senator stepped aboard and peered at her. His southern voice boomed:

"Smile! That's what my daddy always used to say to me! Smile!"

Surprised, the woman asked him, "How did you react? When somebody yells at me like that, I just freeze. I can't smile."

The senator told her, "My father was a six-foot, two-hundred-pound gorilla. When he said, 'Smile,' I smiled."

Jesse Helms in his sixties is a domineering figure, but more by political stature than personality. When he was a child, he himself was dominated by Jesse Helms, Sr., the tall and powerful "gorilla" he talked about. The father became police and fire chief in Monroe, North Carolina, a prototypical southern small town, with all the virtues and prejudices of its time and place. Through the son, that time, that place, and that father have had an emotional, polarizing impact on America in the last quarter of the twentieth century.

In 1921, North Carolina's new governor took office with a summons to "the forces of progressive democracy" to "war for righteousness with the reactionary and unprogressive forces of our state." As if in response, Jesse Alexander Helms, Jr., was born that fall. Eventually he would plunge into and exploit that ongoing war—over who and what are progressive and righteous, unprogressive and reactionary in American life.

Most of the superficial aspects of his family and childhood should have been reinforcing to the young ego that drove him to leave home and take on the world. His ancestors were farmers among the Scotch-

Irish pioneers in Union County in 1742, nearly a decade before Monroe was settled. The ornate county courthouse of today sits on their original farmstead. Their progeny never were great landholders, slave-owners, or memorable Civil War heroes. This was small-farm cotton country, where the Piedmont lifts up from the Coastal Plain. But the vigorous family spread and thickened until it was more numerous than even Smiths and Johnsons. By the 1980s, more than five hundred Helmses would occupy column after column in the local phonebook. But in 1912 when Jesse Helms, Sr., married his distant cousin Ethel Mae, telephones were not that common in a country town of three thousand people. And when Jesse, Jr., came along on October 18, 1921, following a brother named Wriston, the family's economic standing was unimposing. Some who passed the Helms house thought of the Helmses as poor, even by the modest standards of Monroe in the twenties; young Jesse himself never did.

"Mr. Jesse," as the chief was known, was even bigger than his son described him on the Senate subway. Others have called him six-four or six-five. Either way, he was an imposing figure by both title and stature. For representing law and order in Monroe, the town paid him twenty-five dollars a week.

Current memories of Monroe in the twenties credit it with five churches, four Republicans, one pool hall, and one whorehouse. Charlotte lay twenty-six miles west, an upwardly mobile city, ambitious to be the biggest in the Carolinas. But Monroe was the center of its own social and business universe. Its chamber of commerce sang of its location at the junction of the Seaboard Air Line railroad from New York to New Orleans and the Seaboard Line from Rutherfordton to Wilmington. Monroe's lighting plant, the chamber bragged, "illuminates many blocks of white way." The town had seven miles of paved streets, "paralleled by cement sidewalks." It had a Rotary Club, a Kiwanis Club, and a Woman's Club. It had "local organizations of all the leading fraternal orders"—from time to time including the Ku Klux Klan, which was not mentioned by the city boosters. Monroe proudly excelled in its "native born, intelligent, satisfied, dependable workmen."

It also had "a progressive and efficient body of municipal officers," and well down the line below the mayor and aldermen, those included Officer Jesse Helms. Senator Helms's official biography lists his father as police chief, but for most of his life he was one of two or three patrolmen. He was a municipal fixture around the courthouse and firehouse. The family's plain clapboard home was just three doors away. One contemporary of young Jesse remembers that the future senator's father drove the fire department's ladder truck, and one day steered it through the streets with shaving lather on half his face, with no shirt and galluses flapping. "When the bell rang, he jumped," this Tarheel said. Big Jesse had only a fifth-grade education, but his son said he was "the wisest man I've ever known." His friends called him "courteous but firm as a rock." As police officer, "people knew he meant business," and as father, "Jesse didn't argue with him."

"People instinctively trusted him," the senator told me. "I could cite you a hundred examples of how he turned people around . . . I remember one time I was with him and we saw a car weaving around, it almost hit a telephone pole. He pulled it over, and it was a young man from a fairly well-known family. And there he was three sheets to the wind. I remember my father . . . gave him a lecture, said 'You're going to ruin yourself, your family, your children. I don't want to take you and put you in jail' . . . My father said, 'I tell you what I'm going to do, offer you a deal. If you promise me you'll never take another drink, I'll take you home . . . But you've got to promise me you'll never take another drink.' "

Jesse, listening, said to himself, "Yeah, he'll promise anything." But, he recalled, the man never did take that drink.

Many years later, when Mr. Jesse died, "it was a very cold night, sleet and rain, and the custom in our little town was for the family to go to the funeral home . . . I was in the Senate then, my father had sat in the gallery and watched me sworn in. I was kind of relieved at the weather because I thought people wouldn't feel obliged to come on a bad night. But they lined up for three blocks, people came in wet, and we were there till after ten o'clock. That man was considerably older at the time, and he came and reminded me of that night long before, said 'I've never touched alcohol since.' They would have bounced my father if he tried to enforce the law that way today, I suppose. But I think maybe it did a lot more good than otherwise."

As Helms and his boyhood friends tell it, they led a life of un-marred innocence. Jesse remembered hanging onto the rear platform of the ice wagon as it eased down the street. There was the perhaps apocryphal story about the day a ventriloquist came to town and stopped to see a friend who worked at the funeral home. Jesse recalled, "By throwing his voice, he made a corpse 'talk,' whereupon the Negro janitor departed through a screen door without opening it." Jesse and his friends went swimming in Richardson Creek. Occasionally a black child would play with them there. But of course in those days no blacks could sit with them at the Strand or Pastime theater, where the boys paid a dime to watch the great early cowboy stars like Buck Jones and Hoot Gibson.

Mrs. Helms, who was there waiting every day when her children came home from school, was determined to push her children beyond her own limited cultural circle. She boosted them for good roles in school plays, and supervised their church life. She saw to it that Jesse had violin lessons. The Helmses were reliable members of First Baptist Church, and all of them went to Sunday services and Wednesday evening prayer meetings. Jesse's first exposure to group learning was in Sunday school. He told me he was too young to understand any of the political-religious controversy that swirled through the state in those years. But if any of it sank into his subconscious, more than half a century later it all had to seem familiar.

North Carolina, beginning at the turn of the century, had become one of the nation's most education-conscious states. In the twenties it was called "the Wisconsin of the South," in reference to Wisconsin's progressivism under Robert La Follette. But by mid-decade, that progressivism was challenged. In 1925, the legislature in Raleigh took up a bill to forbid teaching of biological evolution. The bill's sponsor attacked evolution as an "infidel doctrine." Its most eloquent opponent was the president of the University of North Carolina. Summing up the situation in a style that would echo in Helms's career, a supporter of the law said, "The professors are lined up against the folks." The professors did not stand alone, of course; there were Constitution-minded legislators like future U.S. Senator Sam Ervin, Jr., a university alumnus, who defended "freedom of the mind" at the state capitol. As historian Willard B. Gatewood, Jr., has written, the conflict raised questions "of science and religion, intellectual freedom, separation of church and state, control of public education and even the future of democracy and Christianity in America. Those who rallied to the anti-evolution standard linked Darwin's theory with secularism, relaxed standards of conduct, disintegration of the family, 'godless education,' communism and a host of other sources of public concern . . . Their war against evolution symbolized their protest against the drift of modern culture . . ."

The struggle roiled pulpits across the state. Big-name evangelists, forerunners of the TV preachers of later generations, traveled from the Smokies to the shore, equating evolution with atheism with communism. One of them, Mordecai Ham, asserted that "the day is not distant when you will be in the grip of the Red Terror and your children will be taught free love by the damnable theory of evolution." The Baptist State Convention specifically was torn by the controversy, with individual preachers and congregations choosing up sides. Churchgoers heard preachers insist on 100 percent fundamentalism, leaving no doubt that anyone who strayed from it also was of suspect Americanism. From the churches the fight spread into town and county politics; candidates for sheriff and applicants for teaching jobs were put to the evolution test.

While the debate was near its peak, William Jennings Bryan made a fool of himself in prosecuting a small-town schoolteacher named Scopes who had exposed his pupils to evolution theory in neighboring Tennessee. That discouraged the campaign in North Carolina. Many who were concerned about Carolina's image outside were relieved when the controversy quieted after the bill's second legislative defeat in 1927. But while it quieted, it did not die. It would flare up repeatedly. More than half a century later, it was part of the fundamentalist reaction against liberties and heresies hardly imagined in the innocent Twenties.

Young Jesse was barely entering school when the anti-evolution frenzy began to recede. It was replaced promptly by another perceived church-state issue in 1928, when the Roman Catholic Democrat Alfred E. Smith ran for president. The church debate was paralleled by the wet-dry argument over liquor sales. Smith was wet and Catholic, and the dry Quaker Herbert Hoover carried the state. It was the first time loyally Democratic North Carolina had gone Republican for any president since Reconstruction, and would be the only time between 1872 and 1968. Like the evolution dispute, that controversy swirled through the church and courthouse world of the elder Helmses.

Boyhood memories stuck with young Jesse, and like all of us he replayed the fun, the sentimental parts. He looked back to "the shady streets, the cotton wagons, the Fourth of July parades and the New Year's Eve firecrackers . . . the stream of school kids marching uptown to place flowers on the Courthouse Square monument on Confederate Memorial Day . . ."

Independence Day, with its flags and patriotic oratory, was special in his memory. He recalled "the honks and shrieks of the town band . . . the chilled lemonade—a nickel a glass . . ." As the parade swung onto South Main Street, "there was a cheer. There were horses . . . prancing and snorting." Some of it stuck with him because of pride that his father had a conspicuous role: there came "both of the town's highly polished fire engines with a multitude of ecstatic youngsters perched atop them; the town's single police car—three sirens in a row in a sort of discordant symphony . . . In the burning noontime sun, men and women—and little boys and girls, too— stood reverently as a prayer of thanksgiving was offered for the 'liberty and freedom' which were God's gift to America. Nobody doubted it . . ."

His friends and teachers think of young Jesse now as having been a good student who did his homework and had polite manners. Early on, he learned that he had a knack for words. One of his friends said he intentionally used a lot of big words to impress them, and sent them to the dictionary to find out whether he was insulting them. "A big vocabulary for a country town," one said admiringly.

He showered retrospective affection and appreciation on all the teachers who guided him then, but especially on three who had a special impact—his first-grade teacher, his high-school English teacher, and his high-school principal.

Miss Lura Heath, he recalled, was "the kind of soul whose life has been dedicated to tender personal relationships with the people around her."

Miss Lura's father had been a major in the Confederate Army, which ever after was the dominant fact in his and his daughter's life. The major used to sit as if built into a high-back rocking chair beside a white column on the Heath front porch. To young Jesse, he was "the South, Robert E. Lee and the rhythm of 'Dixie,' all rolled up in a proud posture of dignity and wisdom." He had been a post-Civil War state legislator, but Miss Lura often said her father only belonged to two organizations, the Democratic Party and the Methodist Church, and he was thinking about getting out of both of them. In Jesse's later perception, the major "became disenchanted with politics when he began to sense a trend toward socialism in this country. He was concerned about what he regarded as the political manipulation of minority groups . . . His wisdom told him that the purchase of votes from the federal treasury would one day be destructive of the very principles of America."

Any mention of Horatio Alger always reminded Jesse of Miss Annie Lee, "as fine a high-school English teacher as ever served the youth of North Carolina." Once in the Senate, when Miss Annie was ill, he halted action on a bill because it had a split infinitive, and persuaded Hubert Humphrey to agree to changing it just for her. Then he called Miss Annie with the good news, and she told him, "Good boy." He also found it significant in later years that Miss Annie had forecast economic chaos if the United States ever went off the gold standard.

Ray House is the most familiar of the usual suspects rounded up by those who go to Monroe seeking background on Helms's upbringing. An outgoing man of formidable memory, he was not only principal, but headed the high-school band, and in both roles became a reliable custodian of Helms lore. He is the source of the most repeated anecdote of all, about how teen-age Jesse overcame his skinny gracelessness and by sheer determination won a state championship.

Jesse was never an athlete; that way into the high school's social in-crowd was impossible for him. But he supported the school teams from the sidelines on the band and the newspaper. As a musician, Jesse was burdened with a tuba. House persuaded him it was a blessing by saying, "Everybody will be able to see you with that thing around your neck, Jesse, even when you're sitting down." Although he had not been playing long, Jesse stood before the judges and dared to try "The Flight of the Bumblebee." As House tells it, "He got going a little bit, then stopped. He started over, but he stopped again. This time he took a new grip on the tuba, looked around for a moment, then looked directly at a judge. He said 'Judge, I'm scared to death.' But then he took off again, and sure enough they gave him the state championship."

Besides carrying papers, Jesse jerked sodas, and got other work to make spending money. His friends say it was assumed all boys would have some kind of part-time job, but Jesse always seemed to have two. He swept floors and covered school sports for the semi-weekly *Monroe Journal,* and later did a regular essay called "The Vagabond Scholar," for a dollar a column. One contemporary remembers him racing up and down the sidelines of high-school football games, typing up play-by-play action on the spot, as if bulletins were being ripped from his typewriter to be flashed to the waiting world. One editor at the *Journal* recalled him as "the overslim youngster who once haunted our shop, eager to learn the trade." And clearly Jesse looked up to those journeymen as role models, long before that term was in common use. He remembered "Mr. Rowland" Beasley, founder of the paper, who "would load his pipe with Prince Albert tobacco and his typewriter with copy paper. With two fingers he would punch out editorials so stimulating and refreshing that newspapers all over the country would reprint them." Jesse's exact words are interesting because that is his own typing style, and because when he wrote those words years later he himself was doing very much what he so admired in "Mr. Rowland."

"I went to college to learn something about newspapering," he said then, "but it didn't take me long to realize that I had learned more under Mr. Rowland's guidance than I could ever learn from a college professor." It may be true, and it may have been Jesse's rationalization of his brief college career. But he was finishing high school at a time when newspapermen, especially in the South, often made names for themselves after going only through "the college of hard knocks," which was considered more essential to small-town journalism than erudition in history and philosophy. As a senior, he listed in the high-school yearbook his ambition to be a columnist. Before making any career step, he listened to advice from Ray House, without which he might never have left home.

House thought of Jesse as "a regular old boy—long-legged and bugeyed" when he was younger. But when his boys neared graduation, he was serious about their potential. Helms attributes to his principal "the most remarkable influence" on his career decisions. "He was the greatest exponent of the free enterprise system," he says. "He taught us that we are personally responsible and accountable. I remember when he called in several from the senior class . . . I was sort of the cow's tail in the crowd . . . He said you can make it in this country. He said it's going to take hard work . . . He said you're going to succeed. He said you'll own your own homes and you'll have two cars and all that. I thought this man had lost his mind."

That philosophy has stuck with Helms all these years, of course —balanced by a negative corollary about what people deserve if they don't work hard enough. House says, "He worked hard, and he made it. And if he could do it, anybody else ought to be able to do it." Out of high school, Jesse took that inspirational advice a shy half-step away from home—to Wingate College, a Baptist junior college just outside Monroe. He went there simply because he could not afford to go farther. But after a year, he was ready for a bigger move. For the fall session in 1939, he enrolled at Wake Forest College, then still at its original site outside Raleigh. It was a long step toward the great world.

Today most of those who knew young Jesse Helms and his family are so admiring of Monroe's most famous son that all any inquiring outsider is likely to hear are these tales of the Helmses' patriotism and piety, of his father's uprightness and universal respect, of Jesse's all-American boyhood, hard work, and honesty.

But those are common characteristics of the young men who grew up white and healthy in Monroe, North Carolina, in the twenties and thirties, who were lucky enough to be exposed to Miss Lura Heath and Ray House and their like. Thousands of other boys were reared the same way in small towns across the South. Those generalities unite them. What separates them is how they turned out afterward. Another Carolina boy named Jim Hunt, a little younger, who grew up outside the tobacco hamlet of Rock Ridge, turned out very different from Helms. They were both from religious families, close to being poor, working for all they ever got. Something made them different; their differences collided in the senatorial election of 1984.

The happy memories that Helms's friends recite for the visiting curious are no doubt true. But they are selective. Others who lived in Monroe, including blacks, remember different details.

As Helms's boyhood pals recall it, "We went to school separate from the Negro children, and we didn't know any other way. It was how we grew up. The black children went to a school down past the ridge, and we went to the main school closer to downtown." It was that simple: no harm meant, no harm done. Sometimes they played with black children, they are always sure to note. As Ray House once said, "We all loved the black people. Of course, we used the term 'nigger,' but we always felt uncomfortable with it, because they were living in your backyards. And Jesse played with them all his life and loved them. They're delightful people to play with." And again, House said, "Segregation was a way of life. We couldn't have done anything. If we would have started a fight against it, somebody would have shot us. You had to live like that. But we didn't have malice."

It is tradition, in a straight line with the old legend of the happy black folks singing on the plantation till the Yankee troublemakers came down to stir things up. Unless he has taken time later to stop and think about that version, perhaps to imagine himself in a black child's place, the southern white man can describe it that way in all sincerity. He is not lying. That is how he saw it, growing up.

To blacks growing up contemporary with Jesse Helms, it was not exactly that way. They remember the White and Colored signs over the water fountains at the courthouse and train station. They remember the difference between the white school and the black school, "down past the ridge." They remember their mothers working for white families, doing jobs white housewives would rather not do. Some of them especially remember the tall policeman named Helms and his son Jesse.

"Big Jesse was hated by the blacks and the aristocratic whites, too," one woman said. "People said he was ignorant, ignorant about being in public, how to deal with the public, treating people fairly. He exercised his power to the fullest, in the wrong way. He especially treated black people in the roughest way he could. He carried a big stick . . . If anybody was drunk or whatever, he'd rough them up.

"The fact is he just favored whites, and he even treated the real poor whites the same as he did blacks. But the poor whites liked him, because he was rough on the black people. That's why he stayed police chief so long. The better-off whites had sympathy for us." The police chief was not himself the town power, but only its representative, said this woman, a contemporary of young Jesse.

Another black citizen, now elderly, says today, "You can tell from his son's attitudes that big Jesse never was much for the poor man. Some people have got a kind of nasty way of talking to people, acting to people. That was him. He was like a typical southern police chief, or worse. There wasn't no gravy for black people back then." One story that survives is that Helms once kicked down the door to a black bootlegger's house and narrowly escaped death when a bullet ricocheted off the shield on his cap. Even a black woman says the Helms family "seemed poor to us. Their house was substandard." But from it, and from his base at the courthouse, "Mr. Jesse" stayed in office at the police and fire departments for some fifty years.

Not all the revealing comments about Jesse, Sr., are intentionally critical, or offered by those who carry a lifelong resentment of how he did his police work. Old friend Ray House, for example, said on one occasion that the police chief "had the sharpest shoe in town, and he didn't mind using it." Another time, House said young Jesse often got left out when the other boys headed out to raise hell, because his father was the policeman. When he was small, "he used to jump up and down because he was so mad he couldn't cut up like the others . . . It was bound to be rough on a little boy. His peers meant more to him than anything else. But he stayed away because he didn't want to embarrass his father."

Thus when Jesse Helms left home that September of 1939, his personal baggage included almost eighteen years of strict upbringing. His boyhood had been outwardly happy but restrained by his father's towering sternness and his own visibility as his father's son. His mother's devotion to her church and its rigid standards of social conduct helped hold back whatever rebellious impulses stirred in him. His feeling of being "just about the cow's tail" among his accomplished peers spoke of the fact that he had never made it into the town's student elite. Being champion tuba player was not quite the same as being champion athlete. He had never been wildly successful with the girls.

He was surrounded at home by the lore of the post-Civil War South. Those born roughly half a century after Appomattox, as he was, were wrapped as children in the romance of the Confederacy. No one questioned the rightness of its cause. In some, that got mixed up with race and religion, and was carried forward as anger toward unfamiliar ideas. In the sons and grandsons of the defeated, there lived on a burning need to get even—with Yankees, blacks, outsiders, infidels. When they headed out into the larger and more complex world, some used their experiences creatively, to shine light on themselves and their society. Others would spend their lives trying to club the world into their version of righteousness.

Chapter 4

Baptism

Jesse Helms's cultivated public image is that of a man quick to disagree, harsh in his judgments, but a straight arrow who would rather die than lie or cheat. Before he was thirty years old, things happened that still cloud that image among many Carolinians.

He arrived in Raleigh that September an innocent, a talented small-town boy eager to get ahead, hardly aware of how politics was played. Less than a dozen years later, he left for Washington. This move up was the direct result of his role in the most calculatedly deceitful statewide election campaign in North Carolina history.

To mention Willis Smith's defeat of Frank Graham in that Democratic senatorial primary of 1950 still stirs bitterness among the losers and evasiveness among the winners. Few campaigns anywhere, not George Smathers's in Florida or Joe McCarthy's in Wisconsin or Dick Nixon's in California, have exceeded it. It was by far the most controversial event of the first half of Helms's life. After his infant years it also may have been the most formative, setting a pattern on which he would fall back repeatedly in his own political future.

In that 1950 campaign, Graham, president of the University of North Carolina, was unseated by an all-out assault of red-baiting and race-baiting. Helms, officially a broadcast reporter covering the campaign, was deeply committed to Smith's side. As much as anything he has done later, since he became a national figure commanding millions of political dollars, Senate seniority, and world notice, that involvement brings into question his inner standards of right and wrong. The question arose originally from the nature of the campaign itself, in which a respected senator was ousted by a program of gross vilification. It has been sharpened by Helms's way of dealing with his role in the thirty-six years since, when he and his political intimates increasingly have maintained he was little more than an interested bystander.

When Helms left home, he possessed neither the skills nor the ideology that would merge so effectively in his later career. Monroe and the Helms family had provided traditions and assumptions, but the nature and direction of Helms's politics were determined in the decade of the forties.

A benevolent character named Jasper "Bull" Memory was the first influence on young Jesse when he arrived at Wake Forest, outside Raleigh. Later Helms would say Memory was instrumental in his going there because "he negotiated an NYA job at $18.75 a month in sports publicity for me." It is surprising, considering his later opinions about government programs and make-work politics, that more than forty-five years later he would acknowledge publicly that it was an NYA job. The NYA, the National Youth Administration, was Eleanor Roosevelt's idea, one of the New Deal's most flagrantly political do-good inventions. Arguments sprang up over radicals in its ranks. It created jobs for young people, many of them part-time assignments designed to help students stay in school through the Depression. One of its beneficiaries was Lyndon Johnson, who was its state director in Texas. Another was Richard Nixon. Another was Jesse Helms. To make ends meet, he combined his job with washing dishes at his boardinghouse and, later, reading proofs nights at the *Raleigh News & Observer.*

Memory was "Mr. Wake Forest," a revered teacher who also recruited students, raised funds, turned out publicity releases, and kept track of alumni. The school's "Demon Deacons" competed in sports then and now with the University of North Carolina, North Carolina State, and Duke, the state's Big Four colleges. Helms still likes to reminisce about his work under sports publicist "Dynamite" Holton. He added another few dollars a month as campus stringer (part-time correspondent) for both United Press and the *Raleigh Times.*

Helms estimates now that "I washed every dish at Wake Forest a hundred times" during those frugal months. But the job that excited him was downtown, in the *News & Observer*'s office near the Capitol. There, reading proofs for fifty cents an hour, he got his first vicarious feel of power on the state's most influential newspaper. It was so appealing to him that when he was offered more direct involvement in it, he decided he did not need to complete college. He moved out of the proof room to take a job in the three-man sports department. Soon he took another step toward the center of things. He switched from sports to city-side reporting, under city editor Herb O'Keef. He was making about twenty-five dollars a week then, and his editors acknowledged his talent. He won a first-place reporting award from the North Carolina Press Association.

Politics was the lifeblood of the *News & Observer,* then as now. The paper was a loyal Democratic organ: Josephus Daniels, its owner and editor, was Woodrow Wilson's secretary of the navy (and thus Franklin Roosevelt's boss during World War I) and later FDR's ambassador to Mexico. Josephus's son Jonathan, who succeeded him at the paper, was a World War II assistant to Roosevelt, then briefly Harry Truman's press secretary and later his biographer. For its time and place, the *N & O* of the forties was liberal. But Helms's friends say that in those days, he was not yet the political animal he would become. He was assumed to be a standard southern Democrat, which meant he was not as attuned to Roosevelt policies as his employer. But mainly he was known as a hard-working, competitive reporter, easy to talk to and joke with. His roommate, Ed Rankin, remembers him as a clean-living Baptist who only once in a while shared a beer with him. In fact, Helms carried with him years later a tale about how firewater got some of his fellow workers in trouble with the owner, old Josephus Daniels, "a gentleman who really hated liquor." Helms looked back on his early newspaper days as the first time "I saw folks really drink liquor." There was a proofreader, "a very fine old gentleman," who could put away a fifth of gin a night, and the managing editor and sports editor "were no pikers, either," though they waited till after the presses rolled. One Sunday morning about three o'clock, Helms remembered, the paper was put to bed and a few staffers were on their knees shooting dice in the advertising department. The sports editor had just taken a slug and was ready to roll when he saw two black shoes appear next to him. He looked up to see old Josephus, just off the late train from Mexico, where he was FDR's ambassador. The sports editor had to absorb a lecture as the price of keeping his job—and, Helms said, "I do believe that was the end of the dice games at the *News & Observer.*" He recounted the incident as if it had a moral.

Helms was not socially adventurous then. But he did make friends at the water cooler with an attractive University of North Carolina graduate named Dorothy Coble. She edited the women's section, and liked to kid herself by describing her job as "cutting the trains off the brides' dresses" in laying out the Sunday society pages. She promptly became Helms's best girl, the only one who figures noticeably in his entire biography.

Helms soon caught the eye of John A. Park, who ran the rival *Raleigh Times,* the more conservative afternoon newspaper. Park offered the twenty-year-old Helms a job as assistant city editor. Helms says, "I guess I'm the only guy that ever left the *News & Observer* to take a job at the *Times"*—because the *Times* was smaller and less influential.

Pearl Harbor came while Helms was in that new slot, and after he was turned down by the army because of a hearing deficiency, he was accepted for limited duty in the navy. He and a young Statesville newspaperman named Harry Gatton were sworn in in March, 1942. They took the train together to boot camp in San Diego. Gatton remembers that it was their first time aboard a luxury train, the Sunset Limited, and Helms was so impressed by the shower, the barber shop, and other first-class accommodations that he got the idea navy life might make a nice career. Then they arrived at San Diego about 1:30 in the morning, and the reality of boot camp set in. The navy then "was desperate for people with public relations talent," Gatton says, so he and Helms were picked to go to recruiter school after boot camp. They were assigned back to North Carolina after recruiter school.

Helms and Dorothy Coble got married that October, two weeks after his twenty-first birthday, and except for a brief stay in Georgia, he spent the rest of the war in his home state. It was the most routine wartime experience anyone could imagine, but in it Helms discovered his future.

One of the courses at San Diego was public speaking, to equip recruiters to describe the glories of navy life to civic clubs, high schools, and radio audiences. On the job, Helms and others in his specialty spent much of their time signing up would-be sailors and writing press releases about their enlistments and promotions. Helms also has said that the navy "lend-leased me" for intelligence duty, an assignment that he has never elaborated. But the part that inspired him was broadcasting.

"I went on the radio and interviewed all over the state. The more I did that, the more I was fascinated by radio," he says. And he was good at it. The microphone gave him the voice he had never had in sports or at school, not even at his typewriter in the newsroom. He had found his instrument.

Out of uniform in 1945, he hurried back to the *Raleigh Times,* and a more senior job as twenty-four-year-old city editor. But he was restless in the city room. "It occurred to me that radio had a lot of potential as a local news medium," he recalls. Up till then, radio had not given much attention to local news. There were famous commentators, and there were a few five-minute news summaries during the broadcast day. But there was no serious effort to put radio's immediacy to work in newsrooms. Helms thought about this as he plugged away at the city desk of the *Times*. Eventually he contacted a friend who owned radio station WCBT in Roanoke Rapids, a cotton-mill town near the Virginia border northeast of Raleigh. "I knew nothing about radio, but I went down there and sort of managed that radio station and changed it to a news medium—and like Topsy, things grew." He tried being a disk jockey, but jive talk was not his strong point. He started using recorded conversations with local newsmakers. He stayed there barely two years, but he learned the rudiments of broadcasting. As 1948 began, he took them back to Raleigh, where the skinny kid from Monroe would soon have a voice to notice.

WRAL, a newly opened 250-watt station in Raleigh, was owned by a forceful conservative from the Carolina mountains named A.J. Fletcher. In time, Fletcher would become "like a second father" in Helms's words, and give him the platform from which he leaped to national prominence. Fletcher hired young Helms as his news director, and gave him loose rein. Long before it became a common sight, Jesse was one of those broadcast newsmen who shows up at every press conference, every city council meeting, every two-alarm fire and three-car wreck, burdened by the equipment of his trade. Then, equipment was more of a burden than now. Jesse's was a wire recorder, which he says weighed sixty pounds. "That technology was a great thing," he recalls. "Everybody told us how they enjoyed hearing the governor himself say something, instead of just being quoted." As for television, "as a boy I never thought it would work. It was like Frank Merriwell stuff to me."

He would remain an admirer of technology, and profit from it, for decades after. But in those postwar years, he was just beginning to see beyond technique to substance. The political virgin who had left Monroe started forming strong, vaguely intellectual opinions atop the standard southern beliefs of his home town and the typical skepticism of the newspaper city room. His first political mentor was his father-in-law, Jacob Coble, a Raleigh shoe wholesaler whom Helms calls "the original conservative," and a fan of such vaunted broadcast opinionators as H.V. Kaltenborn and Fulton Lewis, Jr. Lewis particularly was a venomous critic of Truman and liberalism. There also were examples for Helms there in Raleigh. One was W.E. Debnam, a former newspaperman who did radio commentary on WPTF, the bigger rival station to WRAL. His favorite target for years was Eleanor Roosevelt. Another influence was a young eccentric, a typewriter salesman and sometime radio commentator named Alvin Wingfield, Jr.

Wingfield's autobiographical entry in local newspaper files said he had been on the staff of Army General Lucius Clay during World War II. After V-E Day, it boasted, he had "made three unauthorized visits to the Soviet zone," where he was "twice arrested and once court-martialed" by the Russians. Wingfield said he "speaks Russian and German and subscribes to *Pravda*, a Russian newspaper published in Moscow." Later, some would call Wingfield a Don Quixote. He opposed city parking meters as unconstitutional. In the fifties he would run well back in a multi-candidate Senate primary. His platform included turning over schools and roads to private enterprise, and ending political parties. In 1960, he killed himself. But before all that, in the late forties, Wingfield was taken seriously, at least by Jesse Helms. He guided Helms to the political philosopher the senator often mentions among his early influences, the Austrian-born libertarian economist Ludwig von Mises. Helms himself later urged von Mises' *Human Action* on his friends.

As Helms was taking on this overlay of conservative ideology, North Carolina was making a postwar swing toward liberalism. In 1948, when then-Governor Strom Thurmond of nextdoor South Carolina ran for president as a Dixiecrat, standing beneath the banner of states' rights on a platform of racial separatism, he carried four Deep South states. But in North Carolina, he got less than 10 percent of the vote, running far behind Harry Truman. And as governor, a progressive dairy farmer named Kerr Scott was elected with backing from a coalition of farm and industrial workers. About this time, the political scientist V.O. Key, Jr., published his definitive study, *Southern Politics in State and Nation,* in which he cited North Carolina as a "progressive plutocracy" showing the way for the South. But almost immediately afterward, political chance disclosed the darker elements that still lay beneath that progressive surface.

Governor Scott had hardly begun his populist program when he made a bold decision that set up the bitter, polarizing intraparty battle of 1950. Newly elected Senator J. Melville Broughton died in March 1949, and the governor surprised the state by announcing his appointment of Frank Porter Graham to succeed him. The move was hailed by liberals across the country, but infuriated racial and economic conservatives. Their resentment of Frank Graham had been growing for years, as he ranged out from his base as president of the University of North Carolina, long the target of small-town anti-elitism in the state. Their reaction against Graham's appointment was an outpouring of pent-up anger against national trends and their surfacing in the South: liberal intellectualism, the rise of trade unions, the first threats to the old system of social and political segregation. The spearhead of that change was the university, and its personification was Frank Graham.

Jonathan Daniels, by some accounts the man who urged Governor Scott to appoint Graham, wrote an affectionate description of the university president in his autobiographical portrait of North Carolina, *Tar Heels.* He quoted Graham as saying that the state university system, cooperating with Duke, should become "one of the great intellectual and spiritual centers of the world."

In 1941, Daniels wrote that North Carolina was "the freest university in the South—as free as any in America—but neither it nor its president yet escapes the criticism of those who would put limits on its liberalism . . . 'I know Frank's no Communist but he's trying to protect too many crackpots in his faculty. He ought to get rid of them or get out himself,' a manufacturer said . . . He speaks here, attends a conference there, presides over the committee in another place. He is expected to lead the South as it congregates in black and white rows to discuss its welfare. He is chairman of the new organization which is going, so it is said, to balance the prosperity of the state . . . It is almost a part of the common law of liberal causes, North and South, that his name must be on the board of sponsors . . . Wherever he is, he is the man the reactionaries shoot at in North Carolina when they cry aloud that radicalism in the university is ruining the young . . . I think reactionaries hate him most . . . because he has armed revolt against complacency with patriotic respectability, which they seemed so long to hold in their own name. Calling him a Communist in North Carolina would be an enterprise like trying to prove that the Kremlin was the First Presbyterian Church . . . [His faults] are not important enough to keep him from being the single most important human force for enlightenment in the State."

Daniels's prewar assumptions about the preposterousness of calling Graham a Communist were outdated by the national postwar wave of red-baiting politics. Joe McCarthy, Dick Nixon, and the House Un-American Activities Committee were riding high. When Graham arrived in Washington, Ohio's Senator John W. Bricker tried and failed to block him from taking his seat because the Atomic Energy Commission's security review committee had pointed to Graham's left-wing associations and denied him access to nuclear secrets. And in North Carolina, the conservatives felt they had to do something about the outrageous fact that Frank Graham represented their state in Washington. However, their assumption that most Tarheel voters agreed with their resentment was yet unproven. The test came the following spring, when Graham ran for a full term.

For a while it seemed Graham would not be challenged. Then former Senator Robert Rice Reynolds, a flamboyant isolationist and old-style rebel campaigner nicknamed "Buncombe Bob," announced his candidacy. The state's conservative business establishment worried that with no more serious opposition than that, Graham would walk into a full six-year term. Thus, with its backing, a tall, dignified, blue-chip lawyer, Willis Smith, entered the primary.

Smith had been speaker of the North Carolina House nineteen years before, but that had been the limit of his early ambition in elective politics. He had risen instead as an uptown lawyer, eventually becoming the first president of the American Bar Association from his state. Unlike the small, soft-spoken Graham, Smith looked like a movie senator. His connections allowed him to tap into what little money it took to run a statewide campaign in those days. One of his friends was A.J. Fletcher, Helms's boss, who was an ardent supporter. Another was the ambitious young Helms himself, who had covered a Smith speech at an American Legion luncheon and dropped by later to talk further. When Smith was getting ready to run, Helms told him he would like to help "on my own time." It would turn out to be a significant offer.

Helms, in his unofficial role, had Fletcher's glad blessing to do all he could to see that Smith was nominated. Precisely what he did and did not do is still disputed. But he never disavowed any of it, and was constantly in and around the Smith headquarters. Two of the young men who were there officially became his lasting personal and political friends. One of them was Thomas F. Ellis, a lawyer who had grown up in California but settled in Raleigh after going to college in North Carolina. His nominal role in the Smith campaign was as a researcher. The other was a newspaperman named Hoover Adams. Another young lawyer, Pou Bailey, of a distinguished Carolina political family, also was on the Smith staff and became a close friend of Helms.

The tone of the Smith-Graham campaign was set immediately when Smith formally opened his race by proclaiming, "I do not now nor have I ever belonged to any subversive organizations, and as United States senator I shall never allow myself to be duped into the use of my name for propaganda or any other purposes by those types of organizations. The unwary can do just as much harm as the unscrupulous in the days that are at hand."

That was a restrained version of what Smith's backers put out on his behalf. Ads listed eighteen alleged Communist-front groups with which the Un-American Activities Committee said Graham was associated. Graham, who began by trying to discuss legislative issues, found himself traveling the state denying that he was a Communist. Inevitably, race also arose. Based on Ellis's research, the Smith side accused Graham of supporting a fair employment practices commission, theatening desegregation in the workplace, foreshadowing desegregation in the schools. As the primary approached in May, handbills appeared in rural areas bearing the photo of a handsome black youth named Leroy Jones, whom Graham had named as a second alternate appointee to West Point. It asserted that "no other southern senator or congressman has ever appointed a Negro to West Point." Graham had to defend his choice by explaining that it had been done strictly on the basis of a merit examination, and the first-place appointee was white. Other leaflets and advertisements in scattered county weeklies spread loaded questions and allegations.

Despite all that, when the votes were counted Graham won, defeating the second-place Smith by more than 53,000 votes. But he barely missed a majority, and so was vulnerable to a runoff challenge. Rather than announcing immediately, Smith waited, gathering commitments of support. For ten days, his intention was unclear. He got promises, including some important ones from out of state. But the most conspicuous push came from twenty-eight-year-old Jesse Helms.

Alvin Wingfield put him up to it. The right-wing eccentric phoned Helms at supper one night in early June and urged WRAL to promote a rally at Smith's home to inspire him to run again. Helms quickly got permission from the station. As he retells it, he dictated a commercial to be read by the announcer on duty. It said, "If you want Willis Smith to call for a second primary, right this minute, get in your car and go to Mr. Smith's home." At another point Helms has said he himself "went on the radio, telling folks that supporters ought to go out to his house and encourage him." Others' memory is that he not only exhorted listeners to rally there, he then acted as cheerleader on the scene as the crowd chanted, "We want Willis!"

They got him. And in the second primary, they got a meaner, broader anti-Graham offensive, one that clinched this campaign's distinction among historians as the rawest in the state's modern history. The themes of the first primary were repeated, but intensified. The communist questions and insinuations continued, but were overshadowed by more propaganda promoting racial fear. In this, Smith's Carolina organization had expert help from outside—from Florida, where a political newcomer named George Smathers had just defeated veteran New Deal Senator Claude Pepper in a primary that closely paralleled the Smith-Graham contest. There, the conservative faction led by Ed Ball, a Du Pont in-law who ran that family's interests in the South, financed the anti-Pepper effort. Ball hired a Jacksonville public relations man named Dan Crisp to build up an organization to tear Pepper down. In the campaign, it covered the state with material smearing the man who became known among his opponents as "Red Pepper." That was the primary in which Smathers gave a speech that remains famous in southern political folklore. In it he asked, "Are you aware that Claude Pepper is known all over Washington as a shameless extrovert? Not only that, but this man is reliably reported to practice nepotism with his sister-in-law, and he has a sister who was once a thespian in wicked New York. Worst of all, it is an established fact that Mr. Pepper, before his marriage, practiced celibacy." But there was no sense of humor in the Smith-Graham runoff. Seeing that Smith had failed where his man Smathers had succeeded, Ed Ball made Dan Crisp's expertise available to the conservative challenger in Carolina.

One Smith ad pictured the South Carolina legislature during Reconstruction, when many blacks had been elected, and implied that Graham's election would mean the same thing in Raleigh. One featured a photograph of blacks leaning against a car bearing a big Graham banner, allegedly outside a precinct in the first primary. Some Graham backers maintained that the car and its occupants were posed by the Smith camp. Another ad printed results of voting in the first primary in selected black precincts, showing Graham's lopsided margins there. "Did someone make a deal?" it asked. "Hasn't Dr. Graham raised the race issue? . . . With such mass and class voting, the individual voter must interest him and herself in the second primary, or else find the actual control of their party and state taken over by THIS GROUP. Can we forget so quickly THEIR REIGN not so many years ago? If carpet-bag rule returns it will be because you and I failed to work . . . Vote for Willis Smith and the Traditions of the South."

It and other ads used themes that would become familiar to those who followed Jesse Helms's own political career decades later: "Bloc voting by any group is a menace to democracy . . . Willis Smith represents all the people." Handbills reprinted alleged clippings from black newspapers linking Graham with advocates of "mixed marriages." One warned, "White people, WAKE UP before it's too late. You may not have another chance. Do you want Negroes working beside you, your wife and daughters in your mills and factories? . . . as your foremen and overseers in the mill? . . . using your toilet facilities? . . . Frank Graham favors mingling of the races . . . Do you favor this? . . . If you do, vote for Frank Graham. But if you don't, vote for and help elect WILLIS SMITH for SENATOR. He will uphold the traditions of the South." Signed, "Know the Truth Committee." And the most controversial handbill of the campaign was a photograph of Frank Graham's wife—smiling, perhaps even dancing, apparently alone with a black man.

It worked. The campaign had a massive impact in traditionally conservative, rural eastern Carolina and in the cotton-mill towns of the Piedmont. Smith won the runoff by not quite 20,000 votes. Graham quietly accepted defeat, and later was tapped by Harry Truman as defense manpower administrator.

And although that campaign created enmities some of which last to this day, it was quickly edited out of the public dialogue. The *News & Observer,* for example, had editorialized that Smith was playing with "political arson" by stirring up racial fears. But once he had won the runoff, he was the nominee of the Democratic party, and the newspaper, which calls itself the "Old Reliable," reliably endorsed him and sent a reporter to do a friendly profile of him. It was only much later, when some of the backstage participants in that campaign rose to prominence and became involved in political controversies of their own, that journalists and historians started looking back more closely at the 1950 primary.

What had happened was spread copiously on the record. What was unclear was who had been responsible for it. Reporters questioned everyone they could find who had worked in the Smith campaign. Their main interest was in just what Jesse Helms had done in that meanest Senate fight in Carolina history. And the responses from men of demonstrated intellect, students of politics, men for whom the Smith-Graham election had been their first important public experience, disclosed a disconcerting variety of memory.

Hoover Adams, the Smith campaign press secretary, now runs a devotedly right-wing newspaper in Dunn, North Carolina. He has maintained that Smith got so angry at tactics used against Graham that he threatened to fire his staff and withdraw from the campaign if any of his people were involved. "That stuff about [Smith's] being a racist was wrong, but with a hundred organizations around the state, you couldn't control them all. But there's no question it helped his campaign," Adams conceded. As for Helms's role, Adams told a reporter, "Dammit, Jesse didn't have a thing to do with the campaign."

Tom Ellis, who became Helms's political right-hand man, running his campaigns and his huge fund-raising operations, conceded that he "guessed" there had been dirty tricks in the campaign. "But I don't really see it as being dirty tricks. We researched Dr. Graham's record and that information went to the managers. I reckon they'd make up ads with it. We weren't in charge of anything . . . I was a kid. Nobody paid any attention to me."

To mention the controversy to Ellis today sets off a long, detailed protest that includes denials of things Helms has never been charged with doing. Ellis asserted to me that the whole thing was "hearsay" from "very liberal activists, partisans." He asked why, if Helms was involved, there was nothing about him in the papers at the time. He said Helms was "pure and simple, the one-man news department" of a minor radio station, covering both candidates. Smith was a distinguished man surrounded by senior lawyers, bankers, textile executives, and experienced politicians, Ellis said—"Is he going to have some guy twenty-eight years old, a news reporter for a 50-watt station, running his campaign, telling him what to do?" He called the story "trash and just baloney . . . If a lie is repeated often enough, it takes on its own life."

But of course, Helms has never been accused of running the Smith campaign, only of behind-scenes involvement. As to that, Ellis said to me, "They talk about this doctored photograph of Frank Graham dancing with a black woman." He said anyone writing about it should demand that the newspapers produce a copy of it. "I never saw it," Ellis insists. "If there was any such animal, I never saw it, and I don't believe there was. And if there was, Jesse Helms certainly had nothing to do with it, in my opinion." Again, perhaps accidentally, Ellis was more or less denying something nobody had alleged. The handbill in question did not portray Graham with a black woman, but Mrs. Graham with a black man, and it is clearly remembered by a series of Carolinians with whom I have spoken.

The wording of Helms's own denials has varied. Once he said the "implication" of his involvement had been "picked up and circulated, by whom I don't know." The dirty tricks have been exaggerated, he maintained. "I had no connection with the Smith campaign. I strongly supported Mr. Smith, but I in no way participated in the campaign." Again, he has said he attended strategy sessions and did some writing, but wrote no advertisements. "My connection with the Willis Smith campaign was largely as a supporter and a friend of Mr. Smith," he told the *News & Observer.* "It would be inappropriate to say I had any real connection with the campaign, certainly no formal connection." To yet another reporter, he asserted, "I was strong for Willis Smith, but I never once drew an advertisement for Willis Smith."

Pou Bailey, now a retired judge in Raleigh, has been a personal friend of Helms for almost forty years, but is more outspoken than those who have tied themselves politically directly to the senator. Helms was in the Smith campaign "up to his neck," the judge told me. "He had no official position, but I don't think there was any substantive publicity that he didn't see and advise on. He was deeply involved." Earlier, Bailey had told reporters that Helms wrote news releases and helped with ads. "He contributed to practically every ad that was run, but I don't think you could say he wrote any of them. Before we got through, it was a committee effort." A.J. Fletcher's approval of Helms's role was necessary, of course. "It was sort of like lending his best writer to the campaign," Bailey said.

Dan Crisp, who is still in public relations in Florida, told me his own role in the campaign was at arm's length. "I wasn't on the scene," he recalls, but "we sent them a supply of materials we had used for George Smathers—speeches, radio programs, things typed up. We gave them background material . . . During that campaign we shipped some materials directly to him [Helms]. I don't think we talked directly on the phone, it was somebody else asked me to do the shipping. But it was directly to Jess, is my memory."

The most fascinating recollection I found, because of its first-hand description, came from the late R.H. Carson, the seventy-six-year-old retired advertising manager of the *News & Observer.* Carson had occasionally told others of how the Smith campaign's publicity staff came in to do business with his department at the paper. The first time I talked with him, he spoke freely. When I called back again to confirm the quotations, he asked me not to use his name; once before after he had said something about it, his tax returns had been audited, he told me, and at his age he did not want to stir anything up. He corroborated the quotations, and I agreed reluctantly not to use his name. Since then, our agreement has been mooted—Carson died in the spring of 1986.

"During the campaign I remember Hoover Adams bringing copy in. I'd wait on him at the front counter," Carson told me. "They were anti-Graham ads, seldom as much as a full page. Our policy was cash with order for all political ads.

"Adams sometimes was accompanied by Jesse Helms. Jesse and I were on a first-name basis . . . I knew him when he wrote sports, high school games and so on . . . Often Jesse would alter copy right at the counter. It was never really very professional copy. Jesse would alter it, and one day I loaned him my scissors and he took and outlined around the figure of Mrs. Graham with a Negro . . . He cut out two or three others in the picture.

"I was figuring out how much this was going to cost, four hundred or five hundred dollars maybe. We didn't run that ad in the *N & O.* We set a lot of ads and made mats, sometimes fifty or sixty of them, for them to send to local papers around the state or whatever . . ."

This is not, of course, the version that Helms and his friends have been putting out since the subject arose again during his later campaigns. The outspoken Pou Bailey, for example, who claims to know more about the origin of the doctored photograph than he is willing to tell, is very skeptical of the Carson account. Not only does he doubt that Helms would have done anything so improper, but he adds with a chuckle that Helms did not have the manual dexterity to wield a pair of scissors that skillfully.

Helms himself told me that "Anybody who says he or she knows I had anything to do with that doesn't know what he's talking about . . . I never saw that doctored photo till after the fact, when they started bringing it up." Retelling how he had been offered and regretfully rejected a job with the Graham campaign, Helms said, "I think it's fair to assume that not only did I not have anything to do with such a photo, but I would have repudiated it on the air." In that conversation, he maintained that his only connection with the Smith campaign was that he sat in on some staff meetings at the candidate's invitation. The senator also said he did not recall the name of Florida public relations man Dan Crisp. For confirmation of his denials, he referred me back to his old friend Hoover Adams. Adams was unequivocal, insisting that Helms "had absolutely nothing to do with" the Smith campaign. He also said again that Smith himself "never injected the issue of communism or racism in the campaign," and, when he found out about it, threatened to fire anyone who had been party to it.

That Democratic primary was tantamount to election, as the papers used to say about most southern political contests. After that November, Graham courteously resigned his seat early, allowing Smith to be sworn in ahead of other new senators, thus gaining a few days of seniority. In March, Helms joined him in Washington, as his administrative assistant—the top job on Smith's senatorial staff. It paid substantially more than what Helms had been making at WRAL.

And it broadened his horizons to the national scene.

Chapter 5

Climbing
onto the Platform

Helms occasionally says he went "reluctantly" to Washington. At other times he makes it sound like a dream fulfilled, remembering his first spring there as "splendid days . . . something mystical, like elves dancing on the lawn."

He settled eagerly into Willis Smith's suite 345 in the old Senate Office Building, now called the Russell Building. Next door on one side was North Carolina's senior senator, that courtly, wing-collared caricature of a nineteenth-century southern Democrat, Clyde R. Hoey. On the other was freshman Republican Richard M. Nixon of California, sworn in four days after Willis Smith. Around the corner was "Mr. Republican," Robert A. Taft of Ohio.

These men were national figures, and to meet them was inspirational for a young fellow barely a decade out of Monroe, North Carolina. Freshmen Nixon and Smith especially had a lot in common, and saw a lot of each other. Both were graduates, though twenty-five years apart, of Duke University Law School. Both were devoted anti-communists—ex-Congressman Nixon had slugged his way into the House in a campaign that smeared incumbent Jerry Voorhis for having links with Moscow. Then he had distinguished himself as a principal assailant of Alger Hiss before the House Un-American Activities Committee. And both Nixon and Smith had won their Senate seats the same way: both had consciously patterned their campaigns on the red-baiting offensive by which George Smathers beat Claude Pepper in Florida the previous spring. Where the Smathers campaign had spread the nickname "Red Pepper" for the liberal senator, Nixon's people passed around the nickname "Pink Lady" for the liberal Representative Helen Gahagan Douglas.

Helms remembered that when he worked to midnight and beyond, the typewriters in Nixon's neighboring office would still be clacking.

The older senators said, "Watch Dick Nixon—you'll hear from him as time goes by." Helms admired the way Nixon stood up to attacks as "a target of the left-wing crowd from the very beginning of his political career."

Nixon "refused to submit to the notion that reliable friends could be made of communists, or that communism would mellow, or that it was wise national policy for America to ignore the storm signals of a developing worldwide conspiracy of tyranny and oppression," Helms recalled. "While Nixon was recklessly portrayed as a smear artist, Hubert Humphrey was constantly praised as a humanitarian," Helms said resentfully, years later when Nixon and Humphrey were running against each other for the White House.

Jesse and Dot Helms lived in the modest southeastern reaches of Washington, beyond Capitol Hill. He worked long hours, having with Smith's blessing "a much broader cloak than most administrative assistants have." Helms managed the staff, and is remembered as a considerate boss. He helped with speechwriting—although Smith dictated many of his speeches directly to a secretary, they usually passed beneath Helms's pencil before they were in final form. Jesse also dealt with the press, drawing on his experience in the city room back home for the casual banter that went over well in the press gallery above the Senate floor. And now and then he substituted for the senator in escorting V.I.P. visitors around the Capitol. One of them was North Carolina's own Billy Graham, already a big name in broadcasting the Gospel. "A prince of a fellow," Helms judged.

Willis Smith did not have great oratorical flair, or take conspicuous leadership on the floor or in committee. But he had easy entree among the Senate elders, with his long legal reputation and his stint as president of the American Bar Association. Beyond service to the special interests of North Carolina, Smith's main preoccupation was immigration. The one ringing Smith statement remembered by some ex-aides is, "America is not a dumping ground!"

Helms did little socializing. His friends remember him then as an absolute teetotaler—"I'm dumb enough without it," he would say later—but not a "goody two-shoes." Smith was a model of deportment for him. Helms credited his father first for the fact that he himself didn't even cuss, at least not often, preferring to say "doodle" instead of "damn." And in all the time he knew Smith, he recalled, the senator never said "damn" more than two or three times. Smith also passed up the party circuit that could keep a fun-loving senator busy every evening. Yet interestingly, perhaps out of shared political background, his close friends included his fellow beneficiary of cut-and-thrust campaign tactics, George Smathers, who had North Carolina family ties and was one of the most free-swinging partygoers in Senate history.

Of all the senatorial influences on Helms, however, the one who had the most impact was the leader of southern Democrats, perhaps the most powerful single person in the Senate, Richard B. Russell of Georgia. For almost forty years, the crusty Russell was at the center of resistance to anything that vaguely resembled civil rights legislation. Head back, looking down his nose through his spectacles, he brought down his wrath on legislators and presidents who dared encroach on the cherished principle of "states' rights." He devised the South's parliamentary tactics, and he alone had the stature to cut deals and start or finish filibusters that would carry most of his regional colleagues along.

Smith, abiding by the senate tradition of respecting one's elders, turned to Russell for advice. Helms looked over his shoulder, studying Russell's tactics and philosophy. In time, the Georgian developed "a lot of confidence in Jesse," Helms's friends remembered. In the summer of 1952, Russell borrowed Helms for what could have been a nationally important job, if a lot of things had been different. Helms (like Harry Truman) believed Russell would have become president —if he were not from the South. That big "if" was proven that summer, just after the Republicans had nominated Dwight Eisenhower. Russell went to Chicago seeking the Democratic nomination, and took Helms along to handle his campaign's television and radio arrangements.

Everybody's first national convention is a memorable adventure. Helms remembered a lot about that miserably hot summer in the Chicago Stockyards, the fragrant arena where Chicago conventions were held until the sixties. For one thing, Jesse laughed later about encountering Billy Graham again at the Saddle and Sirloin Club. Well known as Graham was then, television had not yet made his a household name. Graham spotted Helms, and Helms put forth his hand, but the best he could come out with was, "Damned if I'm not glad to see you!" Just then Senator Smith walked up, and before Jesse could prompt him with Graham's name put out his hand and shouted senatorially, "I'll be damned, look who's here!" When

Helms recounted it later, he said, "Billy Graham must have thought Senator Smith's crowd had damnation on the brain . . . I shudder every time I think of it." He seemed at least half serious.

His concern, however, was getting Russell nominated—or, at least, making his message heard. In fact, the Georgian never had a real chance. But he was in the thick of a North-South struggle that began as a carryover from Strom Thurmond's Dixiecrat bolt from the national ticket in 1948. The issue was a party loyalty pledge, which three southern states—Louisiana, South Carolina, and Virginia—refused to accept. That provoked a showdown over their seating, and North Carolina stood solid with the rest of the South in supporting them. Eventually the South prevailed. But then came the choosing of a presidential candidate. Eleven names were placed in nomination on the first ballot. Estes Kefauver of Tennessee ran first, the reluctant Adlai Stevenson of Illinois second, and Russell only five votes behind in third place. After New York and Massachusetts pulled out their favorite sons, Stevenson collected a majority on the third roll call. Russell had started and finished in third place, peaking on the second ballot with 294 of the convention's 1,230 delegates. Then Stevenson picked a less prickly, more progressive southerner, Alabama's Senator John Sparkman, as his running mate. The outcome may have been more disappointing to a young first-timer like Helms than to veterans of convention politics. But even at that, he had heard some rousing oratory, and left with that familiar southern feeling of having fought the good fight, even while losing. Old Major Heath, rocking on his porch in Monroe and reminiscing about Sharpsburg and Chancellorsville, would have commiserated with him.

Dick Russell, Helms recalled, "made men think." He viewed America with "perhaps impossible idealism," where every man could earn respect "on the basis of purely personal traits . . . effort, attitude, responsibility, and achievement . . . He rejected absolutely the kind of politics that preaches that the world *owes* anybody anything." Any experienced listener recognized this as polite euphemism for supporting segregation and opposing public welfare, but Helms then as later found it praiseworthy. Aside from Russell's being from the South, the other personal asset that was a liability to his presidential aspirations was that "he would not consent to compromise with, let alone be controlled by, the political manipulators." Helms liked that, commented on it when Russell died almost nineteen years after that convention, and emulated it when his own time came.

After that adventure, the novelty of running a Senate office did not seem as exciting. Then, in mid-1953, after Smith's sudden death, State Senator Alton Lennon was appointed to replace him. Helms stayed on while Lennon got settled, but he did not have the same personal ties with the interim senator as he had had with Smith. He began looking toward home. Late that year he was told of a forthcoming opening as executive director of the North Carolina Bankers Association. It promised a settled life, prestigious and possibly lucrative connections—and, the way Helms negotiated it, a chance to publish his opinions first-hand, rather than through the politician who employed him. His friend Pou Bailey was counsel to the bankers association. So Helms got the job, and returned to Raleigh. Back home he joined the Rotary Club and started attending Masonic meetings, eventually becoming a 32-degree Mason. He got in more time with his growing daughters. The long work nights endemic in senators' offices became a thing of the past.

The job with the bankers group historically had been typical trade association work—conventions, public relations, lobbying. Helms did all that. One who knew him then said, "North Carolina became a very wealthy banking state with his help. Some of the largest banks in the South grew to mammoth size because he was able to get laws passed liberalizing banking practices . . . All in all, Jesse Helms was a very successful lobbyist. Most people liked him even if they didn't see eye to eye with his positions."

But the role that Jesse enlarged and built upon was editing the association's monthly magazine, the *Tarheel Banker*. It had been a pedestrian house organ, gray with personnel notices and industry news. Helms turned it into his own platform for personal, highly opinionated journalism. Amid the routine tidings of promotions and transfers, he published an editorial page that jumped squarely and controversially into the social and political issues of the day. And opposite the editorials, he began a full-page column entitled simply, "By Jesse Helms."

At that point he began to lay down the immense, documented public record that is both a blessing and a curse for anyone reconstructing his career. In more than three decades since he started as the bankers' man in Raleigh, Helms has become sophisticated in political technology and branched into new regions of world interest. But the foundation of values from which he preaches today was there when he began signing his opinions in his early thirties. There also were occasional signs that he already was imagining his own role in elective politics, at some level, some day.

Helms's first column was about his friend Pou Bailey, who became a North Carolina Superior Court judge but then was practicing law and serving as counsel to the bankers. Jesse wrote about Pou's poker club, meeting for steak supper at a cabin outside Raleigh. He clearly was glad to be included in that informal branch of the capital's establishment, and let people know he had arrived there. He was at last one of the boys, although through the years he would remain unusual among them for his abstinence and difficulty maintaining a poker face.

Most of the time, he used his personal column for chit-chat and nostalgia. His editorials, although they nominally were the voice of the dignified bankers association, were as pungent and often angry as if they spoke for him alone. In his rambling signed pieces he told tales he had heard around town, many of them racially slanted and condescending—not uncommon fare in the South in the fifties, but not usually published in the house organs of the banking industry, either. He often mentioned somebody's chauffeur, referring to him as "the boy," and once told a story about a friend's maid, Mary, who went to Morehead City and on seeing the ocean for the first time exclaimed, "Lawdy, Mr. Smith, it sho' is one-sided!" Like dozens of other such stories, it was intended as humor, and most of Helms's readers probably considered it harmless.

There was a harder edge to his first printed comment on the wave of desegregation litigation that followed the Supreme Court's school decision in 1954. The following year, under a plan drawn up by a commission advised by Helms's friend Tom Ellis, North Carolina joined other southern states in threats to close public schools rather than desegregate. Helms wrote, "Sooner or later, America will learn that there is nothing sacred about a public school system as such. There is the private enterprise way—with private enterprise as the keystone in education, political sociologists would forever be unable to dictate terms and procedures to the people of America regarding their schools.

"Unless our Negro citizens submit more easily than we predict they will, North Carolina does not have the simple choice between

segregated schools and integrated schools. Our only choice is between integrated public schools and free-choice private schools
. . . The decision will have been made by a very small minority of
people who are hell-bent on forced integration."

That premonitory protest was not in isolation; people and politicians were saying things like it all over the South. But appearing
under the masthead of the *Tarheel Banker* gave it the imprimatur
of the bankers themselves. This was not taken lightly in a capital torn
by how to respond to the long-overdue orders of the federal courts.
There was a flurry of reaction, and in firing back Helms characteris-
tically singled out his old employer, the paper that had given him his
start in Raleigh, the *News & Observer*. That paper became the first,
longest-lasting target in Helms's obsessive war against "the major
media." "The *News & Observer* (as frankly we had expected) frothed
at the mouth" against the editorial, Helms wrote. "We can't see why
our editorial upset the newspaper boys so much," because they
should face the fact that continuing public schools inevitably means
integrated schools in North Carolina.

When the paper was disrespectful toward the banking industry,
Helms's response was more indignant. "It is a shame," he wrote,
"that the Capital City of our State does not have a newspaper whose
reliability and integrity are respected by our legislators . . ." He
asserted that for a generation, the bankers had been receiving venom
from the *News & Observer*. He wondered about "the character of any
editor who is unwilling to trust his readers with the unprejudiced
truth."

By the time Helms had been with the bankers association for two or
three years, making influential contacts and speaking up boldly for
the state's established interests, he felt comfortable enough to build
a new home. It was a brick bungalow on Caswell Street in the
comfortable middle- to upper-class Hayes Barton neighborhood.
Next door lived Dot's father, by then widowed, and being there gave
Helms even more chance to talk politics with that "original conservative."

To build the house, he contracted with a Swedish-born businessman named John Danielson, who served on Raleigh's city council.
Helms admired Danielson, he said later, because he stood against
compromises of principle—"he had built his life on absolutes; things
to him were either right, or they were wrong. Religion to him was

based on pure faith, free of squirming interpretations, or it was meaningless." Danielson was a prominent builder, and, as Helms said, he normally did not bother doing "tiny little things like my house." When the job was done, Helms thanked him, and Danielson replied, "Now I want you to do something for me." What was it? Run for the city council yourself, Danielson said. Helms told him, "For goodness' sake, I don't want to be on the council." But it wasn't a very convincing protest. As he told of his council decision later, he found out the filing fee was only two dollars, "and I knew I wouldn't be elected, so I decided to put up the two dollars. Didn't campaign, and lucked out and got elected . . . If I didn't tell the truth, hope to die. That's exactly what happened."

From the day in 1957 when he was sworn in on the city council, Helms rocked the boat. He was one of seven members, elected at large; until just after his service, that at-large system dispersed the black vote and kept the council all white. Despite the fact that he was outnumbered consistently, Helms spoke up and voted against almost every expansion of the city's power and budget, occasionally dressing down the mayor himself. Paul Hoover, an insurance man who served with him, recalls that Helms "stood up for those people who were against anything the city was doing—whether it was eminent domain, taxes, or whatever." Hoover remembers an angry annexation debate, after which one of the losers stood up and said, "My lifelong friend turned out to be a communist. In fact, you're all communists!" Then he leaned over to Jesse and murmured, "You know we're not talking about you, Mr. Helms."

A city official of the time says Helms's attitude was consistently one of, "Who the hell's going to pay for it, why should we do it and put it on the taxpayers?" He was "a tax miser in terms of the public good, quality-of-life questions. He was pretty much a loner on the council." Helms, who became chairman of the law and finance committee, fought establishment of a badly needed urban renewal program. Echoing his mentor Alvin Wingfield's stand against parking meters, he asserted that it is unconstitutional for government to condemn and buy private property for slum clearance. He added that he was against "intrusion by government at any level into the private lives of citizens." Practicing a technique he would perfect in the future, he held up the reappointment of planning commission and school board members until he either got his own choice or extracted promises from the nominees.

Hoover remembers Helms as "a pretty pleasant sort of fellow personally, but not like Ronald Reagan. You wouldn't have said on meeting Jesse, 'This fellow's going to go somewhere.' "

But Jesse was indeed going somewhere, and to help himself along he set a pattern of mixing politics with his other interests in a way that is particularly fascinating to those bludgeoned by his later long-running offensive against "the media." As he continued his job as the bankers' publicist, he became the star nay-sayer on the council, and neither of these roles restrained him from his angry sorties into national and state political issues.

Over and over, that anger was focused on the federal effort to carry out court rulings on racial segregation, which he and other editorialists liked to convert into another Yankee war on their beloved South. Defending segregation had always seemed much more heroic standing beneath the Stars and Bars, while the band played "Dixie." Helms also drew on his 1950 political experience and foreshadowed things to come when he consistently connected desegregation efforts with communism.

During Arkansas Governor Orval Faubus's confrontation with federal troops when the courts ordered desegregation of Little Rock's Central High School in 1957, Helms wrote, "What is happening in America is exactly in tune with the forecasts of Karl Marx . . . The cackles you hear have a Russian accent . . ."

Asserting that many more "race riots" and other such troubles occur in the North, he declared, "These slanders upon the South, these assaults upon the Constitutional sovereignty of the States, this pious sweeping around the other fellow's doorstep should cease . . ."

Helms also spoke out against the black student sit-ins attempting to desegregate luncheon counters in downtown Raleigh. And when Martin Luther King, Jr., the young Georgia preacher who had led the Montgomery bus boycott, came to make his first speech in Raleigh in early 1958, Helms made sure there was controversy.

On the stationery of the North Carolina Bankers Association, city councilman Helms wrote a letter to the city manager, saying he had heard many "expressions of resentment" about the speakers scheduled in a local lecture series. They included King, Senator Hubert Humphrey, and labor leader Victor Reuther. Helms urged special police preparations for possible "physical demonstrations" of protest. Any such incident would be "a blot on the good name of

Raleigh," he said. He got in a dig at the lecture series itself, called the Institute of Religion. The forum "appears to be more political than religious," he said—but added that of course he endorsed its right to free expression.

Such a letter, delivered quietly, might have been considered in the line of duty for a city councilman. But Helms's letter was released to the press. The flap that followed ran a familiar course, with the *News & Observer* editorializing that the letter "was obviously an effort to stir up trouble where none existed." When King came, spoke, and departed without notable incident, Helms's concerns were proven unnecessary. But he had enjoyed a surge of publicity— and the following year, he was elected to his second two-year term on the council.

One of those who admired Helms's strong opinionating most was his old friend and patron, A.J. Fletcher, the radio station proprietor who had encouraged him to help get Willis Smith elected to the Senate. Fletcher had been involved behind one or another candidate in every gubernatorial election since he came to Raleigh in 1919. His son called him "an out-Democrat, a conservative" who never wavered.

In the late fifties, Fletcher took a step that was a major factor in his own enrichment, in the polarization of North Carolina politics, and in the rise of Jesse Helms to national notice. His WRAL got the first television license for Raleigh. That made Fletcher and the station still more interesting to Helms, who had never given up his belief that broadcasting—originally radio, but now TV, too—was the medium of the future.

When he told an anecdote about the seventy-year-old Fletcher in his *Tarheel Banker* column, Helms expanded it into a rich tribute to the broadcasting entrepreneur. It was so flattering it smacked of an indirect job application. Fletcher, Helms wrote, was one of the state's top citizens, though unheralded. He had done more for the state, and gotten less credit for it, than anybody Helms could think of.

More objective impressions of A. J. Fletcher recall that he also was a lawyer, religious layman, and philanthropist—and a very sharp man in a business transaction. One of his beneficiaries said he could quote Shakespeare by the hour, knew the Latin names for all the plants around him, and had a keen sense of humor. One of fourteen children, he came out of the Carolina mountains where his father had been a horseback evangelist for more than half a century. He went to Wake Forest, and later set up a professorship of missions at the Southeastern Baptist Theological Seminary there in honor of his parents. He considered his charities and even his interest in plants an extension of his father's missionary effort. And that missionary zeal applied especially to his politics, which were farther right than those of the conservative candidates he invariably supported.

All of that made him a man to be courted by Jesse Helms, even while Helms continued at the bankers' association. Helms's work with the bankers, his unremitting dabbling in politics, and his ambition for a broadcasting career came to an overdue, probably inevitable collision in the late spring of 1960. In that year's gubernatorial race, the two leaders among four candidates were I. Beverly Lake, a law professor who ten years earlier had been on the other side in the Smith-Graham confrontation, and Terry Sanford, an associate of liberal past-governor Kerr Scott. The emergence of desegregation as the issue of the fifties had pushed Lake rightward. He was against it, while Sanford, a Fayetteville lawyer, was for moving forward. As historian H.G. Jones has written, Sanford asserted that for the state to be first in the South was not enough: "I want North Carolina to move into the mainstream of America." That political shorthand was well understood by the voters. "The mainstream of America" was a place where state officials upheld federal laws. Beyond that, Sanford came out for John F. Kennedy for the presidential nomination. In Carolina's 1960 gubernatorial primary, the issues were clearly drawn, and the four-way primary was so strongly contested that it produced a runoff between Lake and Sanford.

But before it got that far, Helms's brand of journalistic objectivity had put him into new controversy. As he told it, that was the first major election in his adult life in which he had not taken a position. All four of the candidates were his friends, he maintained. It made him uncomfortable. Then, the day of the first primary, WRAL-TV —A.J. Fletcher's station, his own old home base—called to ask if he would help its thinly stretched news staff cover the voting. The executive director of the North Carolina Bankers Association gladly agreed to stick his toe into television journalism.

"Well, I did," Helms recalled shortly afterward. "I tried to be objective. The noise [at the Lake headquarters election night] was terrific . . . I shouted and I screamed, trying to tell the television audience what was going on. Not only could I not hear what I was saying, I couldn't even feel any words coming out." Many listeners did, however. They heard what he said, and felt he was strongly enthusiastic about I. Beverly Lake. Next morning at Sunday school, Helms found people had been making bets on whether he would show up. Monday morning at work, there were unhappy letters calling him names. Sanford's home-town paper contended that Helms, when he couldn't hear his own voice, had made a campaign speech for Lake. Then the president of the bankers' association called to ask what another banker had meant when he inquired whether the association had taken an official position on the campaign. Terry Sanford himself had questions, too.

Helms was angry. He advised those reading his *Tarheel Banker* column that "if you're going to be neutral in a political campaign, be sure to practice your neutrality in your own living room, not before television cameras in a candidate's headquarters. Objective courtesy to the candidate turns out to be partisan support when viewed by supporters of the other candidate." And to sum up his frustration, Helms closed this account of his problems with objectivity by declaring, "In words of one syllable, *I've had it!*"

The italics were his own, and his emphasis on those words was not accidental. Two months later, A.J. Fletcher's son Fred, general manager of Capital Broadcasting Company, announced that Helms would join the WRAL staff as news director of both the radio and television stations.

Looking back on the decision to move, Helms implies there was some uncertainty about it, and that it all came together because Fletcher was pursuing him, although at the very least it was a mutual idea. Fletcher had "mentioned to me about coming out and helping him run his TV station," Helms said, so finally he and his wife Dot talked it over. He was keenly aware that very few TV outlets in the country were running regular broadcast editorials. Forthright opinion was by then common in North Carolina radio, but not yet on television. Helms says he told Fletcher he would be interested in the news director's job if he could do "free enterprise" editorials. That was not a new thought to either of them; more than two years earlier, Helms had recorded in the *Tarheel Banker* his belief that Fletcher wanted his new franchise not merely to be a television station, but "a voice that would speak loud and strong for free enterprise." He noted also that Fletcher was "not the strongest admirer in the world of the Raleigh press, which he feels gives only one side of the news in so many instances."

Helms got a title and pay to justify his leaving the bankers association. More important, he got a platform from which he could legitimately lay out the strong opinions that had been damming up inside him. And A.J. Fletcher got the instrument through which he would see his own hard-right thinking crystallized and laid before the Carolina public.

The fact that Helms was still a member of the city council was no obstacle at all to their plan. He had been a voice for free enterprise as spokesman for the bankers; he was merely moving to a new lectern. From it, he and Fletcher could see far beyond the broad fan of North Carolina to which their station's primary signal was beamed.

Chapter 6

Horatio at the Bridge

Jesse Helms and the sixties collided head-on.

Philosophically, Helms at thirty-nine was fully formed. The political and social beliefs he had laid over his boyhood background were solidified; they would remain the same in 1970, 1980, and beyond. Despite minor, convenient shifts here and there, neither expediency nor principle demanded that he seriously adjust his thinking to the times. Instead, the changing times reinforced his prejudices and enthusiasms.

If the sixties had been quieter, less revolutionary and traumatic, he might have gone on campaigning in a near-vacuum against painful progress and for what he considered the traditional virtues. But the decade accommodated his career. It made him what he is today.

When Helms moved from the bankers' association to WRAL-TV that fall, John Kennedy had just been elected president of the United States and Terry Sanford governor of North Carolina. The New Frontier was just dawning and the Great Society was an unformed concept. Civil rights efforts were still focused on desegregation of schools and other publicly owned facilities; the lunch-counter sit-ins that began in North Carolina had only begun to turn the movement toward private accommodations. The Freedom Rides still lay ahead, as did Birmingham, Selma, and the other sites where stubborn non-violence provoked violence across the South. Riots in Watts, Detroit, Washington were yet to come. The few American soldiers in Vietnam truly were just advisers. Typical college students still went to barber shops and football games. Pot was an exotic commodity. Four-letter words were not commonly used in mixed company. *Playboy* magazine was the hottest publication available at drugstores.

As each of those conditions changed, Helms fought the change. And at each step of his fight, he became a more conspicuous hero to the Carolinians who were angry but seemingly helpless to resist the crumbling of the world they held dear.

Helms was on the air five times a week at 6:25 P.M., at the end of the evening local TV news program. His commentary was rebroadcast the next morning at 6:55, and transmitted by FM radio to feed the sixty to seventy radio stations across the state that made up the Tobacco Network. Eventually Helms also sent out free copies of his broadcast texts to dozens of newspapers, which used them as signed columns.

In his second broadcast, he set one of his major recurring themes: "There is substantial evidence to indicate that many North Carolinians are becoming increasingly distrustful of the major daily newspapers they read, and that respect for the integrity of the newspaper profession may be on the wane," he said, hopefully. "The surest death for freedom of the press lies down the road of unfairness, partiality, and bias . . ."

At the end of only two weeks, he told listeners he had to "confess a sense of pride" at the response such comments already had drawn. Recorded reaction had been "at least a hundred to one in favor of what we are attempting to do," he said. And for those who did not understand what WRAL was trying to do, he spelled it out again: "We have felt for a great while that the vast area served by these stations is entitled to what we call 'another voice,' " he said. "Without being unduly critical of the newspaper media, particularly in the Raleigh area, we feel that the press has drifted into the position of reporting and commenting favorably on only one point of view." The station and its editorials were non-partisan, Helms said: "We don't care which party balances the budget . . . calls a halt to the myriad of give-away programs . . . sets about a program of tax reduction . . . does something to prevent the further deterioration of the dollar . . . first decides to quit playing politics with minority groups for political purposes—just so one of them does." But neither party will do those things, he maintained, "until the people begin to demand them." If we can play a small part in causing that demand, we will feel we are successful, Helms concluded.

He used the traditional "we" as newspaper editorial pages do, to label his comments as the collective opinion of the corporation for which he spoke. But effectively, "we" meant Jesse Helms and A.J. Fletcher. The two of them would meet regularly with Fred Fletcher, the general manager, and Aubrey Moore, the controller. As Fred Fletcher remembers it, Helms would bring his editorial copy in and the conference would look it over and approve it. "It was mostly pro forma," he says. "A number of times I disagreed, but I didn't want to get into an argument with Jesse. He thought his was God's word." More pertinently, it also is possible that Jesse knew his was A.J.'s word, and the younger Fletcher seldom objected because he did not want to be overruled by his father in favor of Jesse. In time, and in important ways, A.J. would would treat Helms more like a son than he did his own offspring.

One former broadcaster, a friend of A.J. who worked at another station in Raleigh, called the old man "a great pirate—I wouldn't say he was dishonest, but he loved to make money. He was very shrewd . . . I wouldn't do the things he did, but I admired him." He believes that whether Jesse was broadcasting his own or A.J.'s opinions is a moot question. "I think each reinforced the other. I don't think A.J. ever contradicted him or switched him off a particular course of action. They didn't fight, although A.J. was never reticent about tangling with anybody he didn't agree with." But Fletcher, this friend remembers, was personally "never very public in his politics." Jesse became his public face, and voice.

Reminiscing about Fletcher, Helms said with admiration that within six weeks of his eightieth birthday, he had remarried. And when a burglar broke into his house, the old man confronted him and said, "Go ahead, you can shoot me, but I'm eighty years old, and I've got this baseball bat"—and the intruder turned and ran. Aside from the fact that A.J. owned the station, that may have been what Helms respected most: Fletcher's fighting spirit, the idea that confronting trouble with a baseball bat could force it to turn and run. Fletcher handed him his own baseball bat—the microphone—and with it, Helms took a full swing at the sixties.

He was good at his trade. At first, he was better at the substance than the style. He had the editorial writer's knack of making one point per piece, rather than cluttering his efforts with a series of morals that left the listener in a fog. He was seldom stylistically ornate, and did not spend much time dredging up instructive quotations from the classics. Rather, he was direct, often sarcastic, more folksy than learned in both message and delivery. He knew his audience, because his target was hundreds of thousands of people in places like Monroe.

He understood their daily conversations—at the service station and supermarket, at the courthouse, at the tailgate of pickup trucks parked in the shade of pine trees beside sandy tobacco fields. When their talk shifted away from the weather, it turned to complaints about the way things were going in Washington, in Raleigh, at the university in Chapel Hill. Helms was the paid spokesman for A.J. Fletcher, a rich old man, once "the best bond lawyer between New York and Miami," a "great pirate" whose station slogan was, "The miracle of America is the free enterprise system." Fletcher's own special interests were a world away from those of the cotton mill doffer, feed store clerk, and truck driver of the Carolina Piedmont and Coastal Plain. Helms connected those worlds, putting together his own scrabbly background with the economic values he had picked up by associating with and serving the wealthy lawyer Willis Smith, the banking industry, and A.J. Fletcher himself. And by playing on their common dislikes and prejudices, he persuaded working people that their needs were the same as those of men whose economic desires were in fact wholly the opposite. That was and is Helms's genius, as broadcaster and politician.

Near the end of his first years as editorialist, a colleague filled in for him, and as in many substitute broadcasts when Helms was on vacation or attending a convention, the fill-in was mostly praise for the absent star. Sometimes it was a colorful character who delighted in boosting him as "Cousin Jesse Jeremiah Horatio-at-the-Bridge Helms." During that first year, an announcer said, literally thousands of pieces of mail had come in response to Helms's editorials, pro and con. Most, he said, had come from listeners politicians like to call "the little people"—"farmers and operators of country stores and small businesses, housewives, schoolteachers, teenagers, and retired people . . . the salt of the earth." He quoted one complainant —significantly from that citadel of liberalism, Chapel Hill—who called Helms "ignorant . . . a liar . . . a John Bircher . . . a McCarthyite." An admirer, the editor of the conservative *Charleston* (S.C.) *News & Courier,* however, found him "a beacon in a dark alley." A preacher in the village of Kittrell said, "We need more men like you who will stand firmly on the fundamentals on which our country was founded."

Helms could be affable, and nostalgic, and overflowing with tender respect for some community figure or old and unthreatening black servant. But his trademark was anger. He felt, with A.J. Fletcher, that what he perceived as an overwhelming liberal bias among other "major media" justified whatever excesses and lack of balance he might display in his own commentary. As a professional broadcaster, he realized that by law he and his station legally were not as free to be biased as an individual columnist or newspaper. But he sought, and thought he had found, justification for his approach to fairness from the very federal establishment he so consistently opposed. He went to Washington for a broadcasters' meeting at which Newton Minow, Kennedy's chairman of the Federal Communications Commission, spoke up to encourage broadcast editorializing. Minow, of course, was the man whose most famous remark in office was about television's becoming a "vast wasteland" of cheap entertainment instead of a force for national enlightenment. Helms was delighted to quote him as saying the FCC stood behind TV editorialists, and recognized that "a station with a strong voice can be a prime target for pressure groups and that the pressure groups might try to put the squeeze on through the FCC." The absence of such pressure "may indicate that your editorials are milk toast," Minow said. "Complaints prove that you are communicating, not toe-dancing with issues."

Helms said the FCC chairman's words were "a matter of considerable relief to us." Since he started editorializing, he had received many critical letters that said copies were being sent to the FCC, and the commission had advised the station of the complaints. But now Minow had reassured him about this. "Don't panic" about those complaints, the chairman said. So Helms, again citing the need for broadcast opinion in the face of growing newspaper monopolies in American cities, told his listeners, "We will now feel a little more comfortable when those who disagree with us take pen in hand to suggest that the government censor us. In any event, milk toast has less appeal for us than it ever had. And we never were very good at toe-dancing."

So he took Minow's advice to heart. It reinforced his natural urge to confront, to polarize. But despite his approval of what Minow had said, the following year Helms went to Washington and testified before a House Commerce subcommittee that the vagueness of the FCC's fairness rules discouraged broadcast editorializing. He turned his testimony into an attack on the *News & Observer* and its parent company's acquisition of the afternoon *Raleigh Times,* converting the state capital into a monopoly-ownership newspaper town. He joked about the *Times*'s dropping of the conservatively slanted "Little Orphan Annie" comic strip, saying, "People are still angry that Annie doesn't live in Raleigh any more." Of course, at that time Helms was the outspoken voice of another local monopoly, Raleigh's only television station. He said the station was hospitable to opposing opinions but had never been asked for equal time by anyone who wanted to rebut an editorial.

Back home, he tried to provoke reaction, and succeeded. Seldom was he willing to attribute good will to anyone with whom he differed. Week in and week out, he was against "Red China," legislative redistricting, "socialized medicine," federal aid to almost anything, foreign aid to almost any country, wheat sales to the Soviet Union, the war on poverty, the boycott of Rhodesia, Supreme Court Justice William O. Douglas, federal requirements for desegregating North Carolina schools, tax-free foundations, the National Council of Churches, the United Nations, Congressman Adam Clayton Powell, the professors at Chapel Hill, and the deal John Kennedy made with Nikita Khrushchev to get Soviet offensive missiles out of Cuba.

But he was not against everything, not quite. Repeatedly, he spoke admiringly of the *Richmond News Leader* and its editor, James Jackson Kilpatrick, who was clearly a source of inspiration for Helms's editorials. He seemed to visualize himself playing the role in Carolina and broadcasting that Kilpatrick had taken on in Virginia and newspapering: vigorous leadership, heard across the South and the nation. Helms also liked and quoted another kindred spirit named Thurman Sensing, who headed the anti-union Southern States Industrial Council in Nashville and who used his position to editorialize much the way Helms had done with the bankers' association.

Helms has had a weak spot for certain charities, which has led both his friends and enemies to agree over the years that he can be full of compassion on a personal level while seeming coldly cruel to the needy when they come in groups demanding help. The most noted example was his adoption of a nine-year-old Greensboro orphan afflicted by cerebral palsy. He read about him in a news story. The boy said what he wanted for Christmas was a mother and father. Touched, Helms and his wife set up a meeting with him at the zoo. Jesse and Dot liked the boy, and began adoption proceedings although they already had two girls of their own. While the paperwork dragged on, they gave Charles some baseball gear. "If you won't keep me," the boy is said to have asked, "Can I keep the glove and ball?" Of course they kept him, and after a series of operations he has much improved physical control. He went to North Carolina State and now, past thirty, holds a job at R.J. Reynolds tobacco headquarters in Winston-Salem.

Helms retained an ongoing affection for the people who had helped Charles to function normally. Dr. Lenox Baker of the North Carolina Cerebral Palsy Hospital at Durham became a close friend. He held Dr. Baker up as an example of why physicians should take more, not less, part in politics. Repeatedly, Helms called on listeners to buy tickets for the annual Carolina-Duke freshman football game, whose proceeds went to the cerebral palsy hospital. And often, his emotional descriptions of the afflicted children and the seeming miracles performed for them stirred generous public response.

Two of Helms's other favorite charitable causes were a little Baptist college at the town of Buies Creek, south of Raleigh, and a Baptist youth camp on Lake Gaston, where he himself had built a weekend home.

Campbell College attracted him because it was one of those schools whose administrators appealed for private support by conspicuously refusing government support. Such schools serve "primarily people of modest means," he said as he gave a plug to Campbell's fund-raising efforts. (Later, with Helms on its board, Campbell College would be Campbell University, an outpost of Baptist conservatism in a state whose higher education, and indeed government, had been dominated so long by graduates of the liberal state university. And its president, Norman Wiggins, also for a term president of the Baptist State Convention, would become a Helms friend often mentioned for statewide office with the senior senator's blessing.)

Lake Gaston, on the Roanoke River just below the Virginia line, inspired Helms occasionally to wax poetic about God and nature. He spent strictly private weekends at his house there with his wife and children, then his grandchildren. And he met a young Baptist preacher named Erbie Mangum and his wife, Linda, who were trying to create a youth camp "to serve God's purpose." It faced hard going, but in time and with Helm's help, it grew. Helms quoted Erbie Mangum as giving all credit to the Lord, and asked, "Who can doubt the effectiveness of such faith?" He himself was on the camp's board, and his personal backing showed up regularly on his Senate financial disclosure statements.

To cite these evidences of private and public softness, however, is to note them as exceptions to Helms's five-day-a-week drumfire of protest against what was happening in the world. No single thing so angered him as the civil rights movement, which gathered momentum in the early sixties. Gradually, it swept into county after county, town after town across the South. In August, 1961, it struck home for Helms when violence flared in Monroe.

The movement, in Helms's home town, was largely embodied in another angry man, a black named Robert Williams. He was the local president of the National Association for the Advancement of Colored People, but he defied the NAACP's national leadership and its policy of non-violence. In 1958, he had enlisted New York leftists and black separatists in his protests over a briefly celebrated "Kissing Case" in which two black boys, eight and nine years old, were sent to the reformatory for allegedly forcing a seven-year-old white girl to kiss them. The next year, two white men were acquitted on charges of assaulting black women in Monroe, and Williams was quoted as saying blacks might have to meet "violence with violence" and "lynching with lynching." For such indiscretions, he was suspended by the NAACP from his post as local president. But he was not quieted. He visited Havana and praised Fidel Castro, and reportedly flew a Cuban flag from a pole in his yard until a black paratrooper on leave tore it down. He published a paper that described racial conditions in Monroe so dramatically that demonstrators at the United Nations carried signs calling the town "America's Angola." True, the Ku Klux Klan had surfaced in surrounding Union County. True, the town's authorities had closed the municipal swimming pool because its chlorinator suddenly broke down when Williams led blacks demanding admission. But blacks had been voting in Monroe for years, and the eccentric Robert Williams had even run for mayor. So Monroe was not dramatically better or worse than most other small towns farther south, which were being thrown into a fright by the realization that desegregation was now inevitable. They had not yet learned that it would be much less traumatic than politicians had predicted for so long.

With the provocative Williams still being heard, the nominal leaders of the Freedom Riders who were going back and forth to the Deep South had ordered their people to bypass Monroe. But in late

1961 a busload stopped there anyway, and its young blacks and their bearded white colleagues began picketing the courthouse where Jesse Helms's father had spent his thousands of days. After a week, hundreds of whites gathered there for counter-picketing. It has never been decided whether the Klan organized the turnout. But it was in that spirit. One car kept circling the courthouse square with a big sign saying "Open Season on Coons." As both sides began straggling away, violence broke out. There was flailing and shooting. Some of the Freedom Riders were arrested. One policeman was wounded. And afterward, when a white Union County couple drove into a black neighborhood, they were taken from their car and held for a few hours in Robert Williams's house as hostages for the release of blacks arrested downtown. Next day, Williams disappeared, and charges of kidnaping were brought against him and two followers. Eight years later, Williams returned from abroad as president of a separatist group called the Republic of New Africa. His case became mired in an extradition dispute and was never prosecuted.

Helms was in Monroe in 1961 on the weekend of the incident, visiting his parents. As a WRAL newsman, he went to Williams's house the day before the violence. As if describing a brave venture, he recalled later that thirty or forty Negroes and a few northern white college students were there, and Williams was "hostile, often belligerent." Helms interviewed him ineffectively, asking, "Are you a Communist?" and being told, "I don't want to discuss that . . . It's none of your business what I belong to." Next day, Williams skipped town. Helms editorialized that "the great majority of Monroe Negroes resent the trouble stirred up by Williams," and blamed the whole thing largely on the press. Reporters came seeking "bigotry and hatred," he said, when "if they would look for the real story of the true South, and report it fairly and honestly, there would be millions around the world who would change their minds about race relations in the South."

And then he went into a line of thought that came to characterize his attacks on the civil rights movement and its leaders. He laid out the alleged Communist ties and criminal records of men and women who had come to Monroe to help defend the black boys in the "Kissing Case" and others arrested in the Freedom Riders violence. The eccentric Williams gave credibility to Helms's theory, since he turned up afterward in Havana, and later Peking. But Helms ranged far beyond Williams and his associates in his effort to paint the civil rights drive as a suspect movement led by people who were not only "professional agitators, opportunistic charlatans, and political phonies," but Communists, or criminals, or both. He referred back and back again to a Communist "master plan" of the early twenties which looked ahead to dividing and conquering America by instigating racial violence. He relied heavily on reports from the House Un-American Activities Committee and the Senate Internal Security subcommittee in alerting his listeners to "Communist infiltration of the civil rights movement in every section of the country." Over and over, he hammered at Martin Luther King, saying some of his important associates "can be labeled and proved as communists and sex perverts." Some of those who followed his broadcasts through those years heard him develop a snarl as he pronounced his angriest charges. And as he did, his following grew and grew.

Everyone who tuned in was not charmed, however. In Chapel Hill, especially, he had the fascination of a cobra to university students and particularly faculty. His broadcasts excited luncheon conversation and classroom discussions. The feeling was mutual. To Helms and many of his loyal listeners, the university community always had been a different world, more in tune with Washington and New York than with the cotton mills and tobacco farms that paid the taxes to pay the professors who were considered "just a bunch of pinkos."

Resentment of the university went back further than the anticommunist wave of mid-century, however. It included a populist anti-elitism rooted in the farms and small towns that had watched Chapel Hill alumni run the state government and most of its institutions for decades. Helms came out of that resentful element—out of Monroe, out of little Wingate College and Wake Forest, where he had never won a degree. The fact that a nest of genuine left radicals made Chapel Hill their base gave critics like Helms a rationale for lumping together university liberalism and communism. A homegrown, avowed Marxist named Junius Scales, grandnephew of a former governor, published a radical sheet there until he was convicted in 1959 and sentenced to six years in prison under the federal Smith Act. In 1962, John Kennedy commuted his sentence. All that preceded a wave of student and faculty demonstrations against segregated public accommodations in Chapel Hill, which Helms and friends naturally charged were inspired by Communists and other radicals welcomed on campus.

Helms climbed on Governor Terry Sanford for saying there was no need to worry about Communist influence at the university as long as J. Edgar Hoover was still head of the Federal Bureau of Investigation. His choler rose as agitation and speechmaking continued at Chapel Hill. The campus, he said, "has welcomed just about every conceivable type of extreme left-winger." Not only that, Helms complained, but the student newspaper, the *Daily Tar Heel,* had given left-wing visitors extensive coverage, while a story announcing a speech by commentator Fulton Lewis III had gotten only two inches of type. (When Lewis, Jr., died, Helms eulogized him on the air: "At a time when most men in radio wished to cling to the serenity of non-controversy, Fulton Lewis proved that the public was hungry for expressions that were at once provocative and informative . . . He dared to be different. He was willing to risk unpopularity. And because he was, he became one of the most popular and magnetic personalities on the air . . .")

Helms kept after the campus communism issue, week after week. He joined hands with the Chapel Hill post of the American Legion, which had passed a resolution calling for an investigation of alleged communist infiltration at the university. "Either the questions ought to be cleared up, or the university cleaned up," he declared. "Let us not be deceived: Where they are able, the Communists impose their ideology by force and terror. Where they cannot do this, they seek to destroy freedom through subversion, through espionage, through poisoning the intellectual climate and the educational system . . . We should not kid ourselves. This is happening . . ."

Suddenly, his alarms took effect. On the day before the state legislature adjourned in June, 1963, it received and passed without formal hearing what became known as the "speaker ban," or "gag law." It forbade "known" Communists and pleaders of the Fifth Amendment on loyalty questions to speak at state-supported institutions. Thus Carolina became the only state in the nation that felt its students needed a law to protect them from subversive speakers. Amid the resulting ridicule, the controversy heightened after the surprise bill was law. As historian Thomas C. Parramore has written, critics "feared the loss of university accreditation, the flight of distinguished faculty, and a precedent for further abuses of academic freedom. Not since the controversy over teaching evolution had a public issue so divided North Carolinians or emphasized so sharply the perennial antagonisms between academicians and the general public."

Although the speaker-ban law was softened during the term of Governor Sanford's successor, Dan K. Moore, it still could not withstand constitutional challenge. It was thrown out by the federal courts in 1965, with Helms still complaining bitterly that its opponents "have let nothing stand in their way in conducting their fight. They have felt the restraint of neither logic nor common courtesy."

One reason he was bitter was that his unremitting commentaries had indeed finally stirred a vigorous backlash. Like Helms's entire broadcast journalism career, this exchange among the editorialist, his critics, and the federal government is worth close inspection in view of his own assertions earlier and later about fairness in media.

In 1964, despite Newton Minow's assurances that the FCC endorsed lusty editorializing by broadcast stations, the commission had taken seriously a formal complaint from Carolinians contending that WRAL and Helms were too one-sided. The FCC held up renewal of the company's licenses while it looked into those charges. It concluded that Helms's "Viewpoint" editorials had addressed many controversial issues without giving opponents adequate chance to reply. WRAL maintained that Helms's opinions merely sought to balance those of the liberally oriented networks. But the commission said the "fairness doctrine" governing broadcast outlets dealt with specific issues, not generalities. It said the station had not given opponents the opportunity to reply to Helms on the particular controversies he addressed. It added that many of the subjects on which Helms commented were local and so in those cases the station's claim that he was balancing network opinion was irrelevant. In view of all this, the commission concluded that the station had not fully complied with the fairness doctrine. Nevertheless, it decided to renew WRAL's license. It credited the station with "honest mistakes" and, more important, recognized that in the midst of the FCC investigation, WRAL had ordered a new policy of soliciting dissenting response to Helms's editorials.

When the commission's decision came down, the local papers commiserated with WRAL for all the trouble it had gone through. Helms said thanks, but could not quite bring himself to accept the sympathy graciously. "It would have been somewhat more comforting, perhaps, if these newspaper colleagues had pondered the implications of the inquiry during the eight months that we were saddled with the red tape and the expense and the torment of proving ourselves innocent, before an unseen jury, of vague charges made by accusers whom we were not permitted to face," he said. While declining to "assign nobility" to himself and the station, he hinted that that might be appropriate. "In a way, it was a fight for personal survival. But in another, it was a fight that we were willing to make for the industry of which we are a part," he said. "A guinea pig was needed, and we were willing to be it." Later that year, A.J. Fletcher himself stood in for Helms on the occasion of the station's one-thousandth editorial. The old man said that "when we were under investigation . . . we pulled no punches, even though the commission maintained a sizable corps of investigators here in Raleigh and elsewhere in this area for a number of weeks . . ." Restating WRAL's editorial goals and warning against the evils of government, he promised that "This station, having placed its hands to the plow, is not turning back . . . We will continue to do the best we can for what we believe to be right . . ."

But that was not the end of Helms's and the station's troubles with the federal regulators. Under siege by the FCC, Helms had announced WRAL's policy of seeking response by saying, "We stand back to watch the fur fly, promising that our own fur will not be ruffled by criticism. Our hide is thick and our intentions are good." In practice, however, the way the station carried out that policy was criticized in the final hours of the 1966 congressional election. The complainant this time was Representative Harold D. "Seab" Cooley, veteran chairman of the House Agriculture Committee. Cooley told the FCC that WRAL had made available to his opponent film of a campaign debate that was artfully spliced and edited into a last-minute commercial that did him in. He said WRAL-TV broadcast it, and it was "distorted, fallacious and misleading, and a fraud on the public." Cooley complained further that a Helms editorial had attacked him on election eve, and although he tried, he was unable to get his response on the air till too late to do him any good. On this point, he was joined by three North Carolina State professors who had been on the debate panel, who said they too were attacked in the last-minute editorial and not given the chance for timely reply. Not only that, Cooley said, but the station had intentionally biased its news coverage of the campaign to torpedo his chances at reelection to a seventeenth term.

While the commission considered this case, Helms's ally, James J. Kilpatrick, came to his aid in a *Washington Star* column asserting that Cooley was just "a poor and graceless loser." The complaint's true purpose, Kilpatrick charged, was "to strangle the leading conservative voice in North Carolina—indeed, almost the only conservative voice in North Carolina." Helms, he said, "offers about the only competition for miles around to the liberalism of the *Raleigh News & Observer.* There is never any question of where Helms stands. He stands slightly to the right of John C. Calhoun."

In the end, the FCC's finding this time was a somewhat more favorable version of its earlier "yes, but." It said the station was not at fault in making the debate film available, that it could not have been expected to "censor" the resulting paid commercial, and that overall its news coverage had been fair to Cooley. However, it found WRAL "remiss" in not making possible a timely rejoinder by Cooley and the professors to Helms's slashing election-eve editorial. Despite a dissent by one commissioner who was unsatisfied about the station's role in the "carefully cut and spliced series of filmed sequences" in the campaign commercial, the FCC finally rejected the complaints, and again renewed the station's license.

Helms clearly considered it a license to do more of what he had been doing. Before, during, and after the legislature's speaker ban and his adventures with the FCC, he kept raising the level of his sarcasm and bombast. He returned repeatedly to battle against Chapel Hill. Well after the speaker ban was overturned, he resentfully called the university "a costly kingdom which the taxpayers have been forced to build and maintain . . . a closed shop, presided over by closed minds," where "no North Carolinain—from the governor on down—who finds himself apprehensive is allowed an opinion. The word from Chapel Hill is: Send money and shut up. This is the measure of 'academic freedom' as it is practiced there."

In the middle of his running campaign against the university, there came along what seemed a godsend to his cause. A fan sent Helms a copy of the university literary magazine, the *Carolina Quarterly,* which was a rather typical showcase of the excesses students and young faculty thought necessary in those days to assert their freedom of speech. As Helms described it, the magazine "resembled amateurish scrawls of four-letter words on a third-rate men's room wall . . . the mark of a sad-sack society, a morally depraved bunch of apathetic do-nothings who think they're being smart when they scoop up filth from the gutter and slap it on a piece of paper." The item that excited him most was a story "which spells out the details of a sordid bit of fornication on a hundred-pound block of ice." The magazine was edited by an English teacher named Michael Paull, and in the response to Helms's first broadcast comment on it Helms heard more about young Paull.

In teaching English literature, Paull had exposed his students to Andrew Marvell's classic poem, "To His Coy Mistress." He had asked them to do papers paraphrasing Marvell, or reflecting on his theme, or something—exactly what he assigned was part of the resulting controversy. Helms contended that Paull told the students to write about how to seduce a woman. He righteously assailed the teacher's "preoccupation with sex," and asserted that the boys in the class "no doubt enjoyed the vicarious frolic of talking about erotic matters in the presence of the five girl students . . ." He pounded at Paull in three, four, five editorials. The university appointed a faculty committee to investigate, and the chancellor accepted a recommendation to suspend Paull while the inquiry went on. Helms praised this as a reassuring step for those who had been concerned so long about "lack of administrative backbone at Chapel Hill." He criticized coverage by "the left-wing press," which in this case meant the *New York Times, Life* magazine, and of course the *News & Observer,* charging that there was "an epidemic of degeneracy throughout the large daily press." But eventually the university did not let Helms down. When its investigation was done, it reinstated Paull to his teaching duties. Helms seemed almost relieved when he could accuse the English faculty committee of "a rather miserable whitewash job," and tell his listeners that the chancellor after all had shown "he would rather switch than fight." Helms came out of the scrap bravely declaring that despite losing, "this station does not fret at the attacks upon it."

And indeed it, and he, did not. Those attacks from "the left-wing press" and its ideological allies served as advertisements for Helms in the right-wing circles where his reputation was spreading beyond Carolina. His extravagances were admired, particularly in the deeper South where resistance to the advance of civil rights was most unyielding. Almost from the start of his editorializing, his arguments had been followed in Mississippi, for example, where the militantly segregationist White Citizens Councils were headquartered. The Citizens Councils were an organization with chapters across the South, dedicated to upholding segregation and fighting federal intrusion. Some critics called it "the country club Klan." The group considered Helms a prize discovery, and prominently reprinted many of his editorials in its magazine, the *Citizen*, alongside treatises by outright advocates of "scientific" white supremacy. A typical Helms piece was headlined, "Nation Needs to Know of Red Involvement in Race Agitation!" It was just what the Citizens Councils liked to hear, and pass on.

Helms adroitly found ways to support extremist groups like the John Birch Society and the Ku Klux Klan without quite putting himself flat on the record as doing so. He suggested that critics of the Birch society used "hit-and-run tactics" and that the group and its founder, the millionaire Carolina-born eccentric Robert Welch, had been "indicted and all but tried and convicted by the press." When the Birch society cropped up investigating school textbooks down the road in Kinston, he maintained it was just a branch of "a nationally known study group." It was doing locally what needed doing all over America, he said.

The Klan found a hospitable reception on some back roads of North Carolina at the height of the civil rights confrontations in the mid-sixties. The House Un-American Activities Committee's hearings on the subject did not get the Helms cheer that greeted many of its other inquiries. In late 1965, a committee investigator found the state "the happiest hunting ground of the reborn Ku Klux Klan." Helms, however, considered the Klan an outfit unduly put upon by Carolina's law enforcement authorities. He neatly equated its hooded night riders and cross-burners with civil rights marchers. When the state got a court order blocking a KKK rally at Lumberton, Helms saw "one group of citizens on one side of an emotional public controversy being denied their right of free assembly at the very moment citizens on the other side were marching and parading up a public highway." To him, it was "a somewhat disturbing pattern of one-eyed justice."

Helms did not limit himself to commentary, however. Just as he had continued to serve out his city council term after starting his editorial career, he jumped with both feet into new ideological-political associations that might have been passed up by an ethically more sensitive journalist. In 1963, when civil rights marchers seemed everywhere across the South, a wealthy Raleigh businessman named A. E. Finley sponsored a group of about fifty Carolinians who joined to defend "constitutional rights." Helms told his listeners he "sat in" to watch this "response to a call for courage." "This is when the men are separated from the boys, the Nervous Nellies from the stout-hearted stalwarts," he said. He commended the meeting for banding itself into "Citizens for Preservation of Constitutional Rights," and told his audience where to write to join up. Two weeks later he reported that "the mail count is running in the thousands; financial contributions are flowing in." He quoted a fifteen-year-old boy who had sent in five one-dollar bills he earned mowing lawns, and promised to send all his earnings. A mother of three bemoaned the Supreme Court decision against school prayer, and asked, "Where are the Christian mothers and fathers who have allowed a minority group to bring this decision to pass?" That fall, Helms said he had "checked in" with the group, and found out it was bringing to Raleigh a renowned speaker. He told where to send checks for tickets.

The speaker was Clarence Manion, the ex-dean of Notre Dame Law School, a John Birch Society stalwart who ran a widely syndicated broadcast forum. Predictably, the Raleigh papers criticized his appearance. And predictably, Helms came to Manion's defense. Manion had been called a "right-wing extremist" and "intruder in the schools" when local teachers were given free tickets to attend his speech. Helms called him instead "a respected constitutional lawyer and historian," and said the press attacked him because he "preaches a doctrine that the newspapers studiously suppress." As so often, the contact Helms made by his editorial stand grew into a lasting relationship that won him wider notice in the frustrated but growing ranks of radical conservatives. (Years later, Helms would put Manion's son on the U.S. Senate payroll.)

Manion came and went, but Citizens for the Preservation of Constitutional Government, which affiliated itself with Americans for Constitutional Action in Washington, went on—at least for a while. When the university speaker-ban controversy was boiling, CPCG sent out a fund-raising letter promising to support the ban. And on the advisory board listed on the letterhead was none other than—Jesse Helms, the editorialist who had done such avid cheerleading and fund solicitation for the group. Along with him there were his boss, A.J. Fletcher; his friends, Dr. Lenox Baker and Tom Ellis; and Ellis's law partner, Armistead J. Maupin.

As a ranking officer of Capitol Broadcasting, Helms also found it reasonable to take active part in the Raleigh Rotary Club—and he brought ideology along with him there, too. One ex-friend says that when Helms's own turn in the club presidency came up in 1969, he brought in "the damnedest speakers" for the club's luncheon meetings that this colleague had ever witnessed. They were recalled as right-wingers, a series of them "so conservative the members were talking, asking 'Why in hell do we have to have this kind of speakers?' " The club's board reportedly took quiet exception to this campaign by its enthusiastic new president, and after a few weeks things settled back into a more predictable Rotary pattern.

From the beginning, as a purported balance to not only the local papers but the networks as well, Helms's editorials had spoken with as much certainty about national politics as about events in Raleigh and Chapel Hill. He liked Barry Goldwater and George Wallace, he disliked John Kennedy and Lyndon Johnson. But Helms had mixed emotions about Richard Nixon. The progress of his public reaction to those strong personalities of the sixties tells much about his own sure progress toward the most fateful personal political decision of his life.

After ripping at John Kennedy's programs and his agents' support of civil rights marchers for three years, Helms still was able to offer him a graceful eulogy a few hours after he was killed in Dallas. But as far as his fans could tell, the sentiment lasted exactly five minutes.

Ten months later, Barry Goldwater came to Raleigh pressing his "in your heart you know he's right" campaign against Johnson. He drew a wildly cheering crowd, and spoke a message that went straight to Helms's heart. "If he accomplishes nothing else in this strange and frustrating year, he has at least brought to life in North Carolina a heretofore slumbering and virtually motionless two-party system," Helms said. A major reason was that Goldwater had voted in the Senate against the historic Civil Rights Act passed that summer, which had been fought by Helms and most southern politicians. Speaking up for the operator of a segregated Raleigh restaurant picketed by demonstrators, Helms said, "Far too few saving hands are being stretched forth today to restrain the balled fists which are pounding at the liberties of all men of all races." Obviously he considered his own hand such a restraint, as he labeled the pending rights bill "the single most dangerous piece of legislation ever introduced in the Congress."

Goldwater, in Helms's view, was politically blessed by opposition from what he always called "the massive bloc vote"—his code phrase for blacks. That bloc vote, Helms said, "breathes its antagonism at the very mention" of Goldwater's name. And so, when the GOP nominated the Arizonan, it stirred an "awesome and bewildering upheaval" in Carolina politics, and across the South. "The fight no longer is pitched on party lines, but on sharply contrasting principles and ideals," Helms said. Just over the line to the south, his friend Strom Thurmond saw it that way and officially switched to the Republican Party. So, unofficially, did millions of southern voters; Goldwater's candidacy made it socially acceptable for them not only to vote for a Republican, but to brag aloud about it.

Except in the South, Goldwater himself was crushingly defeated, but not his cause. As the next presidential election approached, Helms remembered the northern inroads made in the 1964 primaries by that other anti-civil rights, anti-Washington renegade, George Wallace. When Wallace ran his wife Lurleen to replace him as governor of Alabama, Helms applauded. Wallace may not be perfect, he said, but he clearly is "a vastly better man than his liberal critics" would have the world believe. As Helms watched Lyndon Johnson fade and Eugene McCarthy, Robert Kennedy, and Hubert Humphrey fight for the Democratic nomination in 1968, Wallace looked better and better. When Wallace brought his independent campaign to North Carolina in September, Helms said the ovations confirmed major-party fears that the state might go overwhelmingly for him. "There is a general feeling among an increasing number of citizens that if nobody else will pledge to clean up the mess in Washington, then let George do it," he asserted. Wallace later expressed his appreciation for Helms's help, saying the editorialist was "a gracious man who had views similar to my own." Wallace, Helms maintained, presented the best possible argument for a realignment of the major parties. But the issue went beyond personalities, he insisted. He warmly endorsed the idea that there should be one continuing party anchor point for conservatives, and another for liberals.

In the end, Helms gave his listeners a rationale for voting for Wallace that bespoke his own priorities: it was, he said, the best way Carolinians could help Nixon see that Humphrey did not reach the White House. And that is how it turned out. Wallace outdrew Humphrey, allowing Nixon to carry the state. Helms's opinion of Nixon had gone up and down, beginning with the good times when he and

Willis Smith had shared friendship with the Californian in their Senate office. He believed Nixon had lost his comeback bid in the California gubernatorial election of 1962 because he had been insufficiently conservative, tried to be all things to all people. But then in 1968, Nixon rose again in Helms's book. One reason was his choice of Spiro Agnew as his running mate. Welcoming Agnew to Raleigh, Helms applauded his firm and fearless stand against the same enemies he himself had been chastising so long. And after the Maryland governor was elected vice president, he leaped to his defense against the old familiar "left-wing press and radio and television commentators" who would "tear his reputation to shreds."

The fact that Nixon was elected further confused Helms's approach to him. As the man in charge in Washington, he automatically became the focus of much of Helms's criticism. But because he also became public enemy No. 1 to campus radicals, anti-war demonstrators, and liberals in general, Nixon rose in Helms's estimation. Gradually, despite strong disagreement with some of the new president's policy initiatives, especially in foreign affairs, Helms's dislike for Nixon's critics proved stronger.

With rising anxiety, Helms had railed against "this time of the fast buck and the 'New Morality'—the age of apathy and indifference, the season of disdain for simple virtues and common honesty . . ." One of his principal villains was the National Council of Churches, a "pretentious and deceptive political mechanism" which he condemned for allegedly endorsing the lowering of the drinking age to eighteen and other outrages. He contended that liberals had "scoffed at patriotism, at thrift, at personal responsibility . . '. demanded that prayer and Bible reading be eliminated from the schools . . . argued that society, not the individual, is responsible when evil men rape and murder and pillage and riot . . . insisted that young people should not feel obliged to follow any moral code, but feel free to do whatever they want on a given occasion." When police seemed unable to close an X-rated bookstore in downtown Raleigh, Helms mourned that "now there are no standards—we are living in an age of anything-goes." He urged citizens to "raise Cain together" so they "might cause the hands of the police to be united, and the judges to convict some of the polluters of the mind . . ." Alarmed afresh by anti-Vietnam war demonstrations against "the establishment," he said, " 'The Establishment' is America, and America is The Establishment. The mobs in the streets demand that it be brought down. They had better think twice. And so had all the rest of us."

All this was amplified nationally as Nixon and Agnew stumped the nation in their aggressive "law and order" campaign for GOP congressional candidates in 1970. That September, Nixon appeared at Kansas State University and, in Helms's version, "sounded call after call for the very things for which a fed-up America has been yearning for years . . . rebuked America for tolerating lawlessness and violence, on the campus or anywhere else." Furthermore, Nixon was given repeated standing ovations by the student audience. That seemed to impress Helms as much as the content of the speech, in which Nixon "in this happy instance devoted his attention and his gratitude to the majority, and dismissed from his mind the motley minority . . ." The whole performance gave Helms hope that "the soul of America can yet be preserved."

By his later testimony, it also helped nudge Jesse Helms into a decision he compared to a man's changing his religion.

As Helms said often, although he was a registered Democrat he had "never voted for a Democrat nominee for president." He always said "nominee for president," which left plenty of room for the fact that he had often supported conservative Democrats in local and state races, and doubtless also favored nominal Democrats who were running for president without their party's nomination, men like Strom Thurmond in 1948 and George Wallace later. But in the sixties, the party "veered so far to the left nationally, and was taken over by people whom I'd describe as substantially left of center in North Carolina." Although Goldwater was soundly beaten in the state, he opened Republican horizons there. And then Nixon's law-and-order rhetoric further polarized the parties and, Helms said, "persuaded me that maybe the Republican Party in North Carolina and in the nation had a chance to restore the two-party system."

Just after Nixon's Kansas State speech, Helms's daughter Nancy was about to get married to a young army captain. She asked her father to go to the courthouse in Raleigh with her to get the marriage license. As they were coming down the elevator there, Nancy said, "Daddy, I was twenty-one this last February and I haven't registered. Do you register in the courthouse?" Helms told her yes, and led her to the Wake County registrar in the board of elections office.

Nancy filled out the form and checked her preference for the Republican Party. Helms asked her why. She turned to him and said, "Will you tell me why you're staying as a Democrat? You never vote for a Democratic nominee." That, Helms recalled, was a challenge, and in response he went over on impulse, took a slip, and changed his registration to Republican.

"That was it," he said.

He makes it sound simple, an impulsive move, almost as if the idea had never occurred to him before. He says he switched "quietly," with no thought at all of ever being a political candidate himself. But it is interesting to go back over some of the editorials he delivered to his faithful audience—voters of North Carolina—in the months before and after he made that switch.

Through the years, Helms had taken an occasional slash at the state's junior U.S. senator, B. Everett Jordan, a restrained conservative who voted with the Dick Russells and Strom Thurmonds on matters of special southern interest, but a team Democrat who kept himself in good standing with Jack Kennedy and Lyndon Johnson on party-line politics. One of the ways he had done so was in chairing the Senate investigation of the scandal around Johnson's protégé, Bobby Baker. Of that, Helms roared, "If ever a mountain labored and brought forth a mouse, the senator's committee certainly did it during the long and bewildering months when it was supposed to be investigating the lurid details of the charges of Bobby Baker's wheeling and dealing in the highest circles of government . . . It is a wonderful thing, perhaps, to preside over such an odorous affair and never smell a thing." Later he added, "Every day or so there is a mention of Senator Jordan's 'influence at the White House.' Without fail, someone says, 'Why not? Look at what Senator Jordan did for Lyndon Johnson in the Bobby Baker 'investigation.' "

Those listening to Helms across the state were not told the rest of the story. As Everett Jordan approached decision time on whether to run for re-election in 1966, there had been speculation that he might retire. Some of Helms's friends, Tom Ellis and other conservative nominal Democrats, came to see the broadcaster, urging him to run. The episode was related by William D. Snider, the former editor of the *Greensboro Daily News,* in his *Helms and Hunt: The North Carolina Senate Race, 1984.* Snider was told by one of those friends that they considered a Helms candidacy a sort of "fire insurance" in case Jordan did quit. They sent out a letter seeking support for their idea, and were impressed when they got back some fifteen thousand favorable replies in only three weeks. When Jordan decided to run again, the idea was dropped, but not forgotten—either by Helms or his friends.

Helms came back to slice up Jordan now and then in his editorials after the senator won re-election. When Jordan went with the Democratic majority in cutting back U.S. support to South Vietnam, Helms said the vote was "painfully typical of his twelve-year career in the Senate, a career which has become only occasionally conspicuous by his defaults of judgment." The senator has provided great joy to Moscow and Hanoi, he said, and so "North Carolina may one day decide that she deserves better representation in the Senate than that." After Helms switched parties, as Jordan approached the end of another term, the broadcaster accused him of contradictions that had "the growing appearance of a man willing to tamper with his own principles in order to hear, just once more, that last triumphant hurrah along the campaign trail."

Two months later, Jesse Helms announced that he himself was running for Jordan's seat in the United States Senate.

Chapter 7

Coattails I

It was far from a sudden decision.

Helms said later that as soon as his switch of parties became known, "delegations of citizens, most of them Democrats" started urging him to run for the Senate—"and I laughed at them."

"The idea seemed absurd to me in terms of any real possibility," he said, and so he sent them away with his gratitude. Still they persisted, through seventeen months while he got in more editorial licks at the incumbent Democrat, Everett Jordan. Each of his editorials, as always, sounded like a campaign speech. As Helms listened to his suitors privately, on television he discussed what was wrong with the Senate in his absence.

Once "the world's highest and noblest deliberative body," he said, it "has fallen under the domination of a loud minority who constantly use it as their personal arena of picayune political hypocrisy." The "left-wing extremists" had made "outrageous accusations" in examining Nixon's Supreme Court nominees, he charged. The nominees were persecuted "because they do not believe in forced busing, because . . . they have doubts about the constitutionality of many items of legislation having to do with the forced integration of the races in America."

About the first of January, 1972, Helms has said publicly, a group of Democrats and Republicans called on him and pressed him so hard that he gave ground. In departing, he said, one of them asked, "Well, would you object to our sending out some letters to test what might be the strength that you would have?" Helms replied that they would be wasting their time and postage money, but they could go ahead as long as it did not mean any commitment from him. The group sent out letters asking recipients to solicit three or four friends each to join them in sending "a dollar or two," as Helms put it. "I thought that was the end of it," he said, but in about two weeks some fifteen-thousand letters and nineteen or twenty thousand dollars arrived.

"Money came in clipped to little pieces of paper from little old ladies in nursing homes," he said. "Then I began to look at it seriously, and ultimately I got into it."

Little old ladies may have had some effect on Helms's decision, but it is clear that he was never all that reluctant. One who watched him closely through his years at WRAL says, "I think Jesse was working on his own politics all that time." And it was not little old ladies, but one persistent man who put on the pressure that counted. That was Helms's old friend Tom Ellis, who ranks with his father and his boss, A.J. Fletcher, as a major influence on the senator's life and career. Some still today say Helms is just the front man for the wily, ideologically driven Ellis.

Thomas F. Ellis and Helms had been close since they were involved together in the Willis Smith campaign nearly twenty-two years before. Ellis, born in California, moved to Delaware as a boy, and met North Carolina friends while vacationing at Virginia Beach. They interested him in the university, and he studied banking and finance as an undergraduate at Chapel Hill. Ellis told me his own conservatism originated mostly with his father, a Republican business executive. Young Ellis's political thinking was jolted when he came home once during a labor law course and told his father about how "management oppressed all the workers of the world." His father "sat me down and said, 'You've got the wrong idea,' and told me what the score was," Ellis said. After serving in the navy during World War II, he went to law school at the University of Virginia, and shortly after returning to Raleigh signed on for the Willis Smith election.

Somehow, native Californian Ellis became more southern in his thinking and accent than many a Tarheel born and bred. A portrait of Robert E. Lee dominates his office wall. "I spent my first twenty years here being called a carpetbagger," he tells visitors. Obviously, with that handicap, he had to work harder at becoming socially and politically acceptable. He had both the brains and personality to make it seem easy. He has gone beyond mere acceptability to be a powerful adversary in both law and politics—an approachable, pipe-smoking character to some and an "arrogant, insufferable, opinionated" force to others. In 1960 he became a partner in the Raleigh law firm of Maupin, Taylor and Ellis, which made a lucrative specialty of lobbying the state legislature. Since then it has had major clients like the Seaboard Coast Line railroad, big insurance companies, and important out-of-state firms exploring moves to North Carolina because of its favorable labor climate. (It is the least unionized state in the nation.) The firm has made a reputation as an anti-union instrument, representing companies that have the same reputation, such as J.P. Stevens, which fought bitterly for years against organization by the Amalgamated Clothing and Textile Workers.

But while Ellis became professionally successful, his political drive never let up. At first it seemed he was laying a planned foundation for a public career. During the early fifties, he was an assistant U.S. attorney for the eastern district of North Carolina—by patronage of Senator Willis Smith. Then he served as counsel to the blue-ribbon commission appointed by Governor Luther Hodges as a delaying action against school desegregation. The commission recommended state grants to parents who pulled their children out of public schools to send them to private, all-white schools—an idea promoted by the Carolina bankers association's spokesman, Jesse Helms, and approved in later variations by the president of the United States, Ronald Reagan. The state legislature approved the scheme, but eventually it was ruled discriminatory by federal courts. Later it would turn out that Ellis also lent his name, less publicly, to other racially controversial groups.

In 1956, he made his only excursion into politics on his own when he ran for the state senate. He ran an all-out states' rights, anti-communist race—and lost to a more moderate Democrat. After that, he moved behind the scenes, working for segregationist gubernatorial candidate I. Beverly Lake in the 1960 campaign—the effort for which Helms became so enthusiastic that it encouraged him to quit his frustrating, nominally neutral job with the bankers association. Through the sixties, Ellis was managing or otherwise involved in almost every conservative candidate's campaign. He switched to register as a Republican in 1970, the same year as Helms, but says the two decisions were unrelated. And his crowning achievement, even if he himself should strike again for high office and succeed, was the creation of Senator Jesse Helms.

One night after a poker session at Pou Bailey's, Ellis leaned on the fender of Helms's car in the driveway and bluntly put the question. "You've got to be able to tell your grandchildren you tried," he said.

Ellis told me that Helms asked him to do three things before he committed himself: 1. Find out whether conservative five-term Republican Congressman James Broyhill planned to run, in which case Helms would not challenge him in a primary; 2. talk to A.J. Fletcher to make sure Helms would still have a job if he was not elected; and 3. test the waters to see whether he had any substantial support.

Ellis said he consulted Broyhill and told him of Helms's interest, but got no answer. (When Broyhill, by then an twelve-term congressman, decided to run against Ellis's candidate in 1986, Ellis made it clear he still held a grudge about that incident fourteen years earlier.) Then Ellis, effectively acting as Helms's business agent as well as political adviser, arranged with Fletcher for Helms to have an inside job at WRAL while he campaigned, and his editorial spot back in case he lost. Finally, Ellis organized a direct-mail solicitation from proven conservative donors and admirers who had written Helms fan letters. More importantly, he also tapped individual sources of serious money to guarantee that Helms would have all the financing he needed. (Helms told me Ellis had "kept nagging at me to run," but said he only found out later that Ellis had "orchestrated a lot of those delegations that came to the station urging me to run. They weren't as spontaneous as they seemed.")

Helms went through a period of public pseudo-agonizing that January, teasing his backers by telling the papers he was reluctant, then he wasn't sure, then he was leaning, then he was 95 percent decided. On February 1, he wrote a letter to Everett Jordan saying, "I wanted you to know that in the event I do file, it will not be the result of any personal pique with you . . . I shall be seeking to win the office, not to bring personal defeat to you . . . It will never be my intent to speak disparagingly of you . . ."

Then, with all the bases covered, on February 18, 1972, he made his public announcement. "I cannot and will not try to be all things to all men," he said—the people had had too much of that from mere politicians. He said he had gotten "a deluge of mail" that persuaded him the people of the state agreed with him. Literally thousands of pledges of support had come in from those whom other politicians call "the little people," he said—the many who are not little at all, but "the big people, the great people, the people who can build a better America if somehow their voices are heard where it counts— in the halls of Congress."

That evening, A. J. Fletcher himself appeared in Helms's usual spot after WRAL's local news. He told Helms's fans solemnly that "we have come to the end of an era." Helms, he said, had been granted a leave of absence to run for the Senate. He described how WRAL would fill Helms's editorial slot with guest spokesmen for various points of view, augmented when needed by commentaries from the famous conservative voice of Paul Harvey.

One who knew the inner workings at the TV station believed Fletcher's were crocodile tears. The old man "acted like he was upset when Jesse changed parties, and feigned hitting the ceiling when he announced he was going to run. But A.J. was a great actor. He complained he was going to lose Jesse, but I knew he was pleased." In his way, of course, Fletcher had been building Helms up for a plunge into politics for all those years. Merely providing the daily platform—on television, on the sixty or more radio stations of the Tobacco Network, and through the editorials distributed for reprinting as columns in dozens of newspapers—gave Helms the chance to make himself a figure of household familiarity among voters across the state. And almost every time Helms took one of his few, short breaks from the daily grind, his substitute used the time to tell listeners what a great man their absent hero was. Sometimes that substitute was a staff announcer who would read from Helms's piles of fan mail. Many times it was a folksy lawyer and after-dinner raconteur named H.F. "Chub" Seawell, Jr., from the little sandhills town of Carthage.

"Cousin Chub" liked to come on quoting Will Rogers, saying "all I know is what I read in the newspapers," and so launch into his commentary on the day. He called himself "an old-fashioned, deep-water, missionary, pre-millennial, born-again, Bible-believing Baptist," who pounded the "atheistic liberal officials" who had "changed us from a republic of free and independent states to a socialistic dictatorship." That testified that he was in tune with Helms, but he took it further. While Helms purportedly was in the throes of indecision about running for the Senate, it was Seawell who praised him as "Cousin Jesse Jeremiah Horatio-at-the-Bridge Helms . . . a conservative, a patriot, super-dooper." He had been building him up that way at every opportunity for years. "Who is this man?" he asked. "I ain't seen a straight shooter in this country like this since Davy Crockett was killed at the Alamo." When a listener wrote that he and Helms seemed to be members of a mutual admiration society, he admitted that it was so. "It's hard not to admire some man like Cousin Jesse who cuts with a sharp blade and hews to the line of truth with the broad steel ax of the facts, and lets the chips and sawdust of ignorance fall where they may," Chub said. He told of a man who approached him at the courthouse and said, "Chub, go in there and see if you can't get the judge to adjourn this court. He's going to keep fooling around here and cause us to miss Jesse [on TV], and nobody with any sense wants to miss Jesse." Out in the county seats where Helms's fans were thickest, it had the ring of truth. And with that kind of year-after-year buildup, Helms was the front-runner from the moment he filed in the Republican Senate primary.

His primary competition was negligible. The Republicans had not elected a senator from North Carolina for generations. The approach of another election year did not bring out a host of eager applicants for the job. Helms ran against a legislator from Concord named James Johnson, and a school-board member from Charlotte named Bill Booe. Helms refused to appear with his rivals at joint candidate functions, saying, "I've never heard of a front-runner yet who challenged his opponents to a debate." Looking beyond the primary, he concentrated his campaigning against liberals, not other Republicans, and not Democrats as such. He made a point of seldom mentioning his challengers, and never ever saying anything uncomplimentary about them. Wherever he showed up, people shook his hand and told him, "I've watched you on television many times and enjoyed every minute of it. You let the chips fall where they would." Accompanying reporters heard it over and over: "I'm a strong Democrat, but I'm sure going to vote for you because you used to tell it like it was . . . I've listened to you time and time again. I've said it didn't make any difference what you run for I'd vote for you."

"Bless your heart," Jesse would reply.

The primary was a cinch. Helms won easily, drawing strength from every direction. He said then, "I sense that the Republicans of North Carolina today extended their hands to citizens of all political persuasions in an invitation to unite in a great bipartisan effort to restore stability to a troubled state and nation," and he pledged to "resist with all the strength I can muster the destructive tactics of the Teddy Kennedys, the Hubert Humphreys, the Muskies and McGoverns—and all the rest of the wrecking crew now dominating the United States Senate."

But primary day also brought its surprises. On the Democratic side, the mood of the electorate rang clear when moderate ex-Governor Terry Sanford's favorite-son presidential effort was embarrassed by George Wallace, who beat him by 100,000 votes. It was an auspicious sign for Helms. And for the Senate, a young and vigorous congressman from Durham, a relatively liberal Democrat named Nick Galifianakis, beat the incumbent Everett Jordan. All those Helms editorials bruising Jordan over the years may have helped. But Helms had not had the foresight to turn his scathing editorials full force on Galifianakis, who was more a regional than statewide figure until he emerged in the primary. Helms and Ellis would make up for that in the general election ahead.

That spring and summer, Helms had to do something he always maintained he was too shy to do well—go out and meet strangers, campaigning first-hand. He was a master of politics once removed, at the microphone, persuading those who wanted to be persuaded that he was appointed to speak their indignation to the world. It was not so easy in person. Sometimes people disagreed with you when you stuck out your hand in a general store. Conceivably they might even fail to recognize you. But that did not happen to Helms. Everybody knew who he was. And that recognition reinforced his confidence as he learned how to do what is now called "retail" campaigning. As time went on, with Ellis's help he would become the country's leading elected practitioner of wholesale politics, through canned commercials and mass mail. But in 1972 he conquered his native shyness, while retaining some of the lanky awkwardness of his youth. That very awkwardness seemed appealing to those who wanted to like the man who had come into their living rooms every evening for so long. They were not fans of the chic and trendy. To them, squareness was a virtue.

In campaigning, Helms forced himself to go into places he did not normally visit for pleasure. Chapel Hill, for instance. There, he sat for a long interview with the *Chapel Hill Newspaper,* now a daily, then a rather iconoclastic weekly. He insisted on tape-recording every word, a practice he has stuck to through the years. Out of that sitting, the paper's J.A.C. Dunn produced a wonderful portrait of Helms on the brink of national celebrity:

"He wears seersucker, short-back-and-sides and the sort of scholarly spectacles that give a man the appearance of not ever having much fun. His hands are surgically clean and beautifully shaped. His thinning gray hair knows its place and keeps it. He has a certain elegance, but not the easy, unconscious, unshakable noblesse of an L. Richardson Preyer or a Braxton Craven [both well-born state

politicians of the time]. Jesse Helms's elegance is slightly off-target
—his blue striped shirt is just a tad wrong, worn with seersucker; his
accent has a bit too much eastern flatness, and, like many old civic
soldiers, he wears a lot of insignia: a tie clip with a Rotary emblem
on it, a Rotary pin and a little gold tobacco leaf on his lapel, and a
Masonic ring . . .

"Among the glittering little bits of symbolic hardware with which
he is bedecked is a bracelet, on his right wrist. 'That's a POW
bracelet,' he says solemnly. 'I've worn that ever since some POW
wives came to see me' "—and then he went on to talk about how it
was too bad the country was not in Vietnam to win, as it was in "the
war I was in, World War II."

Brandishing all those symbols, Helms set out in his shrewd squareness to stump the state. Part of his shrewdness was the ability to get
righteously mad, and let people know it. It was a quality he shared
with that freewheeling fulminator, Spiro Agnew, and he was glad to
share a platform with the vice president when he appeared in Charlotte. About twenty-five long-haired anti–Nixon-Agnew demonstrators paraded outside the recreation center where a big, enthusiastic
crowd had gathered. The demonstrators jeered each state Republican candidate as he was introduced, but saved their best for Helms.
"Racist!" they screamed, among other things. Helms reddened with
anger. Looking at the neatly scrubbed youthful singers who had
preceded him on the program, he said, "Isn't it nice that the majority
of young people are represented by them"—and then he turned
toward the noisemakers—"instead of by that!" The crowd screamed
its agreement. Getting still redder, Helms said into the microphone,
"And that one with the real long hair—that's George McGovern!"

It may not have been the best line of his campaign, but it was the
bottom line of his campaign strategy. George McGovern was the best
thing he had going for him that fall. When the Democratic contender
mentioned going on his knees to Hanoi if necessary to end the
Vietnam war, and every time his denigrators described his platform
as "acid, amnesty, and abortion," the prospects of anyone, everyone
on the opposition ticket rose. That was particularly true in the South
and Southwest, and more particularly in North Carolina, where
Helms had spent much of his lifetime drawing the contrast between
his own beliefs and those of the McGoverns of this world.

Both Helms and Galifianakis, and their managers, fully understood the public opinion polls about the national Democrats' looming disaster. Both candidates—the commentator who had criticized

Nixon as often as he praised him, and the congressman who had recorded repeated votes against him in the House—did their best to link themselves to Nixon. Galifianakis's job was infinitely harder, and Helms and Tom Ellis drew on the campaign expertise they had stored away in the Willis Smith election to make it impossible for him. They ran full-page newspaper ads turning "McGovern-Galifianakis" into one word. "McGovernGalifianakis welfare giveaways," they said. "McGovernGalifianakis cut and run." "When Mr. McGovern attempted to tie President Nixon's hands in negotiating a Vietnam peace settlement, Mr. Galifianakis followed Mr. McGovern's lead on four separate occasions—voting to cut and run. On the vital issue of keeping America strong, Mr. Galifianakis was closer to Mr. McGovern than any other Congressman or Senator representing North Carolina." The ads carried tiny footnotes explaining exactly which votes had been selected to prove those assertions, but the fine print was beside the point. So were Galifianakis's efforts to remind voters of all the times editorialist Helms had dusted off Nixon, as when he accused him of "appeasement" of Communist China. "Selling out again to communism is a tragically wrong and shameful thing for this nation to do," Helms had protested against Nixon's diplomatic opening to Peking. But Helms as campaigner ran on the idea that "Nixon Needs Helms," and in the home stretch, when his own re-election was a certainty, Nixon flew in and testified to the skeptical that he and Helms were indeed old friends, and he could hardly make it through another term without Jesse's help.

That link, combined with Helms's own statewide high profile, was all the broadcaster needed to win. But he and Ellis had learned one way to run a campaign, and they pushed on beyond what was needed. On the air and in print, they hammered home a slogan, "Elect Jesse Helms—He's One of Us!" It could have meant a lot of things—he's one of us Baptists, one of us conservatives, one of us hawks. To Galifianakis and his supporters, what it clearly meant was that the young congressman was not "one of us," and it was intended to raise questions about Galifianakis's name, the fact that his father came from Greece. And that was not all. In other big advertisements, Democrats with well-known political names avowed their support for Helms because "Jesse Helms is for America," among other things. The implication was that Helms was a patriot, but Galifianakis—a big, personable, Carolina-born ex-Marine—was not.

Years afterward, Nick Galifianakis, practicing law in Durham, was reluctant to stir up all that again. Prodded, he said Helms "used low-cut tactics. In rural areas they had people saying this is not Greece, they used commercial tapes with language sounding like Russian, made gibes about giving aid and comfort to Russian bureaucrats. They said 'vote for Jesse Helms, he's a good Christian,' as if I wasn't." When Galifianakis told me this, he had just seen a late-night showing of the old movie, *Tail Gunner Joe,* about Senator Joe McCarthy. "There were some interesting parallels," he noted.

In going for the kill, Helms and Ellis used overkill. Famous outside conservatives were brought in to boost this new recruit to their ranks. Strom Thurmond crossed the border. James Buckley of New York, then in the Senate, stood by Helms at an airport and told Tarheel voters that "we want a mandate so strong that no stragglers will remain to haunt us in 1976." A Carolina reporter saw it clearly: "They don't want just a victory . . . they want an annihilation." To get it, Helms genially let it be known that he was "very comfortable" with the support of erstwhile George Wallace voters. "If it hadn't been for George Wallace, the message about busing wouldn't have reached Washington yet," he said. "I admire him for that."

Late in the campaign, another Helms advertising spread attacked Galifianakis for his allegedly weak record on anti-drug legislation. It said it was sponsored by "Doctors Against Drug Abuse," although Helms headquarters freely conceded that the campaign had paid for writing and publishing it. The ad asserted that Galifianakis had missed "100 percent" of four crucial congressional votes on the issue of drug control, and that his absence showed a lack of concern about illegal drug traffic. It turned out that there were at least ten pertinent votes on the issue, and Galifianakis said the four he missed while campaigning were on unimportant procedural questions. As soon as the ad was printed, two of the three doctors whose names were used denied that they had any connection with or prior knowledge of it. A brief flap followed.

Helms, as he did after the 1950 Willis Smith campaign, and repeatedly when asked about questionable campaign language or tactics in the future, took a position of ignorant innocence. The ad was the work of a number of people, he told reporters. "I was on the road. I didn't see it . . . I would have researched it more . . . You get all sorts of advice. I think now we've got that situation straightened out." Tom Ellis said, "All I know about the doctors committee is what its purported chairman told me. I had no reason to doubt him then or now because he's an honorable man. The point is the facts in the ad were correct . . ."

And so the Helms campaign sailed on, propelled by heavy contributions from big-name and previously obscure conservative political financiers, in and out of Carolina. Textile executives were prominent among them: Hugh Chatham of Chatham Mills, for example, and Roger Milliken of Deering-Milliken. Chatham had been quoted recently as threatening to close down his plant at Elkin if the Textile Workers Union won a pending election there. Milliken, finance chairman of the South Carolina GOP, had been prominent in the Goldwater campaign and was listed by the John Birch Society on its Committee of Endorsers. Other Helms money came from such conservative political angels as millionaire Los Angeles oil developer Henry Salvatori, a key backer of California's then-Governor Ronald Reagan, and Pittsburgh's generous bankroller of right-wing causes, Richard M. Scaife.

When it was over, Helms reported collecting $648,293, and spending $699,744. Galifianakis spent $403,006. The discrepancy between Helms's income and outgo would be the basis of a post-election fund-raising campaign that eventually turned into the biggest money-making machine ever built around an individual politician.

Nixon carried ninety-eight of the state's hundred counties with 69.5 percent of the total vote, losing only rural Northampton, which has a heavily black population, and Orange, seat of the university. A young traditional Republican named Jim Holshouser beat Helms's boyhood friend from Monroe, Hargrove "Skipper" Bowles, for the governorship. And Jesse Helms got 54 percent, defeating Nick Galifianakis by 120,000 votes, less than a fifth of the margin by which Nixon carried the state. The papers attributed his win to Nixon's coattails, and even Helms himself acknowledged their help. But as he hung up the phone after taking congratulations from Nixon and Agnew, he thumbed his nose at the papers yet again, this time with a special, victorious twist. "It means the people of North Carolina are sick and tired of the pap that is being fed to them by the editors of the major newspapers of this state," the senator-elect insisted.

It would not be the last time that a combination of rough campaigning and fortunate timing would boost him through an election.

Chapter 8

Nobody's Republican

As he raised his hand to be sworn in, Jesse Helms looked up at the Senate gallery where his father sat watching. Tears welled in both men's eyes.

From that day, Helms stood out. He was not going to be just the most conservative Republican in the Senate, not just the rightmost member of Congress, regardless of house or party, but the most outspoken, unyielding hard-liner in the nation—in or out of office, wearing any political label.

It is astonishing how quickly it happened.

He did it with the utmost calculation, in three arenas. One was the Senate itself. Another was the broad range of right-wing conservative organizations—reputable and disreputable, Old Right and New Right, domestic and foreign. The third was back in North Carolina, where Tom Ellis put together on Helms's behalf the most formidable personal fund-raising and propagandizing machine in the nation.

At the Capitol, there was a leadership vacuum on the far right. Barry Goldwater, who had opened the way for Republican conservatism in the South eight years earlier, was tired. Helms's friend Strom Thurmond, who had flown the Stars and Bars during the civil rights showdowns of the previous decades, had read the changing voter registration figures in South Carolina. Since the Voting Rights Act passed, over his objections, in 1965, black registration had soared. Aside from taking a nubile Miss South Carolina as his new wife, in his political reincarnation Thurmond demonstrated that he was up with the times by moderating his rhetoric about racial questions, and even hired some blacks for his Senate staff. Although James Buckley was the only man in the Senate wearing an official capital-C Conservative Party designation, he was a mutation, produced by a freak situation in New York's 1970 election. The newer hard-line conservatives from the South and West were still few, and had yet to show the national scope and daring required of leaders on more than specific bills or regional issues. Jack Kemp, Newt Gingrich, and the other blow-dried TV performers on the House side were not yet heard from.

But there was one man, a tall, drawling, colorless Democrat from Alabama, who impressed Helms in a particularly senatorial way. He was James Allen, an ally of Helms's old comrade in arms, George Wallace. Allen was hardly known beyond Congress itself. He had no charisma at all, and his views, though predictably conservative, were not stated outrageously enough to inspire headlines. However, he knew the rules of the Senate, and he used them to obstruct and frequently soften legislation he could not defeat. In this, he reminded Helms of his idol of two decades back, the crusty Dick Russell of Georgia. Helms attached himself to Jim Allen. The newcomer was ninety-fifth among one hundred senators in seniority. But he saw in Allen that neither seniority nor key committee position was necessary to make an impact, if the desired impact was negative. The traditionally respected arts of coalition-building and compromise could be ignored. Behind-scenes logrolling was unneeded. Seniority and tradition could be leapfrogged, right out on the Senate floor with the world looking on. The way to do it was by working the infinitely complex Senate rules. Jim Allen was their master. Helms made common cause with him, and studied his tactics.

Allen was not one of the Senate's elders. He had no clout in the committee system. Neither did he have the cajoling, deal-cutting talents of a Lyndon Johnson or a Bob Dole. He could not squeeze his anti-civil rights, anti-social welfare measures out of committee. So he bypassed all that, and presented them as irrelevant amendments to urgent or politically attractive bills moving toward passage on the floor. He did not merely offer one amendment, as a gesture; he offered a half dozen, a dozen, dozens. A certain amount of debate was demanded before a vote on each one. Very seldom did Allen win on those votes. But the prolonged tedium he created could wear down his colleagues, could push majority leader Mike Mansfield into huddling with him to determine just how many more amendments he might have, and just what might be the price of dropping them and getting on with the business of the Senate.

Helms spent much of that first year watching floor proceedings from the chair nominally belonging to the vice president, occupied most of the time by a junior member assigned to preside. He won a Golden Gavel, given to those who spend as much as a hundred hours in the chair in a single year. He was presiding when proceedings were interrupted to announce the death of Lyndon Johnson, and when Spiro Agnew resigned from the vice presidency rather than face criminal charges. One of his great satisfactions came the day Allen took on a bill bearing the name of the gentleman from Massachusetts, Ted Kennedy. He pinned on this amendment, then that, changing words, deleting commas, tying paragraphs into knots. Toward dusk, facing yet another roll call, Kennedy wearily surveyed what was left of his proposal and asked the Alabaman: "Is it my understanding, Senator, that at this point in time I will vote against my bill whether I answer 'yea' or 'nay'?" Allen just smiled.

Helms was not as reticent as tradition said a new senator should be. Before being sworn in, a few days after being elected with the benefit of the president's coattails, he announced his independence. "I'm not a Nixon Republican," he declared. "I'm nobody's Republican or anything else . . . If the president's right, I will support him . . . But I think when I disagree with him, he'll know it." By the end of that first year, he totted up his score: ninety-six bills and twenty-one amendments introduced, 138 speeches on the Senate floor, 19,963 phone calls and 71,930 pieces of mail received, twenty-five trips home to Carolina. He had stood up and put himself on the record on every passing issue, usually in words blunter than anyone else used. A quick study, he had started dropping bills and amendments into the hopper—note that his scorecard recorded how many he had introduced, not how many had been passed. But the statistic that spoke best to how he had spent his year was his 96 percent presence for roll-call votes. It quantified how much time he had spent on the floor, most of it watching, then imitating Jim Allen.

One December day he was standing up for Allen in the Alabaman's effort to attach a rider blocking federal financing of elections to the necessary annual bill to extend the nation's debt limit. Allen had been accused of thus filibustering the debt ceiling measure. Not so, Helms cried. "If anything is crystal clear above the fog of pious oratorical obfuscation which has clouded this chamber in recent days, it is certainly clear that Senator Allen has been ready to vote, from the very beginning . . . This Senate ought to be ashamed of itself

. . . We ought to commend Senator Allen for his efforts . . . I admire him. I support him. And I hope that he stands fast . . . The majority is not always right." Then Helms throttled back for a moment, in the mock courtesy at which he excels, to say that "As a freshman senator, wishing to be properly courteous and deferential, I nevertheless am obliged to wonder why the majority in the Senate are so fearful of the due processes of this body . . . I believe this Senate owes Senator Allen its gratitude for his very proper, very courageous stand . . ."

Jim Allen died in 1978. Long before then, Helms had replaced him as the Senate's most persistent obstructionist. That same December when he was so praiseful of Allen, Helms himself took the lead against legal aid for the poor, calling it "a political mechanism from bottom to top." He suggested that he had, oh, perhaps a hundred amendments he would submit to make his point. He skillfully played on the issue of "forced busing" and the energy crisis by pushing another amendment that would forbid busing for purposes of school integration as long as there was a fuel shortage in the nation. It came within one vote of passage.

But most of his efforts did not come anywhere near that close, and he knew they would not before he introduced them. He attached an amendment to the Health, Education and Welfare financing bill that would have made it legal for car owners or dealers to disconnect the anti-pollution devices newly required by law. He lost on that one by 85 to 3. He repeatedly tried to slip anti-abortion amendments into other legislation. Each of his amendments was like another WRAL editorial, drawn up to make a point, not to win on a roll-call vote, not even primarily to delay or weaken bills whose passage was imminent. They were aimed beyond the Senate chamber and the strict purposes of legislation. He was reaching out to a national constituency, to frustrated Americans among whom his hard-line tactics stood for courage and leadership rather than obstruction and obfuscation.

His act was solo. He was "nobody's Republican," as he had promised. Yet Helms led the entire Senate that first year in percentage of voting support for Richard Nixon. He did it despite the spreading stain of the scandal called Watergate. Most Democrats and a few sensitive Republicans began to distance themselves from the president as the Senate began investigations of Watergate, chaired by

Helms's colleague from North Carolina, the irrepressible sep-
tuagenarian, Sam J. Ervin, Jr. Helms had run ads during his own
campaign maintaining that his presence was needed in Washington
to support the popular Ervin; to elect his liberal opponent, Galifianakis, would merely cancel out Ervin's conservative presence. Ervin
was, in fact, a constitutional conservative. He had won Helm's admiration in the previous two decades for standing against civil rights
legislation, although he usually did so in calm legal terms, rather
than the nasty, racially tinged tones of which Jim Eastland and
Strom Thurmond were capable. However, when it came to civil
liberties, Erwin's constitutional conservatism cut the other way, and
that put him and Helms increasingly on opposite sides.

The month after he arrived, Helms voted grudgingly to approve
creation of Ervin's Watergate investigating committee, while grumbling that it should have an equal membership from each party. Soon
afterward, he was minimizing while criticizing Watergate as "the
dumbest, most inept performance in American political history,"
and asserting that past Democratic improprieties "make Watergate
look like a Sunday school picnic." Then he joined delightedly in the
Nixon White House's campaign to blame the whole thing on the
press. He said in a Senate speech that he was "deeply distressed by
the lack of professionalism and balance" in coverage and comment
on the scandal. The press, he said, "is driven more by bloodlust than
by the public interest . . ." He spoke of "the fruit of a bitter enmity
that has been growing unchecked . . . irresponsible and venomous
reporting based on half-truths and allegations."

Gradually, like many other Nixon admirers, he began to concede
that somebody had done something wrong, but not of course the
president himself. The administration has been crippled, he said,
because it "allowed misguided, unintelligent, and fanatical amateurs
to roam around Washington exercising power in the name of the
White House." As the probe searched deeper, he momentarily broke
his pattern of support for Nixon on a matter of ideology, not loyalty,
by speaking out and voting against the president's move to transfer
Henry Kissinger from national security adviser to secretary of state.
(Democrat Ervin approved the nomination; Helms was the only
conservative to oppose it. Kissinger was confirmed, 78 to 7.) But
Helms's pattern of backing for Nixon stretched around and beyond
that. He opposed Ervin on a series of questions spelling out congressional prerogatives against Nixon's assertion of executive privilege.

He supported the president's firing of Archibald Cox and Elliot Richardson in the "Saturday night massacre" of too-persistent Watergate investigators.

Typically, he bucked at being placed on the defensive, and tried to justify the Watergate break-in as provoked by the "traitorous conduct" of anti-war activists. As the Nixon tapes unwound, Helms complained that "we have the tapes with Wheaties for breakfast, the tapes with lettuce and tomato for lunch, and the tapes with potatoes and gravy for dinner . . ." It was all a press/liberal plot, he suggested: "This emphatic rejection of liberalism [in the 1972 election] was a bitter pill for some to swallow. Through a process of selective indignation, Watergate became the lever to reverse the judgment of the people . . ."

But in the final days, as the evidence mounted and GOP stalwarts one by one faced the truth, Helms was little heard from. When it was over, he said only Nixon's "fear of malicious criticism" had led him into doing wrong. Soon afterward, Helms heard a sermon at church in Alexandria, about the loneliness of man. It spurred him to write a sympathetic note to Nixon in California. Nixon gratefully telephoned to thank him. Helms would not say just what they had talked about.

He was happy to change the subject, to turn his attention ahead to Nixon's replacement in the White House, Gerald Ford. Much as he had disagreed with Nixon on foreign policy—especially the opening to China and détente with the Soviet Union—Helms had long personal ties with him, and was indebted to Nixon for helping get him elected. He had no such links with Ford, none at all beyond wearing the same party label. He was free to let his ideological instincts run. The day after Nixon resigned, Helms came out for Barry Goldwater for vice president under Ford. After him, he recommended California's Governor Ronald Reagan, Virginia's Senator Harry F. Byrd, Jr., Republican national chairman George Bush, and—strictly as a gesture—North Carolina's young Governor Jim Holshouser. He reportedly said Nelson Rockefeller, whose name was much mentioned, "stole another man's wife," and "right-to-life" groups were spreading the word that as governor of New York he had once sponsored abortion legislation. Helms got on the phone to drum up opposition to Rockefeller, warning that the move to nominate him would split the Republican Party. (Later Helms denied saying the part about wife-stealing, but Paul Clancy of the *Charlotte Observer* stood by his story, insisting, "He said it. I was there and taking notes.") Rockefeller had, of course, divorced his first wife and married again. When Ford chose him to be vice president, Helms testified against the New Yorker before the Senate Rules Committee, and was one of seven senators, including three Republicans, who voted against him on the floor. The other two Republicans were Goldwater and Virginia's William Scott, who became famous for calling a press conference to deny a magazine article that labeled him the dumbest man in the Senate. So Helms was in the minute minority, but he was comfortable there.

In fact, Ford's choice of Rockefeller merely clarified intraparty matters for Helms. Loyalty to Nixon had been awkward for him. Now, Rockefeller's presence made it that much easier for him to accuse Ford of inadequate devotion to the principles Helms held dear. There were thousands of frustrated right-wingers eager to cheer him on.

During his first year, Helms urged fellow conservatives to band together, to present a united front on the right. The moderate-to-liberal Republicans had a regular get-together they called the Wednesday Club. Helms joined the party's hard-line conservatives in starting their own Wednesday luncheon group, called the Republican Steering Committee. At first, Nebraska's Carl Curtis was its chairman. But everybody knew who was its driving force; soon it was referred to as "the Helms gang." On occasion about twenty-five senators attended—more than half the GOP minority. The group hired its own staff and coordinated speeches to lay out a complete case on high-intensity issues. It confirmed Helms's respect from his ideologically driven colleagues only months after he arrived among them. But that was not enough for him. He was looking beyond the Senate.

Helms had been there little more than a year when he made a significant speech urging the scattered partisans of the right to merge into a unified political movement. At a Washington tribute to that dean of the Old Right, the elderly, physically fading TV personality Clarence Manion, he told his kindred spirits just what they wanted to hear, but had not heard from fainter hearts in public office.

Pointing to a national poll that showed Republican Party affiliation at an all-time low in the depths of the Watergate scandal, he noted that nevertheless those identifying themselves as conservatives stood at an all-time high. He concluded that many of those avowed conservatives were registered Democrats. Clearly, most Americans would choose a conservative in elections if given the chance. But, he said, they have not had such a choice. (He did not mention Goldwater ten years earlier, and what happened to him.) Now is the time, Helms suggested in May of 1974, when the American people may be ready to form new political parties—giving them an honest choice between liberalism and conservatism, so they "will know *what* they are voting for, instead of merely whom." "Conservatives in both parties feel that they have no place to go," he said, so—what might happen if suddenly there were "a movement that offered the majority of Americans, the conservative majority, an opportunity to unite? . . . What's the proper starting point?" He suggested an independent platform convention, to which delegates would be selected by conservatives in every congressional district in the land. Candidates would then be picked from those who first agreed to that conservative platform—in that order: principles first, candidates second. What a memorable tribute to Dean Manion that could be!

It was a sensation among the true believers who heard him, and a mini-scandal among a few GOP loyalists who felt he was abandoning their president in time of need. But Watergate still dominated the news, and across the country Helms's challenge was little noticed as Nixon slipped closer and closer to the edge.

Before and after Nixon went over, Helms kept up the Senate tactics that infuriated the liberals, exasperated the party leaders trying to keep legislation on schedule, and built up his own heroic status among the right wing. He filibustered against continuing federal legal aid to the poor. He made repeated moves against providing food stamps for striking workers. He cast the only vote against expanding a federal juvenile delinquency program. He put in a bill that would keep coming back, his effort to strip the courts of authority to determine the constitutionality of school prayer. He filibustered against the federal consumer protection agency. He opposed amnesty for Vietnam war "draft-dodgers" until U.S. prisoners and missing in action were fully accounted for. Sometimes, rarely, he succeeded on the floor, as when he put through an amendment restricting use of foreign aid funds for population control programs that included abortion. With each conspicuous gesture in the Senate, his standing beyond the Capitol rose. He became the champion of the right, the speaker without whom no gathering of the movement was complete.

Ford's celebrated healing quality, after the trauma of Watergate, included a turn toward political moderation, angling away from the new president's twenty-five years as a typical midwestern conservative congressman. After the party suffered heavily in the 1974 congressional elections, the feeling spread among traditional Republicans that the way back ran through the center. This trend inflamed Helms's fans, but played directly into his hands. A whole array of frustrated right-wingers was listening when he spoke to the Conservative Political Action Conference on Valentine's Day in 1975, elaborating his theories of how to unite a conservative majority.

He described again opinion polls showing the public's low regard for political parties—and for the government then in place. And for a change, he said the press was not entirely to blame. "The people all too often correctly understand what the leadership of the Republican Party is doing," he declared. He assailed budget deficits, borrowing, increased spending for foreign aid and food stamps, negotiations to "give away" the Panama Canal. He did not pussyfoot around about who he was criticizing. "Too often the president's program is so bad that even Republicans have difficulty supporting it," he said. "Under the Republican Party's present course, the party is out of tune with its own rank-and-file membership, and out of tune with the growing conservative majority. It is out of tune with the majority that is fed up with both parties, and is looking for politicians who will stand on issues and deliver what they promise. Is there such a majority?" he asked, and once again drew on opinion polls to say of course there was.

Citing the number of citizens who said they had lost faith with their government, he said, "I think we will find our majority by presenting our views in terms that are easily understood by persons who are worried about what is happening to them, but are outside of active political participation . . ."

Whether they are called Democratic and Republican or something else, there should be two parties, he said—liberal and conservative. Conservatives should form a coherent structure—"not only our trusty band of ideological conservatives, but non-political people who are grappling in their own communities with issues such as pornography, the right to life, school textbooks, community control of schools," as well as those affected by economic policy. "We must stop talking to ourselves in our own code words, and talk to people in language they understand." As a first step, he revived his call for a conservative platform convention, a "second Declaration of Independence" in the bicentennial year of 1976.

At first, not all those listening understood the significance of Helms's insistence that "we must work in different ways, with different groups, with different constituencies. No one organization has the base that we need, and some of the organizations that will help us are not even in political action at present . . . We must not forget that the most fertile ground for political action lies with the millions who are completely disgusted with both major parties."

He was, it is clear in hindsight, summoning up the coalition of issue-based, technically sophisticated, often religiously motivated groups that today is called the New Right.

Helms urged that his call be met by concrete action, "to have acceptable candidates ready and able to run for office, not excluding the presidency itself, in the event that the major parties continue in the direction they are now going."

It was not an announcement that he himself would run for president on a conservative platform, but a lot of people heard it that way. And Helms did nothing to discourage them. When the *New York Times* three days later reported that his staff considered him an alternate candidate for the White House, one Helms aide noted that "that sort of talk doesn't hurt you." When Jerry Ford said the GOP should be broad-based, a generality with which almost any politician could agree, Helms called it "a bunch of hokum . . . if the Republican Party continues trying to be all things to all men, it will come out a poor second choice." When House GOP leaders circulated a loyalty pledge for Republican signatures, approving Ford and promising to work within the party, Helms rejected it. He said it "was drafted by big-spending Republicans who in concert with liberal Democrats have brought inflation and recession upon the American people. This is no way to unify the party . . ."

He swung with angry calculation, on domestic and foreign issues. He thrust at Ford through Henry Kissinger, calling on the secretary of state to quit because "his diplomacy is in ruins, his credibility with the Arabs and Israelis has collapsed . . ." He pointed to "the crumbling of NATO . . . the disaster of his negotiated peace in Southeast Asia and now the failure of his Mideast peace initiative" as evidence that "it's time for a change."

During this unremitting pressure on Ford and Kissinger, Helms began a brief but passionate fling with that tower of Russian genius and ego, Alexander Solzhenitsyn. There is room for doubt about whether Helms himself had studied *The Gulag Archipelago* and Solzhenitsyn's other works, or whether he was put up to this fling by one of his more bookish aides. It hardly matters. All he needed to know was that Solzhenitsyn was anti-communist, and in time he turned their flirtation into another embarrassment for Ford and Kissinger.

When Solzhenitsyn left Russia in early 1974, Helms introduced a Senate resolution directing Ford to make him an honorary U.S. citizen. He wrote to the author in Zurich to invite him to visit North Carolina and after resting there to come to Washington. Solzhenitsyn turned him down "regretfully," but Helms did not give up. Twice, the Senate passed his resolution offering honorary citizenship. But twice, the House ignored it. Eventually, in the summer of 1975, Solzhenitsyn came to America. After the Russian toured the hinterlands, Helms invited him to his home in Arlington. Language prevented their communicating, so they repaired to the home of a Helms associate, another Russian emigré, named Victor Fediay, who interpreted for a three-hour conversation. They discussed Helms's letter to Ford, suggesting that it would be "appropriate" for Solzhenitsyn to visit the president at the White House. At first, Helms said later, White House aides said that sounded fine, but then their enthusiasm waned, and finally Helms was told, "No way." When he asked whether Kissinger was responsible for the turnaround, he said, the presidential aide replied, "Please don't press me."

Helms angrily took to the Senate floor to lay out the whole exchange. He asserted that "advisers to the president of the United States recommended that he not extend the courtesy even of a five-minute visit with the distinguished author and Nobel Prize-winner . . ." He told of Solzhenitsyn's emotional plea to him that the American people not ignore the threat of communism, not fail to realize that World War III was already over, and the Communists had won it by taking over fifteen or twenty nations in the past twelve or fifteen years. "This country has come to a sad impasse when the president of the United States of America must tremble in timidity and refuse to see a man dedicated to freedom," he declared. After Helms went public in the Senate, even some liberal commentators accused the president of faintheartedness for not seeing Solzhenitsyn. The White House made a series of efforts to right the embarrassing situation, but it only got worse.

At a Capitol Hill reception for the author, Helms and Senator Henry Jackson were chatting with him when the White House called to ask whether Solzhenitsyn could come there two hours later. Solzhenitsyn said no. He said he might go if the president sent him a written invitation. The White House said no to that. Kissinger was indeed behind it all, of course. Eventually, to take some heat off the president, he admitted it. He said a Solzhenitsyn appearance at the White House would be "disadvantageous." In fact, he was afraid Soviet President Leonid Brezhnev would be offended if the famous Russian emigré and critic of the Kremlin were feted by the president. Thus, in the end Solzhenitsyn's visit to Ford was sacrificed to Soviet-American détente, then all the rage. Behind his anger over the treatment of his hero, Helms was delighted by the embarrassment to Ford and Kissinger. But at the biggest Washington event in Solzhenitsyn's honor, Helms, who had appointed himself the visitor's guide and sponsor, was shut out. The vigorously anti-communist AFL-CIO president, George Meany, played host for 2,500 people at a banquet for the author, but Helms was coldly uninvited—because, Meany's spokesman quite accurately explained, Helms "is not a friend of labor."

For no publicly stated reason, campus speaking engagements Helms had arranged for Solzhenitsyn at Wake Forest and the University of North Carolina also were canceled.

Following up his call for conservatives to organize before the next election, Helms began legal research that spring of 1975 on how to get an "additional party" on the ballot in all fifty states. He said he hoped that would not be necessary, but "the die is cast if the Republican Party is going to try to be the party of discount Democrats . . ." Liberals like Senators Jacob Javits of New York and Clifford Case of New Jersey had pushed the party too far to the left, he contended. That caused voters to stay home in the 1974 elections and "turned Congress over to the wildest-eyed bunch of liberals in history." The fact is, Helms said, "the Republican Party is a dodo already."

But despite pronouncing what sounded like the last rites for the party, he retained some suspense in his moves—even as he formalized them in a group called the Committee on Conservative Alternatives. Publicly, its aim was to make common cause among the scattered right-wing factions and to complete ballot research. Privately, Helms and his ally, New York's James Buckley, hoped to use this threat to force Ford to run on a rigidly conservative platform —and if he would not, to make good their threat by nominating Ronald Reagan, George Wallace, or someone else to replace the president.

When Barry Goldwater was mentioned, he wanted no part of it. Ford is president, he is a Republican, and this is the wrong time to talk about third parties, Goldwater said. By July, Helms also relented. He let it be known that rather than pushing further for a third, sufficiently conservative candidate, he would devote himself to a known quantity named Ronald Reagan as the Republican Party's candidate in 1976. Hardly coincidentally, talk of Helms as a possible vice presidential nominee stirred at about the same time.

To some, the deal seemed sealed when Reagan came to Raleigh for a fund-raiser in July to help pay off Helms's remaining debt from the 1972 campaign. It was one of the first events run by the Congressional Club of North Carolina—later merely the Congressional Club when it went national—organized on Helms's behalf by his friend Tom Ellis. Its smashing financial success made it typical of the club's later projects.

A thousand people came to an advance reception for the highest rollers, and 2,500 were said to have paid $100 each for dinner. Helms introduced Reagan as "a man who, faced with the choice, would rather be right than president. But I know it has not escaped your notice that there is a very good chance he can and will be both." A little later, Helms urged Reagan to get cracking as a candidate, saying that if he ran, he would support him.

But his own name was still bouncing about on the right. Tom Anderson, chairman of the American Party under whose banner George Wallace had run last time, said Helms and New Hampshire's right-wing Governor Meldrim Thompson were possible presidential choices for the party next time. "We're talking," Anderson said, and soon afterward Helms agreed that they had indeed talked, but added, "I laughed it off."

That a freshman senator could casually flirt with people who wanted to run him for president, and make a sitting president acutely uncomfortable while he exchanged compliments with other contenders, does not happen every four years. Roosevelts and Kennedys, occasionally ex-governors of major states, sometimes extraordinarily handsome and charismatic men have leaped this quickly into presidential politics. Reagan, for example, had all those advantages— name, background, personality. But Helms had none. He did it with boldness, stubbornness, one-track devotion to the causes of the hard right.

While he was issuing ultimatums to Ford and counting the money raised by Reagan, in the Senate he led the attempt to kill the Voting Rights Act because, he said, it was unfair to the South. He was the only legislator in the North Carolina delegation, House or Senate, to vote against extension. He kept submitting anti-busing amendments, to appropriations bills, to whatever vehicle seemed handy. He led a filibuster against the on-site picketing bill favored by organized labor, until the Senate voted cloture to cut him off. He alienated millions of Americans—who were never going to vote for him anyhow. At the same time he fired up the already intense admiration for him in the blossoming New Right movement.

That October of 1975, he ended any doubt about where he would commit his national following and his growing political machinery in North Carolina. Although Ronald Reagan had not yet made his candidacy official, Paul Laxalt, who headed the national Citizens for Reagan, was out organizing for him across the country. He announced that Helms would be Reagan's North Carolina chairman, and his closest ally, Tom Ellis, would coordinate Reagan's campaign in the state. Their move came after Ford headquarters had disclosed that North Carolina's moderate Governor Jim Holshouser would head the president's campaign in the South. That set up a head-on contest for control of the North Carolina Republican Party. And that, in turn, gave Helms and Ellis even more incentive to see that Reagan carried North Carolina in the March primary.

Supporting Reagan, for Helms, was not merely a matter of settling for the least objectionable alternative among the leading party choices. The two men were hardly intimates, and the circles in which they lived their professional lives could hardly have been more different. But Helms had been attracted by Reagan's politics for many years, beginning before the Californian ran for governor, back when Reagan was a traveling after-dinner speaker and TV host, and Helms was doing his WRAL editorials. The Tarheel had gone down to Southern Pines to hear a Reagan speech, shaken his hand, and thereafter called him friend. Shortly after he was elected to the Senate, before he was sworn in, he had gone to California and sought advice and inspiration from then-Governor Reagan.

And despite the contrasts between Reagan's Hollywood years and Helms's two decades living next door to his father-in-law on Raleigh's Caswell Street, there was an interesting parallel in their backgrounds: Both were striving small-town boys of modest family, who had gravitated to sports reporting and then into radio. Later both became TV spokesmen for big business and free enterprise, and rode their broadcast careers into right-wing politics.

Thus there was affinity as well as calculated confidence in Helms's prediction that Reagan would carry North Carolina against Ford. Laxalt told Tarheel audiences that Reagan planners were pointing toward New Hampshire, Florida, and North Carolina as decisive target states. But their confidence was shaken when Ford edged Reagan in the opening primary in New Hampshire, then ran an unbroken string of further wins that gave the Florida voting crucial importance. Both men campaigned heavily there, and gradually opinion surveys showed Ford pulling ahead. Gloom swept Reagan's entourage. Money was running low, and there was talk of pulling out altogether. In the final days in Florida, as Reagan barnstormed down the traditionally Republican Gulf Coast, I asked his press secretary and long-time political adviser, Lyn Nofziger, if this looked like the end of the road. "Wait till North Carolina," he said.

The polls were right. Ford whipped Reagan again in Florida. In Raleigh, Governor Jim Holshouser asserted that "the preconvention battle is about over. Ronald Reagan has had his chance to win and obviously has failed." He urged uncommitted voters to back Ford and thus help unite the party. Helms replied that if he were president, he would be humiliated at getting "only" 53 percent in Florida. But as he spoke, he and the rest of the nation realized that for Reagan, it was North Carolina or never.

Helms and Ellis had exactly two weeks after the Florida voting to intensify the drive in their state. They persuaded Reagan to spend almost the entire final week in Carolina, and to sharpen his attacks on Ford's foreign and military policies, especially the proposed "giveaway" of the Panama Canal.

Ellis's tactics again reminded old political hands in the state of his and Helms's role in the bitter Willis Smith campaign of 1950. He prepared and distributed a leaflet charging that Ford was considering a black to be vice president (Massachusetts Senator Edward Brooke had indeed been mentioned). Reagan heard about it and ordered that the leaflets not be passed out at his rallies. But another Ellis move was a decided success. Against the doubts of Reagan's own staff, he urged broadcast across the state of a thirty-minute Reagan speech delivered in Florida. It, with the fund-raising and get-out-the-vote effort Ellis had mounted, combined with Helms's own campaigning in conservative eastern Carolina to give the Reagan drive a visible boost. Ford did his bit by coming in only twice in that final week, and devoting his main appearance in Charlotte, Carolina's biggest city, to a defense of the nation's homemakers. "I say—and I say it with emphasis and conviction—that homemaking is good for America. I say that homemaking is not out of date and I reject strongly such accusations," the president thundered. The Reagan-Helms camp was puzzled but pleased—and more pleased when three days later, Reagan whipped Ford in ten of the state's eleven congressional districts.

Richard Viguerie, the right-wing political entrepreneur who has been a Helms admirer and collaborator in his fund-raising campaigns, expressed what that victory did for Reagan, and for Helms's and Ellis's standing in the emerging New Right. "In the dark hours for Reagan," he wrote, "two of America's greatest and most important conservatives, Senator Jesse Helms and Tom Ellis, came to his rescue and saved him from having to retire from politics. His conservative friends wouldn't let him quit . . . When conservatives woke up on the morning after the primary to hear that Reagan had beaten Ford by 52 to 48 percent, it electrified conservatives nationally . . . New life was breathed into the Reagan campaign. It became a close fight again." Lou Cannon, Reagan's biographer, wrote that Reagan's career had reached a critical moment. And "without his performance in North Carolina, both in person and on television, Reagan would have faded from contention before Kansas City, and it is unlikely that he would have won the presidential nomination four years later."

Tom Ellis called it a major victory for Helms, and even the Carolina newspapers agreed. It gave the senator the upper hand as the Tarheel delegation organized for the national convention at Kansas City. Ellis, who would be delegation chairman, said mildly that there would be no move by Helms to take over the state party, that the senator believed the party belonged to the Republicans of North Carolina. Then, at district conventions where remaining delegates were picked, the Helms forces refused Holshouser's request that they be split in proportion to the primary vote—and then refused even to give the governor a seat in the delegation. Helms himself was not a delegate either, but with his man Ellis as chairman, he did not need to be.

Helms had won the right to play at the national level in Kansas City. He could see himself as kingmaker, or at the very least as the man who forced the Republican Party to stand up for his kind of conservatism. But before he got there, something happened to sour his enthusiasm. It was an ingenious maneuver by Reagan's campaign strategist, John Sears, with whom Helms and Ellis never had gotten along. Counting delegates as the convention approached, Sears prevailed on Reagan to announce that if nominated, he would ask Pennsylvania's liberal Senator Richard Schweiker to be his running mate. It was either a bold or silly gamble, depending on who described it. Sears hoped it would shake loose enough liberal or uncommitted delegates, those uninspired by Ford, to give Reagan a chance at nomination. It threw right-wingers into a fury, especially any who imagined they had earned a chance at the vice-presidential position.

Helms thus had both ideological and personal reason to be outraged. He called the selection of Schweiker "offensive." He said he was committed to Reagan, but not to Reagan's choice for No. 2. He asked the Reagan headquarters to hold off on announcing that he would second Reagan's presidential nomination. Tom Ellis said he was hearing talk about nominating Helms or Senator Jim Buckley of New York instead of Schweiker. Helms himself joined the speculation about putting up Buckley's name. But all around him, as the delegates arrived, his fans were distributing five thousand buttons that said "Give 'Em Helms."

Meanwhile he used his position as disappointed Reagan stalwart and possible troublemaker to exact hard-right pledges in the party platform. (His key man on the committee was a relatively unknown East Carolina college professor and future U.S. senator named John P. East.) Working with Reagan's backers, Helms forced through strong language on Panama, China, and especially the need for U.S. military superiority over the Soviet Union. On the floor, they won on an amendment called "Morality in Foreign Policy," which condemned almost everything Henry Kissinger stood for.

That helped mollify Helms, and he modestly agreed to allow his own name to be placed before the convention for vice president. After Ford was nominated over the protesting din of thousands of airhorns brought by Reagan backers, Helms had his chance. He took the rostrum to withdraw in favor of Ford's choice, Senator Bob Dole of Kansas. But he made a rip-roaring speech that stirred the same kind of noise that had praised Reagan. He got 103 delegate votes despite his withdrawal—and left the faithful with a memory of one man who had stood up for the Right against Kissinger and compromise.

Helms thus departed Kansas City as the recognized leader of hard-core conservatism. Although he went through the motions of supporting Ford in the fall, the president's defeat by Jimmy Carter did not damage Helms's standing. On the contrary, it enabled him to say with even more authority, I told you so. He kept telling them so, whoever they were, wherever they invited him. He was a certified national political figure, and he was available. Sometimes that availability got him into peculiar company.

Chapter 9

Senator No

In early 1977, Washington columnist Jack Anderson told readers that "Senator Jesse Helms, the shining knight of the Republican right, is leading another ferocious charge against another political windmill . . . To the cheers of the right-wing faithful, he has galloped off to slay the dragons that menace their peace of mind . . . Now the indefatigable Helms is leading the crusade to strip the government of its powers to protect the public from fraudulent drugs . . . The consumers should have the right, he insists, to buy worthless medicine . . ."

Helms's cause, this time, was the controversial cancer drug, laetrile. Like so many of his crusades, this one did not succeed in the short run. Like so many, it was considered by laymen to be an enthusiasm of quacks, kooks, right-wing nuts. That is the way the general public thought of the extreme right for decades: dangerous in its thinking, but essentially harmless in action. Rarely, a politician came along who could see that while those groups separately were futile minorities, together they could be a frightening majority, or at least a decisive plurality. As often as not, the politicians who saw and acted on this potential were called demagogues. Joe McCarthy was. George Wallace was. Jesse Helms is.

Jack Anderson and many others thought it amusing to see this "shining knight" tilting at one windmill after another. But Helms knew what he was doing. To be the one spokesman cheered by all the zealots of the right, he had to be willing first to cheer for them and their assorted causes. The hundreds of bills and amendments he has submitted in the Senate have made very little law, but they have made millions of highly motivated friends. As a speaker and signer of fund-raising appeals, Helms was and is undiscriminating. There is no public list of those who have been turned down when they asked him for a speech, a visit, or an article, but the list of those who have received his blessing is formidable.

It includes single-issue groups and broad coalitions, spans the Old Right and the New. When Helms himself was breaking into politics, such distinctions were not yet fashionable, and he still does not bother to pick and choose among them. Others do; to them it seems important to categorize this or that group as New Right or Old. Most would classify Barry Goldwater in the Old Right, for example. Different though he was, he would be there with those who used to spend time arguing over the views of Edmund Burke or Russell Kirk. The group would include William Buckley and his *National Review,* William Rusher and *Human Events,* the Young Americans for Freedom of the fifties and sixties. A more inclusive view also would place there such radical outfits as Dr. Frederick Schwarz's Christian Anti-Communist Crusade, the Rev. Billy James Hargis's Christian Crusade, the Rev. Carl McIntire's Twentieth Century Reformation Hour, Dan Smoot's Life Line Foundation, Clarence Manion's Manion Forum, and Robert Welch's John Birch Society.

Because he started when he did, Helms was then part of an Old Right more loosely defined, one that included Dixiecrats, McCarthyites, conservative intellectuals, and Christian crusaders alike. As he won a reputation, he responded gladly to them when they asked for his wisdom. Thus in the sixties he was a star contributor to the segregationist White Citizens Council's magazine. When he ran for the Senate, he was delighted to accept campaign money from the men and women who supported those radical groups, including members and officials of the John Birch Society. When he hired his Senate staff, his key men came from Strom Thurmond's payroll. One of them, James P. Lucier, had been a frequent essayist for the Birch Society's publication. And when they invited him to speak, Helms was ready, as when he spelled out his independent political views to the dinner honoring Clarence Manion.

Many arbitrarily drop Helms into the New Right pigeonhole because he came to Washington and national notice about the time that movement was beginning to stir, in the early seventies. True, he is identified with the anti-abortion movement, which has largely been subsumed into the New Right, and he is for school prayer, one of the New Right's favorite causes. In fact, his likes and dislikes cover almost every cause fought for by every group beneath the New Right umbrella.

That umbrella covers a movement best described by one of its founders, Richard Viguerie. A Texas Young Republican who went to work for Young Americans for Freedom, Viguerie soon saw that the fund-raising techniques he had used for that organization could be put to work in his own direct mail company. He set himself up in business, his main tangible asset being a list of all those who had given fifty dollars or more to the Goldwater presidential campaign, copied laboriously by hand from House of Representatives records. Using it, he began contract fund-raising for Republican candidates and conservative causes. "I determined to learn how to successfully market ideas to millions," he wrote. Gradually he gravitated more to the right, and took on George Wallace as a client, helping retire his 1972 campaign debt. Some of his conservative friends objected, because Wallace was a nominal Democrat. That disillusioned Viguerie toward those friends, but started his thinking about coalition politics, about common effort by people devoted to separate rightward causes.

Viguerie began to think of traditional Republicans, "responsible conservatives," as "Uncle Toms," eager to compromise with the liberals who owned the national political plantation. Those traditional Republicans felt they "were doing just fine until the New Right came along"—and the New Right was that coalition Viguerie described, a collection of what had been called "irresponsible conservatives." In his book, *The New Right: We're Ready to Lead,* Viguerie responded to that: "We're so irresponsible we don't even mind losing a fight. We fight anyway. Where the 'responsible' Republican tries to appease and compromise, we try to win. Or if we lose, we want to come out of the fight with an issue to use against the liberals in the next election . . . If we chose to be Uncle Toms, we too could be called 'responsible' and 'respectable' . . . But we refuse to make compromises that are really surrenders."

Viguerie wrote it, but it could have been dictated word for word by Jesse Helms. They were a natural pair. Helms already had succeeded in North Carolina at putting together the coalition Viguerie envisioned on a national scale—the old minority of country-club Republicans, citizens angry about high taxes, businessmen who resented government regulation, combined with born-again Christians fuming at sex on TV and in movies, diehard segregationists and parents against "forced busing," anti-abortion crusaders, paranoid anti-communists, and flag-wavers suspicious of the patriotism of anyone to their left. The TV preacher Jerry Falwell described them as "citizens who are pro-family, pro-moral, pro-life, and pro-American, who have integrity and believe in hard work, those who pledge allegiance to the flag and proudly sing our national anthem." Helms felt right at home beside Paul Weyrich, who said frankly, "We are radicals, who want to change the existing power structure. We are not conservatives in the sense that conservative means accepting the status quo." He hitched up with Howard Phillips, the man Nixon had appointed head of the Office of Economic Opportunity and who seemed to see his mission there to destroy it. Helms made his name available to help Phillips form a nationwide Conservative Caucus, and Phillips in turn helped Jerry Falwell form his Moral Majority. Helms also helped young John T. "Terry" Dolan start the National Conservative Political Action Committee (NCPAC). Helms's ideological brotherhood was automatic with these and the many others collected under the New Right umbrella. His contractual ties began when he, like Wallace, turned to Viguerie for the fund-raising expertise to retire his 1972 Senate campaign debt.

One of the easiest ways to determine whether an organization belongs to the New Right is to check its list of officers and boosters for names like those just mentioned; these groups feature interlocking directorates, attend each other's rallies, and sign each other's fund-raising letters. Aside from names, another shared ingredient is an outright or implied religious calling, a perceived moral superiority to everything to leftward. Another is an angry disdain for compromise. But the one that most uniformly characterizes the New Right is not a matter of principle at all. It is a cold, unemotional devotion to technology.

While New Right groups may differ on fine points of ideology, none has any doubt that the computer and the television camera are blessings from on high. The computer stores millions of names of people who have contributed to right-wing causes, or whose membership in this club or subscription to that magazine make them likely contributors. It writes millions of letters, each with the name of the addressee dropped repeatedly, electronically, into the text, to make it seem specially typed by a personal friend. It keeps account of which lists produce best for which cause or candidate, so they can be hit up again and again. And the television camera, of course, puts thirty-second oversimplifications of complicated controversies into the homes of millions of voters. It keeps the Jerry Falwells, Pat

Robertsons, Jimmy Swaggarts, and their brethren on the air Sundays and weekdays, mornings and late. They are always there, live and on videotape, accompanied by the 800 number running across the bottom of the screen, telling where to call to get inspirational literature —and to get listed on the computers that spew out politico-religious letters appealing for money.

Viguerie's specialty is computer-based direct-mail fund-raising. The educational value of the heated prose in his letters is incidental to its pulling power. It is a highly specialized form of literature. When Helms and Tom Ellis started to pay off the senator's 1972 campaign debt, they put Viguerie to work raising money, and all the time they studied his techniques to make them their own. The first efforts paid off handsomely, and they pushed on beyond settling the senator's old campaign debts to start their own, ongoing North Carolina Congressional Club. It was the original political action committee, around which Helms and Ellis in little more than a decade have built a multi-million-dollar array of committees, corporations, and foundations. Helms's steady hail of hot-issue bills and amendments, his angry Senate rhetoric, added to his fund-raising potential. So did his calculated altruism, his willingness to undersign any appeal for almost any right-wing cause.

Terry Dolan of the National Conservative Political Action Committee (NCPAC) said, "Helms for a time was on everyone's fund-raising letters, and helped establish conservative organizations— ours is one of them . . . Any conservative organization with any respectability—from 1972 on, he was signing letters for them: the Public Service Research Council, which opposes public-sector bargaining; the National Right to Work Committee; you name it."

Of course all this was advertising for Helms himself. It created obligations to him among all the groups he helped. It made other big-name conservatives aware of him and what he was doing for the cause. So when the time came for him to raise more money for his own political future, their names and good will were his for the asking.

As Helms looked ahead to a 1978 re-election campaign, he was not sure who he would face. After his and Nixon's sweeping win in 1972, Watergate and Southern Baptist Jimmy Carter had helped hold North Carolina to its old Democratic habits. In 1974 Senator Robert Morgan was elected to replace the retiring Sam Ervin. In 1976, a young and ambitious James B. Hunt, Jr., was elected governor. Whoever the majority party produced to run against Helms, all signs suggested it would be a tough race. Carter and national Democrats encouraged the press in declaring Helms their No. 1 target for 1978. Rather than moaning about that, Helms and Ellis chortled in appreciation. They made it the theme of their fund-raising efforts as election year approached.

Thousands of letters flew out with the letterhead of Governor Ronald Reagan, directed to those who had sent money for the Californian's 1976 try for the White House. Reagan sent along a photograph, saying that "during my recent presidential campaign I was so overwhelmed by the kindness and generosity of people like you everywhere I went that I want to somehow express my appreciation . . . the photograph is my way of saying thank you . . ." But, the letter said, "I must admit I have another important reason for writing . . . Liberal and left-wing elements have launched a nation-wide campaign of unprecedented proportions to defeat one of the most outstanding and dedicated Conservatives we have in the U.S. Senate —Jesse Helms. Senator Helms is a good friend of mine and was a tremendous help to me during my campaign . . . The big labor bosses have made it clear that Jesse is probably their #1 target for defeat in the entire U.S. Senate. I'm not going to sit on the sidelines and let this happen . . ." Carolina will be swamped with labor money, organizers, and phone banks, he predicted. And to fight it, "Jesse will need to raise over $350,000 in the next few weeks . . . So please send your contribution today." It promised that for gifts of twenty-five dollars or more, Helms would send copies of his new paperback book, *When Free Man Shall Stand,* which was a melding of his old editorials and political speeches, heavily flavored with Christian input, issued by a religious publishing house in Michigan. The letter was signed "Ronald Reagan," and had a machine-scrawled postscript: "Ever since Jesse came to Washington he has done all he could to help other conservatives in Congress and conservative organizations. I think now is a good time to help Jesse. Thanks, R.R."

One of those letters somehow went to a Charlotte banker named Luther Hodges, Jr., a loyal Democrat who happened to be thinking about running for the Senate against Jesse Helms. Hodges sent a good-natured reply to Reagan, and made it conveniently available to the press. He said Reagan need not fear that Helms would be outspent. "With all due respect, Governor, I think you may have been misled by traditional Southern modesty that suggested Mr. Helms was a political poor boy who could not get up money here and could not contend with 'out-of-state labor bosses.' I cannot think of anyone he would rather run against than out-of-state bosses. And as for money, you may not have heard of the North Carolina Congressional Club, an organization unswervingly loyal to Mr. Helms. We truly poor Democrats often think that organization can crank up money almost as efficiently as the U.S. Bureau of Engraving."

Indeed, the club and its expertly crafted direct-mail campaign did just that. They brought in $2.3 million for Helms's campaign fund in 1977, before the campaign had even started, before anybody knew who his opponent would be. As 1978 began, the money mill kept running, full speed. With his conservative reputation, organization, and that kind of funding, Helms had no primary worries. He let the Democrats fight it out, much the way Everett Jordan and Nick Galifianakis had fought, to his benefit, in 1972. And the results were much the same, only more so.

This time, the favorite in a field of Democrats was the jaunty Hodges, son of the popular fifties governor who had gone to Washington as John Kennedy's secretary of commerce. As a bank executive, the ruggedly handsome younger Hodges projected competence and stability, and had the kind of blue-chip backing his name and business suggested. His problem was that all that made him overconfident; he went through the motions but did not succeed at rolling up his sleeves and being one of the good old boys at country service stations. I went with him once to an oyster roast in Durham, where he warned me we could expect a lot of "Jessecrats," as Helms's Democratic-registered fans were called by then. They were there, all right, and Hodges could not penetrate their almost sullen politeness. Meanwhile, an underdog, under-financed Democrat was working that element more naturally. He was John Ingram, the populist state insurance commissioner, described in William D. Snider's *Helms and Hunt* as "posing as a David against the Goliaths of wealth and privilege."

In the first primary, Hodges won as forecast, but he missed getting a majority. The folksy, unpredictable Ingram ran second and took him to a runoff. In it, facing only Ingram, Hodges was even more overconfident. But much of the vote that had gone to the other underdogs swung to Ingram. Labor sent out letters backing the maverick insurance commissioner rather than banker Hodges. And in the runoff, Ingram upset Hodges to win the right to face Helms in November.

From that day, the dominant issue of the Helms-Ingram campaign was money. Each contended the other was financed by out-of-state special interests up to no good. Helms kept pounding at Ingram's alleged enrichment by Big Labor, although all its contributions would amount to a tiny fraction of Helms's own swelling campaign fund. The Democrat made a show of returning a $5,000 check sent by COPE (Committee on Political Education), the AFL-CIO's political action committee, saying he preferred to take help from North Carolina only. For all the good the gesture did him, he should have kept it; he needed it. As the Helms camp filed each financial report required by federal law, Ingram and Helms's other enemies labeled the senator first "The $4 Million Man," then "The $6 Million Man." They made much of the fact that a heavy proportion of Helms's contributions came from "the super-rich and the super-powerful," including oil and other corporate interests beyond the Carolina border. The *Raleigh News & Observer* had hammered Helms's Senate record by calling him "Senator No," a title Helms gloried in. He responded that every time he voted "nay" on something liberals wanted, he was voting "yea" on some vital American principle. Before the campaign was over, some of Helms's needlers abandoned "Senator No" and called him "Senator Dough" instead.

Jimmy Carter followed up his promise to make Helms his No. 1 Republican target for 1978, barnstorming into the state twice. But his impact was questionable, partly because it came at the height of a drive by his secretary of health, education and welfare, Joseph Califano, to raise public awareness about the hazards of cigarette smoking. Tobacco puts between $3 billion and $4 billion a year into North Carolina's economy. It not only supports farmers, but many thousands of workers in tobacco processing and cigarette manufacturing plants in Winston-Salem, Durham, Reidsville, and other towns. Hundreds of thousands of jobs depend on it. And before, during, and after the Senate campaign, bumper stickers blossomed all over the state, saying "Califano is Dangerous to Your Health" and much angrier things about the Carter administration's health secretary. In response, Ingram assailed Helms for voting against the U.S. Agriculture Department budget that included money for Carolina tobacco support programs. The argument may have ended as a washout between the two.

Ingram, who had made his reputation as an anti-trust insurance commissioner protecting the little people against the big interests, reminded some Carolinians of Huey Long, who used his seat on the Louisiana Railroad Commission to take on the oil industry and build himself up to become governor and senator. Because of that reputation and his sometimes erratic campaign, Ingram got very little backing from the state's old Democratic establishment. The major newspapers kept him at arm's length; some opted out of endorsements, others were unable to hide their reluctance when they committed themselves—more against Helms than for Ingram. Major state Democratic figures from the past were recruited to dress up Helms's speaking platforms and newspaper advertisements. Helms tried to make something for himself of Governor Jim Hunt's barely audible support for the entire Democratic ticket. Hunt objected, but Helms's point was made: Ingram did not even have the enthusiastic backing of his own party hierarchy.

Whether that was because of Ingram's uncontrolled maverick tendencies or because he had taken on the distinct aroma of a loser is moot by now. The two liabilities went together, and because they did Helms's prospects rose steadily. Plagued by a bad back, he went into the hospital for a disk operation on September 1, and was out of campaign action for more than three weeks. Helms's broadcast commercials rolled on. Pushed by a hundred full-time and fifty part-time paid employees, nearly four hundred headquarters volunteers, and an estimated twenty-five thousand "doing something for him" in the counties, his organization spread and tightened. As his right-hand man and campaign manager Tom Ellis has told me, "Jesse has no real interest in politics as such, in getting down in the trenches. Sure, he's interested in it, but he recognizes that he personally doesn't have the time for that part. That's pretty well left up to us." Sick or well, Helms did not have to bother with the details.

When he came back to campaigning in early October, he was riding on a sea of money and what money can buy. He busied himself acknowledging potential supporters who might have been ignored. Perhaps his vote on the Agriculture budget still mattered to some; he showed up at J. P. Davenport's farm in Pactolus, in Pitt County, standing on a stack of forklift pallets while a respected tobacco grower and old-style Democrat named Bailey Williamson explained to 250 others why his vote would go for Helms. Perhaps fundamentalist churchgoers were insufficiently fired up to get out to the polls;

there was Helms on the PTL Network (for "People That Love," but assumed by most to be for "Praise the Lord"). In the campaign's last days, Helms was PTL's guest in Charlotte, "urging everyone to take up the cross and follow him," in the words of the *News & Observer*'s editor, Claude Sitton.

Sitton's deft sarcasm, Ingram's angry charges, none of it changed what was coming. Helms put on the air and in the papers an avalanche of home-stretch advertising. Ingram's total funding for the whole campaign was only $264,000, and he ended it $33,000 in debt. Helms's high-tech, high-intensity fund-raising made him not the $4 million man, or the $6 million man, as Ingram had charged earlier; he was the $8.1 million man. That is how much he had spent, much of it from almost 300,000 out-of-state donors.

At the time, it was without comparison the most expensive Senate campaign in history. Helms had outspent his hapless opponent by an astounding margin of thirty to one. And when the votes were tallied, he had indeed won a second term in the Senate. But considering the resources brought to bear, it was a less than overwhelming victory. He defeated Ingram by 55 to 45 percent, a margin of 103,000 votes in more than 1.13 million cast. Despite their reservations about Ingram, high-ranking Democrats and opinion leaders had some guilty second thoughts about what might have happened if they had gone all-out to unseat Helms.

Helms himself, however, did not dwell on the figures. He stepped before the crowd at his campaign headquarters and sang into the microphone, "I'm Senator No, and I'm glad to be here!" and they loved it. Some waved signs saying, "Give 'Em Helms in 1980." The suggestion was not lost on the senator. He had been thinking ahead when he prepared his victory speech. Perhaps remembering all those contributors beyond Carolina, he called it "a victory for hard-working Americans everywhere." Thinking of his own role and the movement that had joined in so enthusiastically to re-elect him, he called it "a national victory for conservatives . . . a bipartisan declaration." It also was a painful jab to Jimmy Carter, who would count on states like North Carolina when he was up for re-election two years later.

All that naturally inspired reporters to ask what role Helms foresaw for himself in the 1980 presidential election. "I love the Senate," he said. What about president or vice president? "Nothing appeals to me less than either of those jobs." The always cagey, sometimes more forthcoming Tom Ellis suggested that Helms just wanted to keep his public guessing.

But there was no guessing about where he was looking. The moment he had been elected the first time, he set out to spread his name and his word across the nation. He had succeeded. As a result, the span of groups called the New Right, which he had helped bring into being, had rallied to help him into a second term. Now he was equipped to return the favor. He and Tom Ellis had seen the millions they could raise on his own behalf. Now they were ready to take not just his name and his word to the nation. They had the organization, and with it they would create more organizations, until they ran an unprecedented conglomerate of right-wing fund-raising and propagandizing groups. With it, they set out to whip the United States Senate and the White House itself in line with their philosophy.

Chapter 10

Riding High

The most impressive thing about Helms's re-election victory in 1978 was not his vote margin against a candidate virtually abandoned by the Democratic establishment. What was astonishing instead was Helms's money margin: of the $8.39 million contributed to the two senatorial candidates, almost 97 percent was raised and spent on his behalf. Seeing those figures, campaign specialists everywhere realized suddenly that computer-generated, alarmist letters carrying Helms's blocky, awkward signature were a fund-raising instrument with great potential for the future of American politics.

That realization was strongest in Raleigh, in the never-satisfied political mind of Tom Ellis. "We're bionic," Ellis had said when the campaign fund crossed the $6 million mark and kept going. When the election was over, his imagination kept working.

The day after Helms's victory, the senator told reporters he had no interest in seeking either the presidential or vice presidential nomination in 1980: "The nomination isn't thrust on you, and I'm not going to seek it." But nobody knew better than Ellis that that was what any politician was supposed to say the day after he won re-election. He could see further toward 1980. Whatever Helms did, as candidate or kingmaker, would cost money. So would the spread of Helms's ideology and influence across the country. So would the election of kindred souls to the Senate. To raise that money, Ellis and Helms would erase the words "North Carolina" from the title of the Congressional Club, and make it a national force.

In more than five years, Ellis had seen both the possibilities and the limitations of the club as constituted. He had converted it back and forth from single-candidate committee to multi-candidate committee, trying to legalize the funneling of money first here, then over there. But the political financing laws passed after Watergate, laws

that made all that switching seem necessary, got the club into problems with the Federal Election Commission. Looking ahead, Ellis
saw that his ambitions for the club and Helms were going to be
constantly bumping up against those laws.

The most inconvenient rule to an outfit operating on the Congressional Club's financial level was the one that restricted political
action committee contributions for a single candidate to $5,000 in the
primary and $5,000 in the general election. So Ellis hired one of
Washington's first-rank law firms, Covington & Burling, to find ways
to work around those regulations.

The result was an organizational flow chart that looks like an
innocent business firm after an invasion by hordes of consultants out
of Harvard Business School. The Covington & Burling plan created
four nominally independent organizations in place of what had been
the single Congressional Club entity.

One was the ongoing club itself.

The most important addition was a theoretically for-profit corporation named Jefferson Marketing. It would handle the club's direct-
mail fund-raising and media advertising and absorb much of its staff.

The third group was the Hardison Corporation, a for-profit company to handle the club's accounting and the voluminous reports
required by campaign law.

The last was the Coalition for Freedom, a tax-exempt non-profit
foundation to raise money separately for producing television programs and commercials for right-wing causes.

There were several perceived advantages to this setup. Most frustrating to those who wanted to know more about what happened to
all that money, the creation of Jefferson Marketing and Hardison
Corporation as legally for-profit concerns meant their books were
closed to the public—unlike those of tax-exempt non-profit groups.
That feature screened the details of those corporations' ties with the
Congressional Club.

Not conspicuously noticed until the sheer scale of Helms's campaign funding apparatus dawned on the public, the senator's aides
also had created a string of non-profit foundations based in Washington. Helms said they began when his legislative arguments repeatedly
were blunted by statistics and allegations presented by liberals like
Ted Kennedy. "By the time I found them to be inaccurate or irrelevant, it was no longer news," he complained. "My responses got lost
in the shuffle . . . So I sought a research capability and a parallel

means to distribute this research. The idea sort of became obvious."
The result was the non-profit institutes, which he said "operate
precisely like the think tanks on the other side of the spectrum," and
importantly, "None of them uses a dime of tax money."

Those groups were:

The Institute of American Relations, which with an offshoot
named the Foreign Affairs Council concerns itself mainly with
foreign policy;

The American Family Institute, heavily involved in anti-abortion activity;

The Centre for a Free Society, nominally founded "to encourage the education of future leaders and provide a forum where
people can exchange ideas," but involved in a wide variety of other
interests;

The Institute on Money and Inflation, concerned with the
soundness of the dollar.

Time would show that these outfits, in which Helms's Senate staff
was deeply involved, were doing much more than researching the
issues. But to Tom Ellis in Raleigh, they had to be a distraction from
the hard core of his ambition for Jesse Helms. They were the Washington end of an ongoing rivalry: over here Helms's oldest allies in
Raleigh, those devoted to his political career and his ideals as if they
were synonymous, and over there his Washington crew, to some of
whom issues came first and Helms was merely a vehicle for advanc-
ing their ideology.

I asked Ellis which was tail and which was dog—Raleigh or
Washington? "I reckon it's a two-headed thing," he said cautiously.
"We can't have somebody in Washington unless we do what needs
to be done in North Carolina. Yet we all recognize we've got to have
that kind of leadership coming out of Washington in order to carry
North Carolina . . . In carrying out his functions as a U.S. senator,
they have to deal with certain issues, which they do, and we don't
have any input into that whatsoever . . . I'm sure his office staff up
there helps him in those decisions. That office is independent of
ourselves. We take what they end up with, and try to elect Jesse
Helms, or John East, however what they've done up there affects the
state of North Carolina."

Money, of course, was and is the key for achieving all of that, in
either arena. And Helms's name is the most important gimmick in

raising it. For fund-raising, the variety of organizations under his aegis functions much like the variety of cereal boxes arrayed by one manufacturer on the supermarket shelf. It enables one Helms interest or another to work the right-wing mailing lists constantly, and for all of them together to broaden his market share. A recipient might be annoyed at getting an appeal from the Congressional Club every week. But if he heard one week from the club, the next from the Institute of American Relations, the next from the American Family Institute, and so on, the object of all this heated attention might be kept in the mood to help the club itself again when its appeal arrived in turn.

An amazing number of contributors did just that. In 1979, when Helms's re-election was over and before the club shifted into high gear for its next effort, the money kept rolling in at a rate of more than $1 million a year. The reason was obvious, spelled out in dramatic prose in a cascade of fund-raising letters: the menace of liberalism still hung over the nation, Helms needed help in the Senate, the country needed a certified conservative in the White House, there is always another critical election just ahead.

Helms and Ellis were doubly motivated as they looked ahead to that next test in 1980. One thrust was to elevate Helms's influence on the presidency and the Republican Party nationally. The other was to extend their joint grip on the state of North Carolina.

Publicly, Helms pretended to be aloof from presidential politics. He took the pose of a man to whom others should apply if they wanted him to save the party. His fund-raising list was one of his attractions, of course. "Needless to say, there are a great many political figures around the country who are salivating over it," he acknowledged after the 1978 election. Some of those interested in running for the White House already had been in touch, he said— including Ronald Reagan, Senator Bob Dole of Kansas, and Representative Phil Crane of Illinois. But he insisted, "I'm not going to commit now to anybody."

That seemed to deny his well-known admiration for Reagan and his ideology. But Helms still resented what had happened in 1976, when after he and Ellis had gone all-out for Reagan and kept his hopes alive with his Carolina primary victory, the Californian had let them down at the Kansas City convention. Helms still burned over Reagan's advance disclosure of Richard Schweiker as his vice presidential preference. He blamed that and other mistakes on John

Sears, the Reagan campaign strategist whom he and Ellis simply could not abide. And Sears was still on board. Thus Helms went through the motions of indecision. "I've talked to Ron," he said, but he would stay out of the presidential runup till he saw "how he's going to set up his campaign." "Yep, Sears is the problem," he said bluntly to a reporter. And so for a while, Helms professed indecision between Reagan and the lesser known right-wing favorite, Phil Crane, and perhaps even some darker horse. Obvously the longer he held out, the bigger the war chest accumulated by the Congressional Club, the stronger his bargaining power.

Before the summer of 1979 was out, while Helms himself still insisted he was uninterested, the North Carolina Republican Central Committee passed a resolution urging him to run for vice president. A few weeks later, Tom Ellis announced a committee to promote him for that spot. He said the Coalition for Freedom would use the facilities of Pat Robertson's 700 Club, the politico-religious show broadcast out of Virginia Beach, to produce tapes starring Helms. These would tout right-wing issues across the nation, and do double duty by increasing Helms's exposure to the national electorate. Soon Richard Viguerie's *Conservative Digest* helped that push with a cover story proclaiming "A Draft Campaign: Jesse Helms for Vice President." The article did not have to note that Helms was a major client of Viguerie's mass-mail empire as well as a close ideological comrade.

But why should a man with such a strong personal following, such an overpowering financial base, such uncompromising views, entertain the idea of taking the second job to any other politician? Helms rationalized it by saying that while he found the prospect of being either president or president's flunky unappealing, there was something to be said for the vice president's constitutional role of presiding over the Senate. "You could have the presidency. Just let me run the Senate," he said. "Within the rules of the Senate I would stop whatever I wanted to, all those appropriations bills, and everyone would soon come running to me to work things out. We would get this country straightened out." After a reporter wrote about this rationale, Helms said, enthusiasm for his running spread.

Ellis took the daydream a step further, describing how Helms could counter what he saw as the Democrats' domination of the television dialogue in Washington. "Every time they open the Senate doors, there's CBS interviewing Ted Kennedy," Ellis said. "Now maybe Helms could nuzzle up there, too, and say, 'Well, I feel just the opposite.' " Ellis also theorized that in 1980, after all the fuss over Reagan's vice-presidential tactics four years earlier at Kansas City, the party would break tradition and let an open convention pick a No. 2 candidate. Even he could not foresee the flurry of absurdity that would surround selection of a vice-presidential candidate the following year at Detroit. But the Jesse-for-vice-president drive was one more way to keep contributions rolling in. And it raised Helms's visibility as a man who had to be dealt with by any Republican interested in the White House.

He held that uncommitted posture until late the following winter, after Reagan had whipped George Bush in the New Hampshire primary. Then Ellis announced that the Congressional Club was putting Helms on the air in an "unauthorized" television campaign backing Reagan's primary drive. The first commercial came two days before the next primaries in Florida, Georgia, and Alabama. Ellis explained that the effort was strictly independent of the Reagan organization—a stance that would enable it to spend unlimited amounts of money for the Californian through a loophole of federal law.

Helms himself did not have to bother with the details of this furious maneuvering ahead of the GOP convention. Neither did Ellis. Helms did not have to sign all those fund-raising letters personally; a machine did that. But to keep up the Congressional Club's staff, keep the money flowing, keep up the pressure on the national party, Helms had to keep high his own profile on issues that mattered to hard-core conservatives.

Thus that winter he made his annual appearance before the Conservative Political Action Conference, where he demanded that the United States pull out of the United Nations. He delayed confirmation of Jimmy Carter's nominee to be ambassador to El Salvador. After the aborted mission to rescue the U.S. hostages in Tehran, Helms tried to block Carter's choice of Edmund Muskie to replace Cyrus Vance as secretary of state; he lost on a 94–2 vote, but his point was made. He tried to rally Senate conservatives against Carter's nomination of General David Jones for a second term as chairman of the Joint Chiefs of Staff. Few days passed without Helms's name in a headline.

As the convention approached, he attached it to a fund-raising letter for Americans for Reagan. The next day, a letter went out to round up ten thousand signatures on a petition urging Reagan to pick Helms for vice president. When early arrivals were already in Detroit for platform committee sessions, another letter to delegates warned that choice of another vice presidential "liberal" like Earl Warren, Henry Cabot Lodge, Jerry Ford, Nelson Rockefeller, or Richard Schweiker could lead to another defeat.

That same day, Helms was in Raleigh grumbling that the platform committee chairman, Senator John Tower of Texas, had denied him a final appearance before that group to "see that Reagan's positions are reflected in the platform." He specifically said the draft platform fell short because it was unclear on an Equal Rights Amendment, and not strong enough against abortion and for Taiwan. In fact, his man Tom Ellis was there in the committee room, directing a squad of Helms Senate aides during rewriting of the platform at the Detroit Plaza Hotel. He got rid of the party's endorsement of the ERA and hardened its position on abortion. The platform eventually incorporated more than thirty Helms amendments, and was the most conservative document adopted by the party since the Goldwater convention of 1964. But to seem satisfied so soon did not fit Helms's strategy.

Thus he did not stay home pouting for long. He went to Detroit, where he could do it on television. On arrival, he shuttled from anchor booth to anchor booth as the networks clamored for interviews. With Reagan's nomination assured, the only major question left was who would be picked for vice president. And while Reagan stayed out of the spotlight during the preliminaries, Helms was the only show in town. Fearing that Reagan would pick a non-rightist like George Bush or Howard Baker, he said his own name would go into nomination no matter what decision Reagan made.

He did it in terms that still stick in the minds of some Americans who fear what the White House would be like if Helms ever became president. He said, "If I were lobbying for my own candidacy, which I'm not and which I have not, I would point out that I have strong ties to the evangelical movement, and it's fair to say they are strongly supportive of the idea of my being on the ticket." He reminded of how Jimmy Carter had won four years earlier by carrying the South, and had done so by "a strong appeal to Christian people." After saying this, Helms flew off to California for a joint rally with Jerry

Falwell while his backers continued to blitz the Detroit area with cable television commercials on his behalf.

When he returned, he remained the star in Reagan's absence from view. Middle-aged groupies bounced around him in the crowded corridors. He stopped at an American Conservative Union luncheon to blast the idea of letting Henry Kissinger address the convention. It had seemed Kissinger was a dead issue, out of office nearly four years, with Reagan's nomination assured. But in fact, as Helms spoke Kissinger and other inveterate intriguers were at work behind the convention scenes talking about what would have been the most preposterous vice-presidential deal in history. In it Reagan would choose Jerry Ford, the man he had challenged so fiercely in 1976, the former president of the United States, as his vice-presidential candidate. Pumped up by the news-hungry networks, this scenario got as far as reported discussion of who would have rights to Air Force One when. But it never was to be. That midnight, Reagan squelched it by holding a press conference to disclose that he was picking another of his intraparty rivals, George Bush, as his running mate.

Helms said he was "stunned." But he was hardly surprised. He knew better than others that his own name had not been included on the list of prospects from whom Reagan's people asked background information. He realized, resentfully, that Reagan was moving from the militantly conservative line that had clinched the nomination into an outreach phase, to bring in the wavering Democrats and independents needed to win election. The clear hard-right choice about which Helms sermonized for so long already was being fuzzed up for the fall. But Helms did not shrug and forget it. After going through the motions of conferring with his backers, people like anti-ERA crusader Phyllis Schlafly, Howard Phillips, head of the Conservative Caucus, and Representative Robert Bauman of Maryland, chairman of the American Conservative Union, he did what he had to do.

Joe Louis Arena swelled with cheers of the defiant faithful as Helms stood before the convention to acknowledge Reagan's decision. He said what mattered was not personalities but principles. The millions who backed Reagan "will not be moved by appeals to 'party unity' or by wheeling and dealing in the back rooms of any convention, whether in Detroit or New York," he went on. "The American people are interested only in what is right and wrong." Having recorded his own devotion to principle, without ever mentioning Bush's name, he said he would back the ticket because "they—both of them—have emphasized their faith in and dedication to the platform adopted by this convention." The Helms platform, he might have added.

When the roll was called for vice president, Helms got fifty-four delegates despite his withdrawal. Most of them were from North Carolina. And that is where he turned his attention after seeing the national party off on the right course.

Long before Reagan's nomination for president had been decided, the Republican candidates for governor and senator in North Carolina had been effectively decided by Helms and Ellis. For governor, they had persuaded State Senator I. Beverly Lake, Jr., son of Helms's conservative friend from the days when they were both Democrats, to switch parties and run as a Republican. Lake bore a name that had been involved in top-level state politics for a generation. But the man tapped to run for senator was virtually unknown outside Carolina's political in-crowd.

He was John P. East, a political science professor from East Carolina University. He had run unsuccessfully for office twice before, and later had become GOP national committeeman from the state. But nobody could imagine him as a match for Senator Robert Morgan, the conservative Democrat who had served as state attorney general before going to Washington as Sam Ervin's replacement in 1975.

In the eyes of Helms and Ellis, what East lacked in personal following he made up in ideological purity. When he ran for Congress in 1966, East complained that that old familiar "bloc vote" was being mounted against him on orders from Martin Luther King, Jr., and Lyndon Johnson. Protesting against that "open racist appeal for a bloc vote," he maintained that it showed "the level of desperation to which my opponent has fallen." He lost in the heavily Democratic eastern district, but he said all the right things for his future in Helms's Carolina GOP. When Helms was still a Raleigh editorialist, he spotted East as a kindred spirit worthy of a few kind words. Later, East ran and lost a race for secretary of state. But he persisted. In 1976, he was Helms's man on the GOP platform committee at Kansas City. In 1977 he urged that the Republicans change their party name because in the South it still carried too much negative connotation. When he was put on the national committee, he was recognized as Helms's man.

To most Carolinians, East was a nobody. That made him just what Helms and Ellis needed to run against Bob Morgan. In late 1979, the Congressional Club got the drive started. Letters went out, signed by Helms, about how East was brilliant and courageous. (The Illinois-born East went into the Marine Corps during the Korean war and was stricken by polio at Camp Lejeune, North Carolina.) Helms called him "a tireless, articulate, unshakable conservative"—and said of course that he needed help to run for the Senate against "the stupendous amount of money that will be spent by pressure groups" against him.

That was as positive as any of the Congressional Club's campaign for East was to get. As soon as the candidates were lined up head to head, the club's publicity machinery set out to paint the conservative Morgan, former campaign manager for Helms's friend, I. Beverly Lake, Sr., as a liberal. It did so by distorting his Senate record on a series of selected issues. It charged that he had voted to sell out U.S. interests in the Panama Canal, to aid the Communist regime in Nicaragua, and to scrap the B-1 bomber.

Morgan was nonplussed by this assault, because he thought he had a gentleman's agreement with Helms. They went back a long way together. Six years earlier, when Morgan was running for his first term, Helms had considered him ideologically acceptable. He said he would not campaign much for the GOP candidate because he was too busy with out-of-state speeches. "They are both campaigning as conservatives and both have endorsed a balanced budget," he said. "I'm for Bill Stevens [the Republican], but Bob Morgan has been my friend for years. I just can't get political enough to kick a friend in the teeth." The rest of the story was that Stevens came out of the traditional wing of the state GOP, with which Helms was contending for party domination. The senator was not eager to share senatorial stature with any Carolina Republican who was not his own man. So he served a term with Morgan, until his next opportunity to install his own man at his side in Washington.

Morgan felt that when Helms ran for re-election in 1978, he himself had observed a vague tradition called senatorial courtesy, in which no sitting senator is supposed to campaign outright against his colleague. And so he expected that in 1980, Helms would show the same respect for tradition and not attack him. Morgan should have known better; for all Helms's praise of old-fashioned values, he has respected political tradition only when it fit his needs.

Helms maintained that by speaking well of his opponent, John Ingram, Morgan had spoken ill of him in 1978, so all courtesies were off. His Congressional Club created John East and kept the U.S. mails busy on his behalf. His friends in the evangelical right joined in, although Morgan himself was a serious Baptist layman. So one-sided were they that they provoked an uncharacteristic outburst from Morgan at a meeting of the North Carolina Baptist State Convention. "Religion and church should not be used as justification for dogmatic political positions, propounded from the pulpit, or for condemnation of those who disagree," he said. "Demagoguery from the pulpit . . . is no different from demagoguery on the campaign trail. If anything it is worse, because it clothes itself in self-righteousness, invokes the name of Christ or his church in an appeal to passion, prejudices, and irrationality." Alluding to Helms's friend Falwell, Morgan said, "Across the nation I understand there is a crusade by a group that uses the word 'moral' as part of its name. This implies that anyone who disagrees with any of their beliefs is not moral . . . Millions of dollars flow into the media ministries each week, and I hasten to add that I am sure much is spent wisely. But as Baptists we should be vigilant to insure that such funds, often from the widow's purse, are not used to advocate political beliefs, promote intolerance, and chill public debate by those claiming, as against all others, to be divinely guided." Morgan's protest is interesting now mainly because the demagoguery he complained of so clearly foreshadowed the campaign of 1984. But he was not looking that far ahead; he had a furious time trying to catch up with the Congressional Club's broadcast commercials that made him out to be just another Democrat of the Ted Kennedy mold, rather than a straightline descendant of Sam Ervin and the conservative Carolina Democrats who preceded Jesse Helms in Washington.

He never did catch up. While East's limited campaign appearances were mainly to private audiences of potential contributors, his ads were everywhere. They were reminiscent of every campaign in which Ellis and Helms had been involved. From his record, they would pick one procedural nay out of a series of substantive yeas to prove that Morgan had opposed the B-1, for example. It would take Morgan five minutes to counter what they had alleged in ten seconds, and meanwhile they had moved on to another allegation, on ten other stations, night after night. A year later, Morgan said he remained angry at Helms personally because of the distortions on his behalf throughout the campaign. "He can't continue to skirt the responsibility by saying 'Well, that was done by Tom Ellis down in Raleigh.' " Five years later, a still-bitter Morgan remembered how he would respond to charges in his speeches, and the papers would cover it—but while the papers ran the story once or twice, the East commercials ran over and over. "The only way is to outspend them," he said, and that he could not do.

By November, East had spent almost $1.2 million. And by that time Ronald Reagan had pulled ahead of Jimmy Carter—not only across the nation, but in Carter's South, and in North Carolina. Reagan carried the state by forty-one thousand votes. East defeated Morgan by just over ten thousand—little more than half a percentage point. There was a premonitory cloud in the returns, little noticed in the general euphoria that swept the right wing: the Congressional Club's gubernatorial candidate, young Beverly Lake, had failed in his effort to unseat Governor Jim Hunt. Hunt, standing against the Reagan tide, looked stronger than ever, perhaps strong enough to challenge Helms himself next time around. But for the moment, Helms and Ellis stood back to admire what they had wrought—not only in North Carolina, but across the nation.

The promise, or threat, of the New Right finally had materialized. Nineteen-eighty was the year when the Republicans took the U.S. Senate for the first time in a quarter-century, and the New Right took the credit.

That Reagan's coattails might have been mainly responsible for the election of a squad of right-wing senators was beside the point; after all, the New Right had boosted him, too. But in the Senate races, most attention had gone to the intensive negative campaigns against established Democratic senators carried on by outfits like Terry Dolan's National Conservative Political Action Committee. Dolan, whose manipulations of political records were so ingenious he made Tom Ellis seem meticulously accurate, had targeted five famous liberals—George McGovern of South Dakota, Frank Church of Idaho, Birch Bayh of Indiana, John Culver of Iowa, and Alan Cranston of California. Four of the five were defeated. Helms had urged the Vietnam war hero, ex-POW Admiral Jeremiah Denton, to run in Alabama. The Moral Majority had adopted him as its own, and he won. Other new right-wing candidates came through in New York, Florida, Georgia, and Oklahoma. Helms's Congressional Club contributed to all of them, to twenty-two Senate and thirty-four House candidates.

More conspicuously, the club also spent $4.6 million on the Reagan presidential campaign, and let the political world know it. Helms assumed he had bought into an influential role in the new administration. He deserved a serious say-so over policy and appointments, and he set out to exercise it. He and Ellis also had doubled their representation in the Senate: John East went off to Washington with the Congressional Club's erstwhile chairman, Richard W. Miller, as his administrative assistant. It is the top staff job, a position from which he could oversee every move made by East, whom reporters and politicians there dubbed Helms's clone, or "Helms on wheels."

Out of all this, Helms himself emerged with national recognition as the embodiment of right-wing success, the "high priest" of the movement. *Time* and *Newsweek,* the *Wall Street Journal,* the *New York Times,* the networks splashed his owlish image and detailed his humble roots for millions who had never focused on him before. It was a glorious time.

But along with the glory came unwelcome attention. Gradually, as awareness of Helms's formidable money-raising machinery swelled in the national consciousness, inquisitive reporters had begun looking into where that money came from and where it went. Now, Helms's leap into prominence inspired even more diligent investigations. As he stood tall in Washington demanding that Reagan hold true to the faith, back home there were rising questions about whether the Helms machine had held true to the law, and to the assumptions of the many faithful who had sent in their millions for the cause.

Direct mail is the backbone of the New Right, and of Jesse Helms's political structure. It is big business, based like all selling on understanding the psychology of the sales target. Most political fund-raising appeals are aimed at three human weaknesses: ego, paranoia, and gullibility.

The skillfully written letter is long enough—three pages or more —to persuade the recipient that he is an important citizen. It is computer-personalized, often with his name dropped in several times. Sometimes it includes what look like hand-scrawled postscripts, as if the senator or other busy figure sending it took time out from his full schedule to make this special point to this individual alone. It conveys a spirit of conspiratorial comradeship: sometimes it bears a "confidential" stamp, as on a secret shared only among intimate friends.

The letter arouses paranoia with urgent warnings about what will happen if we fail to act now, immediately. It uses market-tested "devil figures"—names of opponents the very mention of whom is calculated to provoke response among those on a carefully chosen mailing list. Appeals from the hard right, especially, suggest that the only medium that can be trusted is computer-written mass mail itself —that whatever you may read elsewhere, anything sold over the counter, available to the masses, is part of a liberal media conspiracy.

Most people receiving this mail, on lists that may have originated from magazine subscriptions, voter registration lists, or much more exclusive sources, throw it away. Perhaps 2 percent respond to a successful early mailing; then when the list is narrowed to just their names, the percentage is supposed to rise with each follow-up. The best, most expensive lists to rent are those of proven givers. Huge numbers are gullible enough to respond again and again. But to keep them writing checks, the ingenuity of the mailer is taxed to produce a higher and higher note of urgency. It is astounding what wild tales these donors will respond to—and how, after each threatening catastrophe does not happen, even after the phoniness of the appeal is sometimes exposed publicly, they will give again and again.

The first necessity for the direct-mail operator himself is start-up money. Money can rent mailing lists, and buy skill at writing appeals, and technical know-how and equipment to print and mail them. But beneath those must lie a ruthlessness, a cold willingness to take advantage repeatedly of those gullible Americans who worship the very man who is hoodwinking them.

What the law requires for raising and spending political money is infinitely more complicated than what the contributor assumes. But one thing it does not require is that all or any particular part of the money raised must go to the cause for which it was purportedly solicited. By far most of the funds raised by New Right groups go to raising still more funds—and into the salaries and overhead of the fund-raising organization, and the profits of the direct mail agency. The two parties' congressional campaign committees, as well as corporate and professional political action committees (PACs) all commit a far larger fraction of income to the candidate or cause than do the nominally independent PACs.

There are no better exhibits of these generalities of the genre than in the workings of Jesse Helms's political money machine.

The complex of legally separate organizations devised by Covington & Burling for Helms and Tom Ellis raised money and managed elections with such efficiency that it became feared across the nation. But it was not perfect.

Its imperfections became noticeable when, after the 1980 election, some of the country's best investigative reporters started focusing hard on the Helms machine. One of the findings that did not surprise those who have studied mass-mail fund-raising and political campaign management was how little of the total money involved went to the candidates themselves. One examination of the major PACs' finances before the 1978 election showed that an average of only about 7 percent of what they collected was being passed along to the candidates in whose name it was raised. As the increasingly efficient machinery boosted its intake in later elections, the percentage to the candidates diminished. In 1982, for example, when North Carolina had no statewide elections, Helms's organization ran a slate of candidates for Congress in North Carolina as well as supporting hard-core conservatives across the nation. And of the $10.4 million the Congressional Club laid out in that election cycle, only $147,119, or 1.4 percent, was reported as going to candidates. The rest was attributed to other advertising, polling, efforts for other right-wing causes, and for staff and administration of the club itself.

Carter Wrenn, the bulging, technically expert Carolinian in day-to-day charge of the club's operations, reasoned that the mass mailings that seek to raise still more money are themselves advertising useful to the candidates. They hammer at the issues important to conservative campaigns and serve the broad purpose without naming the individual candidate, he explained. More importantly to the club, they also are a way to keep Helms's name before his millions of fans in states near and far.

Two experts in political direct mail told Elizabeth Drew of *The New Yorker* more about the insiders' view of how this technique works. A conservative activist told her, "There is great potential for fraud. There are organizations out there raising thousands and thousands of political dollars, and doing nothing like what they say they will do with the money." One conservative candidate, he said, had to "bleed" to get $1,000 from the Congressional Club. "What happens is little old ladies in Peoria are asked to give money to help national congressional campaigns, but an enormous amount of their money ends up going into Jesse's fight to maintain his power in North Carolina." One specialist who worked for Ronald Reagan said, "If I pump 100,000 pieces of mail into a candidate's district, and it has four pages about the candidate, and a tag line asking for money for the candidate—and it always does—I've helped that candidate by sending the letters and pumping him up. Then I turn around and give him $5,000, which is all I'm legally allowed to do, and my letter is counted as a fund-raising appeal, not as a contribution. And then the press criticizes me for spending all my money on fund-raising, and not giving direct contributions to candidates. I sit there and laugh."

That is precisely the technique and attitude of the Helms-Ellis machine, except that its spokesmen try not to laugh in public. A breakdown of the Federal Elections Commission's figures on how the $10.4 million above was spent suggests that more stayed in the Congressional Club's close orbit than was distributed anywhere, even to the master broker of mailing lists, Richard Viguerie. The biggest item after administration (salaries, travel, etc.) and mass mailing was payments to the club's nominally for-profit sister outfit, Jefferson Marketing, Inc.

The Congressional Club-Jefferson Marketing connection was the most sensitive spot in the Helms-Ellis Carolina machine. Robert Timberg of the *Baltimore Sun* spent weeks digging through records to determine that Jefferson Marketing (JMI) was a way to provide the Congressional Club's candidates with the most modern political services at cut-rate prices. He concluded that JMI, though technically a for-profit firm whose books are thus closed to public inspection, actually was not intended to make a profit. Thus, the club's candidates could save many thousands of dollars by contracting with JMI for expensive services provided virtually at cost.

As Timberg pointed out, U.S. campaign laws prohibit private, for-profit firms from "making any contributions whatever" in federal elections. They also limit political action committees to providing five thousand dollars per candidate per election. Ellis said that faced with that limitation, the club set up JMI to provide services to its candidates for "a more reasonable charge" than elsewhere. He was quite open about how the Congressional Club could give a candidate the maximum of five thousand dollars for a campaign, then through

JMI help him get far more for the five thousand dollars than he could by contracting with others. But Ellis insisted that this did not circumvent federal regulations, although they state that "provision of any goods and services without charge or at a charge which is less than the usual and normal charge for such goods and services is a contribution." They also stipulate that the value of such a contribution is determined by the difference between the price charged and the "usual and normal" fee elsewhere. The difference between what JMI charged a client and what the client would have had to pay someone else amounted to a contribution, Timberg stated.

He also noted that the link with JMI effectively shielded Congressional Club operations because the club's payments of millions of dollars to Jefferson were vaguely listed under headings like "advertising" or "consulting services," and detailed breakdowns were unavailable since Jefferson's books legally were closed to the public. That opened the possibility that the club subsidized its sister "for-profit" company with money contributed to the club.

Others agreed with Timberg; taking off from his investigation, opposition candidates and the Federal Elections Commission itself later brought legal action. Four years after Timberg's research, the case ended when the Congressional Club and JMI finally conceded that they were a single entity, and were ordered to pay a $10,000 fine. Long after maintaining that they were separate organizations, they promised that henceforth they would be. Carter Wrenn and Tom Ellis would have to step off the JMI board. JMI's officers also were ordered to disclose its expenditures for the previous six years. One early investigator of the club's spreading interests commented that all this meant was that Wrenn probably would have to move his chair a few feet. But trivial as the penalty seemed compared to the millions churned through those groups, it was a distinct blot on the record of a machine professedly devoted to law and order.

But the initial glare of investigative attention caused little if any embarrassment to the Helms-Ellis machine. The club and its branches shrugged and kept the Post Office busy, just as they had after earlier stories by Daniel C. Hoover in the *News & Observer*. These reports linked the Congressional Club and Jefferson Marketing with anti-labor activities on behalf of J. P. Stevens, the textile company that was fighting a long, bitter struggle against unionization of its plants—and which also was represented by Ellis's law firm. The apparent tie was through two Charlotte-based organizations named the North Carolina Fund for Individual Rights (NCFIR) and the Southern Employees Education Fund (SEEF).

NCFIR, set up as a legal aid association, had as its executive director H. Joseph Beard, Jr., a Charlotte lawyer and member of the Congressional Club. Both Ellis, the club's chairman, and John East, then running for the Senate, were on its advisory board. Fund-raising and promotion for both NCFIR and SEEF were handled by Jefferson Marketing. NCFIR, one of many right-wing legal advocacy groups set up in the seventies, also had sued to stop Governor Jim Hunt from using public money to promote passage of state water and highway bonds; to stop the University of North Carolina's law school from admitting a specific number of less-qualified black students; and to challenge the state industrial safety agency's rule authorizing inspectors to enter business places without search warrants.

It was not the first time eyebrows had been raised about the Helms-Ellis political connection and the Ellis-Stevens lawyer-client relationship. In 1978, for example, Helms dropped a few thousand good words for J. P. Stevens into the midst of congressional debate. He noted that "the so-called labor reform bill presently before the Congress has been nicknamed by some as the 'J. P. Stevens bill.' This apparently is in reference to the inability of the Amalgamated Clothing and Textile Workers Union to organize the J. P. Stevens Company over the past fifteen years. One of the purposes of the so-called labor reform bill is to make it easier for unions to organize plants and factories which contain a majority of those not wishing to be represented by a union."

"It would not be appropriate for me to take sides in the dispute between J. P. Stevens and the Textile Union," Helms said. Just how inappropriate, he did not spell out. "That is a matter left to the courts," he said. Then, of course, he did indeed take sides. "However," he went on, "one cannot ignore the vicious and distorted propaganda campaign generated by the labor bosses against the J. P. Stevens Company. By the daily hoisting of inaccuracies into the public view, big labor apparently intends to create a climate favorable for the passage of the so-called labor reform bill." Then he laid into the *Congressional Record* two long editorials from the *Wall Street Journal* which he said "put the matter in a better perspective" for those who may have seen only "big union propaganda."

But Helms and Ellis were riding the crest of conspicuous success, and seemed invulnerable either to political defeat or criticism. So well had their principal effort worked in 1980, when they tapped the virtually unknown John East and made him a U.S. senator, that as 1982 approached they decided to strike for a hand-picked North Carolina delegation in the House as well. To do it, they recruited and ran candidates in five of the state's eleven districts, providing them all the financial backing and technical expertise the Congressional Club and Jefferson Marketing could offer—which was more than any other political machine in America.

The cutest ploy pulled by the club that year was its buildup of young Bill Cobey, ex-athletic director at the University of North Carolina, who had run respectably close in losing the lieutenant governor's race in 1980. Looking ahead, Helms-Ellis organized a nominally separate project under the Coalition for Freedom, their tax-free educational foundation based in Raleigh. This offshoot, known as the Taxpayers' Educational Coalition, was chaired by none other than—Bill Cobey himself, out of work after losing his state-wide race. His main function as chairman was to appear in television commercials broadcast in the Raleigh area, soliciting funds for a drive to cut state taxes and spending. In the thirty-second spots, which were almost identical to standard campaign commercials, Cobey's name and face were the most conspicuous feature. In one, his name was mentioned five times and flashed on the screen four times in half a minute. After this publicity drive had run for sixteen months, Cobey resigned the chairmanship, the Taxpayers' Educational Coalition dropped from view, and Cobey announced for Congress in the Fourth District, which includes Raleigh. He had effectively campaigned right through from one campaign into the next, with not only expenses but $43,750 in salary paid by the tax-free Coalition for Freedom. Again, Democrats in the state were outraged.

But despite the Helms-Ellis conglomerate's most intensive efforts, something happened in November of 1982. Amid national economic recession, after a blizzard of negative campaigning by direct mail and television, all five of the Congressional Club's House candidates were beaten. Although Bill Cobey's opponent, incumbent Ike Andrews, had been arrested for drunk driving late in the campaign and top Democrats had considered asking him to withdraw, Cobey still lost like the rest of the Helms-Ellis team. It was the first time Helms and his organization had suffered a net loss since he won his Senate seat ten years earlier. The Democrats gained seats across the country, in line with off-year tradition and the rising unemployment statistics. But five out of five was stunning.

Carolina Democrats blamed it on the excesses of the GOP campaign. Ike Andrews said the Congressional Club had been his biggest asset. "People everywhere rejected extremes," said one Democratic operative. This time, even Tom Ellis could not sound smug. Defensively, he said what his opponents called negative campaigning was "something they'd like to dwell on, and make appear sinister," but "we're putting the guy's record up there, and if that's negative, that's that guy's problem." Looking back, he said the only thing he would change about the campaign was the result.

Looking ahead, he and Helms could see the senator's re-election two years later looming as the supreme political test of his career. It was not just a matter of grass-roots operations in North Carolina. Helms and Ellis were unlikely ever to be outspent or outmaneuvered there. But in Washington, Helms after the 1980 election had stuck out his chest so far it was bound to provoke challenges. His pride led to a stumble. Most Democrats were his natural enemies, for all kinds of substantive reasons. By his manner, Helms also managed to anger men who by party and ideology should have been his friends.

Chapter 11

The Generalissimo and the Troglodytes

Delton Ponder was a maintenance man for a hospital in Hattiesburg, Mississippi, a hard-working citizen whose family barely managed to get by with the help of federal food stamps. Late in the winter of 1981, supporters of the food stamp program found him and brought him to Washington to testify against the Reagan administration's proposed cuts in that program. They considered him a good exhibit because he was southern, hard-working, and white, and so might disarm those who brandished the axe against food stamps as just another welfare boondoggle for lazy big-city blacks who preferred not to work.

The man in charge of the food stamp hearings was Jesse Helms, who became chairman of the Agriculture Committee when the Republicans won control of the Senate the previous November. Helms made no pretense that he was neutral on the subject. He opened the hearings by recalling horror stories about food stamp fraud. "The American people are legitimately resentful about the abuses which they themselves have observed, and which they are expecting us to correct," he said. One South Carolina man, he maintained, had used stamps to buy five automobiles, thirty-two weapons, and marijuana. He said there were criminal rings that bought stamps from recipients for fifty cents and sold them to grocery stores which redeemed them for their full value of one dollar each. He told the committee he had filing cabinets full of evidence of those abuses.

By the time Ponder's turn came, there seemed little chance of softening the chairman's position. The Mississippi father of three told how chronic illness caused his family such high medical bills that they could not make it without food stamps. "We're already eating beans and potatoes and every kind of food that fills you up but doesn't cost much," he said. If his food-stamp allotment were cut, he added, "I just honestly don't know what I'm going to do."

The crowd in the hearing room leaned forward as Helms suddenly put his hand over his microphone and said quietly to the stenographer that his next remarks were not to be on the record. Then he asked Ponder if he attended church. When Ponder said yes, Helms told him he knew some people in Hattiesburg, and he would see what he could do to get him some help.

Then Helms picked up where he had left off, presiding through the testimony of thirteen witnesses in four hours, never missing a chance to take another crack at the food-stamp program. He had begun by saying that he not only approved the new president's aim of cutting $2.3 billion from a projected food stamp budget of $12.4 billion; it was "entirely possible" that he might call for deeper reductions. And he did. He pushed amendments to double the administration's cuts.

Those watching the Delton Ponder incident that day believed they had witnessed a striking public illustration of Helms's double standard—of his "anecdotal" approach to helping others. Like Reagan, he repeatedly extrapolated from some individual horror story to an all-encompassing generality about a program or policy. Because of the tale about the unnamed man who bought cars and weapons with food stamps (and many more tales like it), Helms attacked the program as a ripoff of the public. But when it came to helping those who needed help, Helms's reputation was the opposite: he was willing to exert himself, or his staff, on behalf of the suffering individual, but adamantly refused to generalize that private gesture into public policy.

As it turned out, the incident illustrated only the hard-hearted half of the Helms attitude. Five years later, Delton Ponder had not heard from Helms or from anyone on his behalf. I talked to Ponder one Sunday night when he was on duty as a watchman at a Hattiesburg shopping center. At age fifty, he also was doing free-lance maintenance work in the daytime. His food stamp allotments had been reduced by the Reagan-Helms cutbacks, and only in early 1986 had he started earning enough money to be ineligible for them. His daughter had a birth defect, his wife had undergone twenty-two operations, yet he said stubbornly, "Things are looking better. I think we're going to pull out of it."

However, there are areas in which Helms's stubbornness does melt away. His dedication to principle often takes second place when it confronts the special economic interests of North Carolina.

Helms heartily supported the Reagan administration's campaign against federal spending as budget director David Stockman started swinging his axe in 1981. To be the Agriculture chairman leading the attack on food stamps was pure bliss for him. It fit his ideology and his personal nature. It put him out front in the crusade promised by the conservative president he had championed for so long. In fact, on many issues Helms was out front of the president himself in those early days of the new administration. He found some of Reagan's appointments and policy switches insufficiently radical departures from what had gone before. His reflexes and his past successes had accustomed him to roll out of bed every day to criticize what the in-crowd was doing. Now the in-crowd was his crowd, the people he had thought would be his political soulmates. It was awkward. So, he gradually realized, was being chairman of a Senate committee, the man in charge of moving legislation rather than the free-lancer specializing in quixotic charges and lonely stands.

In his furious assault on food stamps, Helms may have thought he was showing the way things would be with a new administration, with a new Republican majority in the Senate, reinforced by true believers from the New Right. He did not reckon with true believers in the programs he was treating so roughly, with the sensitivities of his colleagues, and with the continuing Democratic majority in the House.

Four days after he had cut up the food stamp program in that hearing in Washington, Helms was back in Raleigh, at the annual meeting of Tobacco Associates, a southern leaf-growers' lobby. About five hundred farmers and warehousemen listened as the chairman of the Senate Agriculture Committee stood before them and said, "Now repeat after me: "There—is—no—tobacco—subsidy!" Lustily, the five hundred chanted the line together. They and Helms had begun to feel the cumulative resentment built up in response to the senator's food-stamp assault and his tactics over the years. By a bare nine to seven, the Senate Budget Committee had rejected a move to eliminate tobacco price supports totaling $23 million a year. Thus, in his keynote address to the Tobacco Associates, Helms led his audience not that once, but five times in chanting, "There is no tobacco subsidy." He was drilling them, and himself, in the line they would take in the future debates to come.

No single issue is more important than tobacco to Helms's Carolina constituency. None so strains his vaunted commitment to the idea that government should stay out of relations between the private entrepreneur and the free market. And from the moment he came to the Senate, expediency prevailed on this one. Because he had to, Helms became the Senate's leading protector of federal price supports for tobacco.

The growing, processing, manufacturing, packaging, and selling of tobacco put about $1½ billion a year directly into North Carolina paychecks. The state is by far the biggest tobacco producer; close to 350,000 Tarheels work at it, full- and part-time, and the livings of many more depend on it indirectly. They are overalled farmers on the sandy Coastal Plain and the red-clay Piedmont; cigarette factory workers in Durham, Winston-Salem, and Reidsville; white-collar clerks and computer operators at R.J. Reynolds; truck drivers along U.S. 64 between Tarboro and Lizard Lick. They are the super-rich, the dirt-poor, and those in between—people like Mrs. Jesse Helms. (She, like thousands of other Carolinians, owns a tobacco allotment —in effect, an exclusive growing permit—which she rents out to others who do the farming and get the federal price support.) Tobacco is as sacrosanct to Carolina politicians as oil is to Oklahomans. Helms was not alone at the head table at that day's meeting in Raleigh: Republicans and Democrats, senators and congressmen, the governor and attorney general, the appointed and the ambitious all were there.

Since New Deal days, the federal government had regularly loaned funds to tobacco cooperatives through the Tobacco Stabilization Corporation (TSC) and the Commodity Credit Corporation (CCC). The cooperatives used that TSC money to guarantee a price for the crop. Whatever tobacco failed to bring at least a penny above that floor price was bought from the farmer by the TSC and held for resale when its market value rose. In a separate program, the CCC made loans to tobacco and other farmers at a percentage rate substantially below the market. Supporters of the programs said the government eventually came close to breaking even on them. But as Helms and his political allies and rivals stood up before the Tobacco Associates that day, the TSC program alone had lost some $50 million in its forty-seven-year history. It was a minor sum by federal standards, but it was an irresistible target to the long roll of senators and representatives who had been offended by Jesse Helms.

That was not the only reason for a close look at the tobacco program. The towering evidence linking smoking with lung cancer and other mortal diseases continued to mount, and be publicized, even after previous anti-tobacco surgeons general were replaced by a man Helms backed for the job, Dr. Everett Koop. Koop was true to Helms's expectations in opposing abortion, but he also stood behind the irrefutable scientific findings on tobacco's lethal effects. And there was a newly fashionable reason for eliminating the tobacco supports: cutting out such programs was a major priority of the Reagan administration, its budget director, and its secretary of agriculture.

With momentum running their way, Senate opponents in 1981 began lining up behind an amendment by Ohio's Howard Metzenbaum, who had clashed often with Helms on other issues. It would phase out the support program over a three-year period. Helms and John East began lobbying frantically for support against it. One congressional aide said in mid-summer, "We're in the worst shape we've ever been in." As things looked desperate, East said, "We are very carefully determining who our friends are, who our enemies are, and who is wavering." Helms and East together made the mistake of sending a joint letter to other senators saying that if tobacco supports were cut out, there might be an effort to end other farm loan programs as well. Coming from the chairman of the committee, that language sounded to some like a threat.

Helms had huge liabilities to overcome in this suddenly desperate flurry of backslapping and logrolling. That was about the time California's Alan Cranston, the Democratic whip, said, "Since Jesse Helms started his warfare against those who disagree with him, there's a meanness in the Senate now that I don't think has been seen since the days of Joe McCarthy." Some of his colleagues said that to Helms, the Senate was not a gentlemen's club, but a jungle. One of the tobacco program's most vigorous opponents had been Missouri's Thomas Eagleton, who was holding firm against it as expected.

But some of its erstwhile friends were of a different mind now. One was Brooklyn's Congressman Fred Richmond, who as chairman of the House nutrition subcommittee had helped maintain an urban-rural coalition that protected both food stamps and tobacco supports. After Helms attacked the food stamp program so ardently, Richmond told Rob Christensen of the News & Observer, "Helms has been so vicious and unbending toward social programs, and he has so antagonized members, that they want to get back at Helms through the tobacco program. Helms is the worst liability you have in the state of North Carolina."

That kind of talk rankled Helms and his friend East. As he was entering a meeting at Wilmington, Helms told a questioning TV reporter who asked about Richmond's remarks, "I'm not going to yield to any blackmail from some loudmouth congressman from Brooklyn—who has a curious lifestyle, I might point out." Shortly afterward, East jabbed at Eagleton by reminding a press conference in High Point, "He was George McGovern's running mate, you know, and then dropped out because it turned out he had mental problems." Newspaper files showed, of course, that Richmond had been charged three years earlier with soliciting a young man for sex. The charge was dropped after the congressman agreed to take part in a court first-offender program. And Eagleton had indeed been chosen as McGovern's running mate in 1972 and later dropped from the ticket after it was disclosed that he had undergone treatment for mental problems. But the fact of those events did not legitimize their use years later in a congressional dispute that had nothing at all to do with either subject.

Helms and East may have assumed without thinking that their fans would applaud such personal attacks. After all, Helms's political prosperity was based originally on the hundreds of TV editorials he devoted to equating liberals and immorality, and both he and East had used McGovern's name in derision in their runs for the Senate. What was one more dig of the same sort? Perhaps, for their devoted fans, it was just political hardball, just the kind of honesty for which Helms and East had been elected. But if that response was there, it was muted. What was heard, in the press and in Washington, was a rising tide of resentment—clearly counterproductive to their cause. Thus, a month after his crack, with the Senate showdown approaching, Helms wrote a letter to the *News & Observer,* publicly regretting what he had said. But the way he worded it was reminful once again of the tactics of campaigns past.

His statement had been "inappropriate," he conceded, although he said it in response to Richmond's "rather personal" criticism of himself. Certainly, he said, "there was no reason for me to refer to his 'curious lifestyle.' " Then, lest any reader not understand that reference, he blamed the news media for elaborating on it by describing "the homosexual activity that led to his arrest." Perhaps, he suggested, "the media and I share a common responsibility in this matter . . . It will not happen again." Political veterans who read his letter could not help but recall the way he had so often used the form of responding to others' remarks to repeat the ritual charges of "bloc voting" against him—and, however tenuously, to lay blame on the press for whatever went wrong. Within days, East had followed him by sending a letter of apology to Eagleton. When Helms was asked whether he would apologize personally to Richmond, he implied that he would talk it over when the two sat across the table from each other in conference committee.

Somehow, despite these lapses of judgment, Helms's and East's furious lobbying and promising and threatening combined with a stroke of luck to save the tobacco program that September. Helms had to vow that he, the Agriculture chairman nominally in charge of passing the farm bill, would filibuster against the whole thing if his pet program was cut. Eventually eight wheat-state senators who at first were counted against the tobacco program returned to support it, and four weary anti-tobacco senators went home for the night before the roll was called. That made the difference. Helms had won what some senators said in advance would be more a referendum on him than a vote on legislative substance.

But his trials were not over. So ensnarled and confused had Helms become in the fight over tobacco that Bob Dole, second-ranking man on the Agriculture committee, had to step in for him and guide the overall 1981 farm bill to passage. As columnist Ferrel Guillory pointed out, Helms had come up against the fact that he serves two separate constituencies—his Carolina voters and his national right-wing following. Too much compromising of the sort that had saved the tobacco program could alienate the New Right. Too much ideological rigidity could bind him in making the deals necessary to protect his home-state interests. "The farm bill put the spotlight on the political dilemmas and vulnerabilities confronting Helms as he is thrust into something other than his role of 'Senator No,' " Guillory concluded.

"Senator No" was the way his opponents preferred him. That fall, looking ahead to the next year's elections, the Democrats started using Helms as a "devil" in their fund-raising literature, exactly the way his own direct-mail campaigns had used McGovern, Ted Kennedy, and other liberals. Mailing to women, one letter said that "with Reagan in the White House and ultra-conservative senators like Jesse Helms . . . the New Right is dangerously close to achieving its goal of putting women back in their place." Pitching to blacks, another said, "Strom Thurmond, Jesse Helms, and their allies in the New Right . . . want to kill the Voting Rights Act." All the way down the list of liberal interest groups, there was a way to appeal to each by holding up Helms as a scare figure. "Basically, his negative appeal is pretty universal," explained one Democratic official. "In certain groups, the mere mention of his name causes concern." He ranked Helms ahead of such other productive scarecrows as Jerry Falwell, David Stockman, and Interior Secretary James Watt. Common Cause, the liberal lobby, also used Helms in a full-page advertisement in the *New York Times.* It asked for contributions to help turn back Helms bills that would strip federal courts of authority on abortion, school busing, and school prayer.

All of that merely certified that Helms had arrived where he had been aiming for so long. But public relations success as figurehead of the radical right did not mean success in the legislative efforts that so alarmed the liberals, or in the fight for his own political survival that was nearing. The rejection of his and the Congressional Club's candidates for Congress in North Carolina in 1982 was a forewarning of how serious the coming fight would be. But that was an impersonal setback, for his machine and its millions of dollars, and might never have happened without the surrounding national economic recession. Other things happened to Helms that year that directly threatened his political stature, both at home and in Washington.

After Ronald Reagan's staff made clear that the president's tax-cutting economic package should take priority over all other legislation in 1981, Helms kept the pressure on Senate Majority Leader Howard Baker to take up the New Right's social agenda as soon as the tax and budget bills were passed. Late that year, Helms and East led the way with measures on abortion, busing, and school prayer. A filibuster by Connecticut's liberal Republican Lowell Weicker already had held up a Helms anti-busing amendment for three months. The next wave of Helms-East proposals collided with others sponsored by their hard-line conservative brethren. Utah's Orrin Hatch had a constitutional amendment against abortion before his Constitution subcommittee. Helms's bill declaring that human life begins at conception and barring federal court jurisdiction was backed by the National Right to Life Committee, while Hatch's approach, to give restrictive state laws priority, was preferred by the

U.S. Catholic Conference. But Helms, insisting he had made a deal with Baker, pushed to bypass the committee process and bring his proposals directly to the floor. It was not that he expected to win on them, especially with proponents split over both substance and procedure. It was that he wanted to put his colleagues on the spot, to get record votes to be churned in and out of the Congressional Club's computers and mass mail machinery.

Thus in January, 1982, the club sent out fund-raising letters over Helms's signature summarizing what it had accomplished in the year just past and what it hoped to do in the year ahead. It said the club had generated more than three million letters, postcards, telegrams, and phone calls to Congress urging passage of Reagan's program; placed commercials on a hundred TV stations reaching ten million homes, collected 250,000 pledges supporting the president. The club had "cut back waste in the food stamp program," partly by running TV ads in the South and Midwest urging people to petition their senators and congressmen. It had collected more than twenty thousand petitions to pressure Congress to "bring back prayer in the public schools." Looking ahead, the club was preparing "a massive campaign to win conservative control of the House in 1982." Soon afterward, it got off another mailing, asking for more money, and enclosing postcards and petitions to be sent to pressure specific senators who had not co-sponsored the constitutional amendment to require a balanced budget.

To say that Helms's colleagues in Congress resented this constant setting of backfires in their home states is gross understatement. But with the crisis over the tobacco support program past, Helms was unconcerned about his colleagues. He was playing to his national audience, and to the Carolina voters he would have to face in two years. That summer, he and East filibustered against extension of the Voting Rights Act, which applied only to a dozen states, including North Carolina. He asserted that the bill was "insulting and degrading" to the South, and warned that he had at least forty-one amendments ready for introduction. Eventually, the Senate broke his filibuster and passed the extension. On each vote, Helms had the backing of only seven colleagues. The whole Senate seemed exhausted by the grueling showdown, but Helms did not let up.

He raised the pressure for action on the high-intensity social agenda. In the summer of 1982, he used the tactic of hitching his proposals to a measure that had to be passed, the annual extension of the federal debt limit. Without it, the government would have to halt—thus, for Helms's purposes, it was the ideal vehicle. "This is the only shot we will have," he told his fellow advocates of school prayer and opponents of abortion. "We had better take our best shot."

While he was maneuvering on the floor, opposing lobbyists were playing rougher than ever against him. They mounted the biggest anti-Helms letter-writing campaign to that date. Some wore a button picturing a coat hanger and saying, "Abort Jesse." They ran a big ad in national newspapers showing a senator in bed with a man and woman, and saying, "The decision to have a baby could soon be between you, your husband and your senator." Helms, on the receiving end for a change, complained bitterly. He got little sympathy. In the Senate, Dale Bumpers of Arkansas said Helms was pushing the amendments just to create new ammunition for the Congressional Club. "His presses are running, his letters are going out," Bumpers declared. "He is going after all the troglodytes in the Senate who are opposed to school prayer." Paul Tsongas of Massachusetts said Helms would be raising money to beat Thomas Jefferson if he were in the Senate. Even Barry Goldwater was adamantly against Helms. So when the Carolinian took his best shot, he was defeated on three decisive votes, and after weeks of hangup, the Senate approved the debt extension and moved on.

New York's Daniel Patrick Moynihan cheered that "the radical right" had been turned back. But Helms and his supporters confirmed what Bumpers and others had said during debate: as Peter Gemma, of the National Pro-Life Action Committee, put it, Helms's power was not in his popularity, but in "getting the job done." "On something like this, we need groundswell support. Jesse Helms gets it for us. We need some hardball tactics . . ." Helms, he said, is "absolutely still the generalissimo of our movement. He's gotten us what we wanted: recorded votes." And Helms himself, although making clear his anger at conservatives like Goldwater who opposed him, put a bright face on defeat. "The liberals have done us a service," he told Rob Christensen. "Our troops all across the country have been very attentive to what has been going on in the Senate . . . [The opponents] have served a useful purpose because they have raised the adrenalin level of the people who want prayer back in the schools and people who want to stop this business of deliberately terminating innocent human life as a matter of convenience."

But Helms, inevitably, also had raised the adrenalin level of those he crossed in that fight. Some believed he had broken an agreement on how his amendments would be brought to the floor, although Helms said it was just a misunderstanding. Afterward, one of those involved told Bill Peterson of the *Washington Post,* "People started to question his word, his integrity. That can be devastating around here." One southerner said, "Jesse has worn about as thin as tissue paper with most members. It's not any one single thing. It's not abortion. It's not school prayer. It's his tactics. It's what he did on tobacco. It's his fight with Tom Eagleton. It's his Congressional Club and how he makes you vote on emotional issues, and then sends a bunch of money into your state and tries to beat you. There are a lot of people lying in wait for Jesse, and not all of them are Democrats."

But it was the Democrats, those in Carolina, who leaped on Helms's most politically damaging mistake of 1982. Among his national fans, it had passed with little notice amid the clamor over their social agenda. But it stirred excitement back home; it was the first major event of the forthcoming Helms re-election campaign, and it was a near-disaster.

It came when Reagan, facing a sure economic recession, bowed to his advisers and reluctantly threw his weight behind Senate Finance Chairman Bob Dole's $99 billion "revenue enhancement"—one of history's biggest tax increases. Helms and East had backed the president's tax-cutting package the previous year, and seemed consistent when they started off opposing the increase. More than consistency underlay their position: the bill would double cigarette taxes from eight to sixteen cents a pack. On the first test, the Reagan-backed bill lost by two votes. At five o'clock in the morning, Helms and East buckled under administration pressure and told Dole they would switch. That turned the vote around, and the tax increase passed. They had done their turn for Reagan, who telephoned the senior senator from Air Force One to thank him. They also had set off a furor in North Carolina. No matter that when they realized this they squirmed and wiggled and eventually switched back to vote against final enactment of the bill. All that was too late. Back in Carolina, Helms and East were suddenly "the Tobacco Tax Twins."

The Democrats focused their gleeful pseudo-anger on Helms, who was facing re-election. From county clerk to governor, from overalled farmer to high-paid lobbyist, those whose living or political fortunes were based on tobacco proclaimed their shock. Helms contended that it was all politics, that the hand of his sure challenger,

Governor Jim Hunt, was behind a "Tobacco Tax Twins" advertisement. But he realized that he had been hurt. He was determined to reverse that damage, at whatever cost to his already diminished standing in the Senate. His next opportunity, as he saw it, was a populist issue that should help him with the farmers and blue-collar workers he had so recently offended. It was the administration-supported proposal to boost the federal gasoline tax by a nickel a gallon.

Helms and the Congressional Club had run a major campaign against a state gasoline tax pushed by Governor Jim Hunt. Now Helms rose against the federal proposal, calling it "another dumping on the consumer." As Congress ground into the final days of its session, with senators eager to spend Christmas at home with their families, he and East led a filibuster against the gas-tax increase. After more than a week, Howard Baker pulled the bill off the floor, but later decided that if he gave in, Helms would be able to tie up proceedings at will when the Senate reconvened the following year. He brought the bill out again, and as the filibuster groaned on, tempers rose.

Helms turned down a plea to desist from Reagan himself. He reminded the president that he had once said it would take a palace coup for him to back such a tax boost. "When did the palace coup occur?" he said he asked Reagan. Then he vowed to keep the Senate there over Christmas if necessary. Finally, Baker filed a cloture petition, and Helms was smacked down 81 to 5. He tried to make light of it, as if he had just lost a friendly game of poker, but the others would have none of that. Helms approached Alan Simpson, the Wyoming conservative who is known for his expansive sense of humor, and stuck out his hand. He obviously assumed Simpson would forget his earlier description of Helms's filibuster as "an obdurate, obnoxious performance," and his prediction that in the months ahead, bills of interest to North Carolina would meet "a veritable phalanx of opposition which likely will be most demeaning and disturbing to the senator's constituency." "Let's be friends," Helms said to Simpson. But the towering westerner kept his seat, staring silently at Helms until he dropped his hand and walked away.

That it was Simpson who spurned Helms's gesture made the incident more significant than if he had been so insulted by one of the Senate's aggressive liberals. (Three years later, coverage of this incident still angered Helms. I asked him whether the press had made any specific mistakes of which I should be wary. He immediately brought up the gas-tax debate. He said he had studied the bill more carefully than anyone else. "It had a post office to be named for Tip O'Neill," he said—"a colossal disaster." Simpson, he insisted, was "one of my best friends in the Senate," and "he got up and he let me have it. He called me obdurate, and so forth. And I bet they printed that sucker ten thousand times in North Carolina during my campaign, which is fine. They said Helms was the most unpopular man in the Senate, he's hurting North Carolina, so forth. I defy you to take a poll and see if that's so . . . Simpson came to me within an hour and said, 'Jesse, I'm the biggest S.O.B. in the world, I'm sorry I lost my cool; forgive me.' I said, 'There's nothing to forgive, forget it.' And that's all there was to it. Then Al Simpson went to North Carolina to campaign for me, and afterward he caught me on the Senate floor and said, 'Jesse, what kind of G.d. press have you got down there?' He said, 'I went down there and they about killed me. They said why are you down here, why are you supporting him . . .?' He told them, with some expletives according to his version, 'What do you want me to do, jump out the window?' Now if that doesn't give you some measurement of bias . . .")

In the wake of the Simpson incident, Helms minimized the loss and the reaction of his colleagues. As usual, his ideological friends found good news in defeat, repeating their belief that in losing Helms had furnished yet another grievance to be used in raising funds.

But as he went to North Carolina for the holidays, Helms had to realize he was ending the worst year he had experienced since he entered politics. He had been beaten down repeatedly on his efforts to push legislation for school prayer and against abortion and school busing. He had embarrassed himself on the tobacco-tax vote. His candidates had been manhandled in the congressional elections. And he had angered even some of the colleagues who by politics and personality should have been most tolerant of conservative excesses. One reporter wrote that Helms's stubborn filibuster had made him "a virtual pariah" in the Senate. A senior presidential aide said that on an admiration scale of one to ten, the Reagan White House would rate Helms at a minus two.

Dismal as all these rebuffs made his immediate past, Helms found little to brighten him as he turned home. There, he faced the most serious political challenge of his career, and he was starting behind.

Chapter 12

Coattails II

To many North Carolinians, Jesse Helms's struggles with the likes of Ted Kennedy and Alan Cranston in the Senate are endearing, even when he loses. With his state audience of voters, as with his direct-mail audience across the country, those noble defeats are useful to enlist more help, more contributions to go back and keep fighting off the alleged liberal threat to American values.

But running against Jim Hunt in 1984 was not the same as running against that symbol of northern liberalism, Ted Kennedy. And more than two years before their confrontation at the polls, many months before either Helms or Hunt officially announced as a candidate, their confrontation was ordained. The two strongest personal and political forces in the state were on a collision course starting when Helms's man John East won in 1980, on the same day Democrat Hunt was winning his second and last four-year term as governor. Hunt was a down-home boy with a background just as humble as Helms's own—a churchgoing moderate raised on a tobacco farm, who had carefully catered to Carolina's special interests while building a political organization that could be challenged only by another force as elemental as the Helms network.

Even as Helms was returning wearily from Washington at the end of 1982, emotions already were running high in anticipation of the Helms-Hunt contest. "This is not the state of North Carolina, it is a state of obsession. Everybody seems to be going nuts over Helms and Hunt, even during Christmas," said a Democratic party worker. "It is a fact that either people love Senator Helms or hate him," conceded a Helms operative—"and those who don't like him are absolutely obsessed with the idea of getting him out of the U.S. Senate. It is their No. 1 driving force."

That it was, and as 1983 began, those obsessed with getting Helms out were in high spirits. He had generated columns of what seemed to be devastating publicity with his gasoline-tax filibuster and the anger it stirred even among other Republicans, including those in the Reagan White House. The criticism did not surprise him, any more than the defense raised on his behalf by his old friend James J. Kilpatrick. "Not since the days of Joe McCarthy and the earlier days of Theodore Bilbo, so far as I can recall, has a member of the United States Senate suffered the kind of vilification and personal attack that Jesse Helms of North Carolina has had to endure in the past few weeks," Kilpatrick contended. "The abuse is utterly undeserved." Even less surprising was the *News & Observer*'s editorial rejoinder to the Kilpatrick column. It escalated the rhetoric yet another notch by asserting that "if Kilpatrick were a North Carolinian . . . he hardly could be very happy about having the vital affairs of his state represented in the Senate by the political version of Typhoid Mary."

But there were more objective assessments of Helms's standing. Public opinion polls, his own and those taken for Hunt, showed the senator running eight to sixteen percentage points behind as the year began. Weeks before, still earlier surveys had inspired Hunt's press secretary, Gary Pearce, to say, "If we don't win, it'll be because we were stupid." Democrats were buoyed by the turnout at a Hunt fund-raising dinner that brought in $250,000, and by response to a hard-hitting direct-mail solicitation that painted Helms as a "right-wing demagogue" feeding on emotional issues. Hunt's Washington-based fund-raising consultant, Patricia Keefer of the Craver, Mathews, Smith firm, explained its success: "You have to have a devil. You have to have someone for people to respond to. That's how you raise money."

Even those Helms should have been able to count on as his most faithful backers were showing doubts. The legislative director of the National Right to Life Committee, the country's biggest anti-abortion organization, wrote an internal memo implying that Helms's unpopularity among his colleagues might make him a liability for the cause he so strongly supported. Helms's standing had fallen to a new low, said the note: "The level of animosity toward Senator Helms has in fact increased steadily during the 97th Congress." Since personal relationships are such an important part of the legislative process, the memo suggested, "pro-life" leaders might consider whether someone else would be a more effective point man for their efforts to ban abortion.

Disclosure of this memo clearly got to Helms. That same week, he spoke to a dinner following the annual "March for Life" through downtown Washington. He said he wished he and the marchers could be celebrating together the total triumph of their cause, but not to quit, because "it will come, it will come . . ." He was cheered when the group, seeming to contradict the Right to Life Committee's legislative director, gave Helms its first Life Award for Outstanding Service. Then the gathering sang to him, to the tune of "Hello, Dolly":

> Just feel the room swaying, 'Cause we're all praying,
>   For the Human Life amendment right away.
> So here's our hand, Jesse, You're our man, Jesse,
>   We need this song to save our families.

It is safe to say it was a rare honor, but it did not change the polls. Trying to start some kind of counter-trend, Helms's Congressional Club already had begun a media campaign against Hunt, but at that point the campaign badly needed an inspiration. As Hunt's consultants pointed out, Helms himself was the necessary "devil" figure for those working to unseat him. But for Helms to mount the kind of campaign that always had worked for him before, he too desperately needed a villain—someone more provocative to Tarheels than familiar, moderate, unthreatening Jim Hunt.

That villain flew into Raleigh that spring, and called at the governor's mansion. He was photographed sitting beside Hunt in an obvious strategy conference. When he emerged, the visitor announced that he would lead an all-out voter registration drive in the state. "With 200,000 more blacks registered, Jesse Helms could be put out of work," he said.

His name was Jesse Jackson. His visit, his registration campaign, and especially the reaction to it were one of the deciding factors in the Helms-Hunt election.

Lamarr Mooneyham was a young preacher then at the Tri-City Baptist Temple, in Durham. The Baptists there are independent fundamentalists, unaffiliated with the mainstream Southern Baptist Convention. In that, the temple was like Thomas Road Baptist Church, in Lynchburg, Virginia, just over one hundred miles north. Thomas Road is the home base of television evangelist Jerry Falwell, who headed the Moral Majority. Lamarr Mooneyham was Falwell's lieutenant in North Carolina, the man who organized the state's Moral Majority network in 1980. He was and is a devoted admirer of Jesse Helms.

Just how much impact the Moral Majority's widely discussed effort to register voters had on the election of Ronald Reagan in 1980 remains uncertain. Falwell bragged publicly then about getting two million new voters on the books nationwide, and openly endorsed Reagan for president. That first venture of the Moral Majority into national politics was a noisy operation, long on televised controversy but short on the mechanics of vote production. Before the 1984 election, the group's officers set about planning quietly to do grass-roots organization. In February, 1983, Mooneyham met with other Moral Majority operatives in Washington, to analyze what would be needed to help Helms the following year in Carolina. They estimated that the voters then registered, though heavily Democratic by party, probably would split down the middle between Helms and Hunt. The way to win was to "create a new pool of voters," as Mooneyham explained it to me—people who previously had been uninvolved in politics, but could be counted on to back Helms. "We figured seventy thousand new voters, roughly, would put it in the bag," he said.

The Democrats, specifically Jesse Jackson and Jim Hunt, were thinking in the same direction. Jackson looked at the registration figures in each southern state, and saw that the number of unregistered blacks more than equaled the margins by which Reagan had carried those states in 1980. Thus he set out on his Southern Crusade, aiming at putting two million new black voters on the rolls. In North Carolina, Hunt had seen this potential. An estimated half-million blacks were eligible but unregistered—and Reagan's 1980 margin there had been just forty-one thousand, and Helms's two years earlier barely over a hundred thousand. The nominally non-partisan State Elections Board mounted a major registration drive, directed at all eligible citizens, not just blacks. Some eighteen thousand persons were authorized as registrars to sign them up. This state drive had brought in 150,000 more voters, seventy thousand of them black, in 1982 alone. It enrolled Tarheels in supermarkets, schools, banks, factories, and in the lines where they waited for driver's licenses. Alex Brock, long-time head of the board, told me then that he could not say how many had been signed up by which political groups. He insisted that "we record male, female, black, white, Indian, and 'other.' Beyond that I couldn't say."

This drive already was rolling when the Moral Majority strategists met in Washington to plan their own effort. At that point neither side knew what effect Jesse Jackson's intervention would have. Hunt clearly wanted a drastic boost to black registration, since all polls showed that almost every black was eager to vote against Helms. But there also was a potential downside to publicity about the strident Jackson's efforts on his behalf. That is why, rather than having a public press conference with lights and cameras, the governor had Jackson in on a Sunday morning, without television, and with limited coverage. He hoped the visit would get maximum play in the black press, which it did, and minimum attention in other media. It did that, too, until Helms and the Moral Majority got hold of it.

Soon after Jackson visited Raleigh and toured the state to drum up enrollment, fliers went out from Helms headquarters with the headline, "Jackson/Hunt Voter Drive Endangers Re-Election of Reagan/Helms." A picture of the Hunt-Jackson meeting was reprinted from a black newspaper, the *Carolinian.* And in early summer, with Helms still trailing Hunt in the polls, Helms, Jerry Falwell, and Lamarr Mooneyham made a tour of the state.

With Helms wearing a "Senator No" wristwatch held on by a red, white, and blue band, and Falwell warning that America was becoming Sodom and Gomorrah, they stopped at Asheville, Raleigh, Charlotte, Wilmington, and Greensboro. Boosting their own registration drive, they used the Jackson effort to fire up the senator's supporters. "We told people what was going on," Mooneyham recalls. "Sure, we referred to Jesse Jackson's registration campaign in North Carolina. We said he had a right to do that, and we basically were doing the same thing. We said, 'Jesse Jackson wants to put Jesse Helms out of work, and you must decide which Jesse you want to represent you.' " Mooneyham also said registration was "the only way to stop a political blackmailer like the Reverend Jackson from acquiring the kind of political clout that he needs to implement his racist agenda."

On that tour, the Moral Majority stars sought to sign up people to become pro-Helms registrars. Then they wrote to fundamentalist churches across the state, asking each of them to set up registration drives. "We put one registrar in each church," Mooneyham says. "We'd go anywhere anybody was interested. It was mostly just conservative churches, evangelical, fundamental, not necessarily Baptist. The common denominator was they were conservative in theology . . . We had a table there every Sunday, out in the hallways where the people would come out after services, or sometimes outdoors when it was nice. That's allowed. Under North Carolina law, a church is like any other place."

Unlike the Jackson Southern Crusade, which often created resentment among local politicians because the charismatic Jackson came and got the headlines and then left them to do the follow-up work, the Moral Majority drive had staying power. Its campaign in the fundamentalist churches went on Sunday after Sunday for almost a year and a half until the election, Mooneyham says.

But the most telling difference in the competing registration drives was the way they were focused. Jackson's effort, aimed at blacks, was clearly directed, but lacked organizational follow-through. The mass drive by the State Elections Board was a broad catch-all. But the Moral Majority effort, concentrating on the white fundamentalist churches, was finely pointed. Mooneyham, the Durham preacher who has moved since to Northside Baptist Church in Charlotte, says, "We believed the majority of the non-registered were conservatives who would vote for the conservative candidate. We never failed to give our personal opinion about candidates when asked, but we were not registering for a party, we were registering them to vote. With the big Democratic majority in this state, we knew if we messed with the party, we'd be in a lot of trouble."

Mooneyham told me that the weakness of the Hunt drive was that "it didn't go to the people who were likely to coalesce as voters, once registered. The Hunt driver's license application thing, we monitored it and found out they were registering Republicans, sometimes by ten to one. It seemed to backfire . . . It's always been amazing to me how they just went to the wrong watering trough . . . But our drive—if you think about it, a person conscientious enough to bring his family to church on Sunday, if he's registered he's probably going to do something about it."

Despite the church-volunteer atmosphere, the Moral Majority drive cost money. Mooneyham says "in excess of $100,000" probably was spent on it. The total may have been much more. It was raised by direct mail. Mooneyham says he started with a Moral Majority mailing list of some three thousand names, and after the election that had grown to more than forty-five thousand.

The public relations aspects of the drive also were handled skill-fully. "To have Falwell come in to accompany Jesse Helms a year and a half before the election is okay," Mooneyham said to me. "A week and a half before the election, it will blow up in your face. They can come from Lynchburg or Chicago or somewhere and say they're going to put your senator out of work, and people say 'No way!' Phyllis Schlafly and those people have to watch what they're doing when they come in here, too, because these Carolinians have a thing that's very unique, they want to take care of their own laundry."

So effectively did Mooneyham's Carolina effort work that in May of election year, he was summoned to the Moral Majority's head-quarters in Lynchburg to help create programs for all fifty states. This was the takeoff of a new organization, the American Coalition for Traditional Values (ACTV), headed by the Rev. Tim LaHaye. It provides handbooks and other aids for church-based voter drives. Mooneyham is proud that the Smithsonian Institution asked for a copy of his handbook for its social and cultural history collection. That National Voter Registration Manual outlines step-by-step procedures for registration by churches. It explains the fine lines across which preachers should not step in political campaigning—essentially, that they can and should speak out and organize for whomever they wish, as long as they stipulate that they are voicing their personal opinion. And it justifies this by saying separation of church and state is "a myth that has become a false political dictum." "Apathetic Christians have distanced themselves from politics and government, and humanists and other amoral and immoral persons have rushed in to fill the vacuum," it says. The manual was sent out with red-white-and-blue posters urging churchgoers to "Protect Your Christian Heritage—Register and Vote," and proclaiming a national goal of two million registrants for the ACTV drive.

Voter registration was everybody's game in those months, and Jesse Jackson seemed everybody's inspiration. If Governor Hunt's auto-permit campaign seemed unusual, it was unimaginative by comparison with the Moral Majority's statewide, then nationwide church-based drive. And that in turn seemed routine beside another effort headed by a man who lived down a lonely tobacco road beyond Angier, south of Raleigh.

"When you get to Angier call me from there," he said, so I did, from a hot phone booth beside the highway. "You come seven miles out

McIver street," he told me. "I'll be waiting for you on the left, in a blue Buick."

Six-point-four miles, actually, past fields of tobacco wilting in the drought, squat frame houses apparently empty, not another car along the road.

He was there, wearing a camouflage dungaree cap, with a boy beside him wearing a Pac-Man cap. A 12-gauge shotgun was propped across the seat within easy reach. "Just follow me," he said, pointing down a side road. We turned left onto the dry, hard yard of a tiny house sided with rustic plywood. He got out and extended his hand:

Glenn Miller, leader of the Carolina Knights of the Ku Klux Klan.

He asked me in, introduced me to his wife and offered me tea or coffee. The temperature inside was worse than out. I thankfully took some iced tea. Three, then four children lay in the heat, watching cartoons on television. The wife sat silent on the screened porch, watching an infant lolling sweating in a baby bouncer.

Glenn Miller himself, camouflage cap still at a strictly military angle, mustache seemingly clipped for inspection, sat stiffly in an easy chair. At his left was a polished M-1 carbine, its ammunition clip in place. Across the door, an M-14 infantry rifle leaned ready against the wall.

One corner of the living room-dining room-kitchen was filled with boxes of leaflets touting a Klan rally near Bennett, South Carolina, each flier wrapped around a copy of *The Thunderbolt,* newspaper of the National States' Rights Party. Stacks of other leaflets loaded the kitchen shelves.

The atmosphere at this headquarters and training center of the CKKK was polite but hardly relaxed. I spoke above the jabber of the TV cartoons: "I've heard about this voter registration drive you're running. Since the popular perception of the Klan is that it doesn't operate mainly through the ballot box, I thought you might tell me more about it."

That flicked the switch. All I had to do was listen. "It's the 'Jews media,'" Miller said. That's why people had that perception. He produced another leaflet, this one purporting to show that all major American news organizations have Jewish ownership and management. He had an epithet to answer every question.

What started him crusading for the Klan? He is an ex-paratrooper and Green Beret. "I got interested in the white movement before I retired, at Fort Bragg. I got educated about what's happening to the white race. It's simple arithmetic. The minorities are taking over. The white race is dying.

"And now we're educating hundreds of thousands of people about it. We're going to educate them to what happened in the Greensboro trial, too. Those heroes are not criminals. They were found innocent on ninety-four criminal charges."

He was talking about the 1979 shootout between Klan and Nazi party members and demonstrators of the Communist Workers' Party, which left five of the latter dead.

"The niggers and the Jews and other minorities screamed bloody murder, and so now they're throwing the white patriots to the bloody minorities to get votes . . . Those hundreds of niggers, communists and Jews . . . were trying to pull women and children into it," he said. "I'm under a gag order from the prosecutor not to talk about it."

Lean, spring-loaded, articulate, he wanted to talk on in that direction. It was hard to turn him back to voter registration.

"Jesse Jackson came in here, and Hunt opened the schools and military bases to him to register the niggers," he said. So his Klan began a counter-drive. "We have probably registered ten thousand to twenty-five thousand already. We've got over six hundred members in fifteen dens around the state. We've had two marches and four rallies so far."

He got up and picked the phone off the kitchen wall, dialed it, and handed it to me. "Listen," he said.

It was his voice on a recording, a racial screed touching all the objects of his hatred. It concluded with an exhortation to register to vote.

"We've got seven recording numbers in the state," he said, "and we're going to get more." He claimed each number averaged ten thousand calls a month—and that two or three times a week he got angry calls from blacks, threatening his life.

"Jesse Jackson encouraged white people to get off their lazy asses —make that backsides—and register," he said.

But what is the aim of all this registration? "We're going to get petitions and form our own American Patriot Party, with a hundred candidates, for governor, lieutenant governor, attorney general, state legislature, right on down." What about senator? "No, not senator. Just state offices."

Whether the CKKK actually stirred thousands of white voters to register was hard to prove. So was the membership of the CKKK itself. It was one of six Klan offshoots in the state. Glenn Miller claimed six hundred-plus members: the editor of the *Smithfield Herald* down the road said he thought it was a one-man Klan. A few days earlier, seventy-two had turned out in camouflage uniforms or Klan robes to march behind Miller in a white registration parade in Benson. (Later, Miller changed his organization's title to the White Patriot Party. Wearing the White Patriot label, Miller himself ran in the 1986 Republican primary for the other Senate seat, and got 3 percent of the vote.)

But Miller refused to say whether his earlier voter effort had anything to do with the Helms-Hunt election. If Jesse Helms was going to benefit from it, I would have to deduce that myself. Miller only hinted at it, implying that his dreamed-of party did not need to run its own senator because it was satisfied with the one already there. He also helped me with the shadings of his disdain for the major parties: "The Republican Party is for the rich and the near-rich. The Democrats are for the homosexuals, pornographers, baby-killers, minorities, communists, socialists, and anti-Christians." It was for me to hear the echoes there of other speeches by other men.

Whether his CKKK had hundreds or only dozens of members, Miller himself was a churning mill of propaganda. The state's newspapers were blitzed by his letters to the editor. An example:

"Jesse Jackson's PUSH, the NAACP, Black United Front, Black Political Caucus, and hundreds of other black organizations are working specifically in the interests of the Black race, while the tens of millions of minorities smile, nod approval, and shout 'Right on!' Meanwhile, Whitey smokes his dope, sips his six-packs, watches as the Blacks play ball on TV, rides around in his pick-em-up truck, and supports the system that makes it all possible, while condemning that ole KKK."

Considering his thirst for publicity, it was surprising that Miller warned me that his "board of governors" had ruled that all out-of-state media would be charged a twenty-five-dollar interview fee. Asked why, he said because they are biased and unobjective. One of my own biases is against paying for interviews. My reflex was to say no thanks. But I decided that twenty-five dollars, paid on the record, was a reasonable price for the armload of CKKK handouts and other hate literature he stacked up for me. So I rationalized the payment and handed him the money.

Only later did I realize how pertinent the material was. There was the *NAAWP News,* organ of the National Association for the Advancement of White People, with its warning that "A dramatic change is taking place in America. Every minute of every day America's population is becoming darker." The NAAWP's principles were listed: "Equal rights for whites, an end to forced busing, total welfare reform, crackdown on violent crime, no more immigration, an end to race hatred in media, preservation of the white race and its heritage, excellence in all things." Its ads listed dozens of "suppressed books," racist and anti-Semitic tracts by authors like Carleton Putnam, Henry Garrett—names familiar to readers of the periodicals where the commentaries of Jesse Helms used to run. There was the *Thunderbolt,* "Defender of White People's Rights," asserting that federal prosecution of the Greensboro Klansmen was a Reagan frame-up to win minority votes. It had a bold-face "NOTICE: Don't blame Sen. Jesse Helms who opposes all of Reagan's liberal policies. Gov. Hunt backs Reagan's pro-minority stand!"

There was Glenn Miller's own *White Carolinian,* with claims of "tremendous success" and nationwide interest in the recent White Voter Registration March, and reminders that "The family that Klans together, stands together." There was a handout announcing a forthcoming CKKK White Unity Rally on Highway 902 south of Bennett. "We'll have a pig-pickin, country-western and white power music, free Klan literature, the marching KKK Honor Guard, Confederate Battle Flags, speeches by Klan leaders, White fraternity and brotherhood, and a KKK 50-foot cross-lighting ceremony at dusk. (No open consumption of alcohol allowed.)" Interestingly, across the top of this invitation Miller had typed a line that apparently carried special weight with his audience: "Mr. Herbert F. (Chub) Seawell of Carthage urges all patriotic citizens to attend." Seawell, of course, was Helms's old friend, soulmate, and frequent editorial stand-in during his years as a Raleigh commentator. He has died since, and I never had a chance to ask him about the significance of his purported endorsement of the Klan rally.

The ice in the bottom of my tea glass had long since melted. As I stood to leave, I noted the cleaned and oiled weapons leaning against the wall. What kind of training did Miller hold out back? "Strictly defensive," he said. "Counter-ambush, hand-to-hand, defensive training, martial arts." Any trouble with the police? "The sheriff came and inspected our firing range and approved it."

On the wall hung a family portrait, a photograph of his father's generation and before. They were lean, grim-mouthed, sunburned people, lined up in a bare flat yard before an unpainted farmhouse that made Glenn Miller's look luxurious. "Look at them," he said. "Can you imagine what they'd think of their family being mongrelized?"

He walked me to the door. The children still lay transfixed by the cartoons. He extended his hand again. "Send me a copy, now," he said. "If you don't I'll come burn a cross in your front yard."

"Wait till the weather cools off, will you?" I said as I backed the car out onto the sizzling road.

I doubt that Jesse Helms ever met Glenn Miller. But I am confident that however many people were registered by Miller's voter drive, that many voted for Jesse Helms against Jim Hunt. The same can be said of almost all those registered by Lamarr Mooneyham's Moral Majority campaign. The most effective motivator for both those efforts was Jesse Jackson. Big, dramatic, fearsome to those who suffered from racial paranoia, he gave flesh to an element that has always been present in Helms's elections. It is harder to stir racial emotions in a general, impersonal way, although somehow it always happens when Helms is running. Given Jackson as a threat, the Helms drive sprang to life. "I owe that man a lot," Mooneyham conceded to me. Lest that drive lag, Helms kept it going.

"What do these radicals and liberals have in common?" asked a flier enclosed with one of his fund-raising letters. It showed Jackson photographed in an angry moment, along with Julian Bond, "black radical activist," who was quoted as saying, "I'd like to see us run a picture of Jesse Helms in the North Carolina papers with a rifle's crosshairs over his chest." Another later Helms fund-raising message mentioned Jackson's name twenty-four times. But Claude Allen, Helms's young black campaign press secretary, asserted that it was Hunt, rather than Helms, who had appealed to race in the campaign. "We have scrupulously avoided bringing up the race issue," Allen said. "We have not targeted any particular groups for voter registration drives, unlike Governor Hunt."

But Helms's most successful reminder to his fans of where he stood on such matters came in the Senate. For a month in the fall of 1983, he maneuvered and filibustered as leader of the opposition to a national holiday in honor of Martin Luther King, Jr. Those who recalled his hammering at King during the civil rights days of the sixties found it all familiar. "The legacy of Dr. King was really division, not love," he said. "Dr. King's action-oriented Marxism . . . is not compatible with the concepts of this country."

Some of his Senate colleagues who had not heard Helms on King at such length became more and more furious. As the debate began, Helms had a 350-page stack of FBI documents on King placed on each senator's desk. New York's Daniel Patrick Moynihan denounced it as "trash" and flung it to the floor. Helms roused Ted Kennedy to a personal confrontation as he invoked the names of Kennedy's dead brothers to support his allegations against King. He brought suit demanding, unsuccessfully, that raw FBI investigative files, including wiretaps of King, sealed for fifty years by a federal judge, be opened at once.

As the Senate struck down his roadblocks and prepared to pass the bill, individual senators stood to explain their votes. Many were critical of Helms. None was so blunt as New Jersey's Bill Bradley. He compared Helms to "Bull Connor and his dogs," who had attacked King in Birmingham twenty years before, and said Helms was catering to "the old Jim Crow." The Senate voted seventy-six to twelve against Helms's motion to recommit the bill to Strom Thurmond's Judiciary Committee. Only three senators from the old Confederacy joined Helms in voting against final passage.

Perhaps some senators were impressed by warnings like the one from a Helms adviser, saying that to oppose the King holiday bill would be "political suicide." Helms knew better. But after the vote, he held a press conference and denied what his colleagues and others had implied during the debate: "I am not a racist," he insisted. "I am not a bigot. Ask any black that knows me, and they will tell you I am not." Then he stood by as the North Carolina legislature, with Hunt's approval, overwhelmingly passed a state King holiday bill. Then he inspected the public opinion polls showing reaction to his latest display. And then, true to form, he used what he had just done to raise money to do it some more.

In a five-page direct-mail appeal that went out a week after the Senate vote, Helms summarized his charges against King, emphasizing that he had opposed the bill mainly because of its cost to the government. He slid from that straight into his need for funds to counter "Jesse Jackson and the bloc vote extremists." "We are scraping the bottom of the barrel right now because we have had to spend all our reserves on our grassroots voter registration drive to try to counter the voter registration drive of Jesse Jackson," he said. "My campaign manager tells me that without new commercials now, we will slip farther behind."

Till that fall, the polls had indeed showed him still trailing Hunt. Both candidates and news organizations had been taking surveys since Helms and Hunt started down the track toward each other. Peter Hart, the Washington specialist who did Hunt's polling, was not only asking who voters would prefer, but why. In early 1982, he found that Hunt was perceived as more effective, more in touch with North Carolina, more likely to improve the state's national reputation, more positive in his thinking, committed to a more balanced approach to problems. Those were assets, but they were soft values. At the same time Helms was seen as having deep convictions, being a strong fighter who operated on a simple right-wrong value system. By 1983, when Jesse Jackson had helped raise race consciousness, these Helms qualities were sounding more positive: Helms was seen as consistent, a man who didn't change his goals, who had the courage of his convictions. The back side of those assets also showed up: some saw him as too outspoken, a bigot, and a few volunteered their impression that he was a racist. But a solid 72 percent said Helms was a man of principle.

Hunt ran well ahead as the campaign started taking shape. In the summer of 1982, he led by 50 to 36 percent. That was before any important money had been spent on advertising by either side. Reagan was down in the polls because of the slumping economy. But even then Hunt already was tagged by some as a political creature, a liberal, and the governor who had boosted the state gasoline tax. As 1983 developed, Helms's performance against raising the federal gasoline tax, which had so enraged his Senate colleagues, showed up as a net plus in Carolina. Beginning in late summer, the surveys had the candidates close, with Helms pulling up. He was spending heavily to portray Hunt as a liberal. That fall, Helms's Senate stand against the Martin Luther King holiday gave him the sharpest upward turn he would get in most of the ongoing polls. At about that time, Tom Ellis and the Helms organization shifted their media campaign into high gear, trying to make Hunt rather than the senator the focus of controversy.

Long before either man formally entered the 1984 race, the Congressional Club and its allied organizations were soliciting money with mail that served the double purpose of tainting whoever might oppose Helms. In mid-1983, there was the letter from Congressional Club executive director Carter Wrenn about how "sleek black limousines rolled up the driveway to Pamela Harriman's mansion" to an "ultra-chic, elegant dinner party that attracted the 'cream' of liberal Washington. High-fashion Washington socialites and super-rich liberal power brokers flowed through the softly lit rooms." Mrs. Harriman, it said, "has become the 'darling' of liberal Washington—she recently returned from Moscow where she met with Yuri Andropov at Communist Party headquarters near the Kremlin!" At her party, the letter said, "the liberals raised almost half a million dollars to defeat senators like Jesse Helms, Strom Thurmond, and John Warner." People like her are teaming up with union bosses to make Ted Kennedy majority leader of the Senate, it warned, and they would succeed unless good citizens sent in their contributions to resist.

With an expertise and cutting edge previously unseen in Helms's opponents, Hunt's backers running the North Carolina Campaign Fund responded in kind. Early on, their direct-mail effort raised the alarm: Helms's "political juggernaut . . . reaches far beyond the borders of North Carolina. He can tap the financial resources of every rabid, right-wing group clear across the country." Ticking off his positions, it said Helms was "an unscrupulous campaigner with a long history of grossly distorting his opponents' records." This mailing did not mention Jim Hunt by name. It noted that early polls had shown Helms trailing "one of his likely challengers" by 19 percent, and thus vulnerable. But that, of course, would require a "generous gift" of support from the out-of-state contributors.

After this barrage, each time Hunt's people complained about Helms tactics, the senator's handlers pointed to the fact that the Democrats too had used strong adjectives and appealed for out-of-state money. As the campaign intensified, it would become clear that Helms inspired extremism in his opponents, and the vigor of Hunt's counterattack eventually worked in Helms's favor. Such politics was expected of Helms and his Congressional Club; it was not expected of Hunt and those who had charged for so long that Helms ran dirty campaigns. In many voters' minds, Hunt's shift to such uncharacteristic aggressiveness helped reinforce what became Helms's most effective campaign line: "Where do you stand, Jim?"

That theme was devised by a bedridden young man named Bob

Harris, a behind-scenes operative for Helms's Congressional Club who was unknown to the public until Mike Wallace later put him on CBS's "Sixty Minutes." Tom Ellis and others maintained on the air that Harris was the brains behind the whole Helms operation. Many who saw Harris's frail figure on television, his voice electronically amplified, his mother at his bedside acting as interpreter, assumed this was just a put-on. They could imagine Ellis trying to make Wallace and CBS look foolish by feeding them a tale about how Harris had been calling the shots since 1976, when he was in his teens. CBS played the story straight, perhaps thinking it was so surreal that it would make the Helms political headquarters look appropriately weird. In fact, Harris was a dogged researcher and idea man, lying abed and reading through newspapers and records, seeking weak spots in the backgrounds of those who opposed Helms and his allies. By putting Harris forward for "Sixty Minutes," Ellis not only gave him some deserved credit, but in Claude Allen's words, "softened the public image of the Congressional Club, making it not just a bunch of mean, nasty people, but with a human aspect—probably to Mike Wallace's chagrin." Allen told me "the whole strategy of the '84 campaign, the flip-flop strategy, was from Bob Harris . . . He had a catalog on every move Jim Hunt ever made, from the way he tied his shoes to the kind of hair spray he used."

Digging into Hunt's eight-year record as governor, Harris found a rich lode of material. As a result, the Helms campaign accused Hunt of shifting his position on a nuclear freeze, out-of-state campaign contributions, school busing, school prayer. Hunt's projected image as a moderate came out seeming wishy-washy. Helms began calling him "the windshield wiper candidate—first one way and then the other." Coming after Helms's anti-Martin Luther King performance, this "Where do you stand, Jim?" campaign was a key factor in bringing Helms from a twenty-point deficit in some early 1983 polls to "dead even" in Peter Hart's survey in March of election year.

By that time, the heated Democratic presidential primaries dominated the national news. Walter Mondale's rivals were helping the Republican cause by painting him as too liberal, or too committed to "special interests." As the May North Carolina primary approached, Hunt kept an officially uncommitted stance, but everyone knew of his earlier backing for Mondale. He also attempted to keep hands off the state's spirited gubernatorial primary, but all he earned for that was near-unanimous resentment from the contenders. Helms stepped up his hail of thirty-second commercials and direct-mail appeals for money, linking Hunt with Mondale as soon as it was apparent that he would be the Democratic nominee. And as the Democrats approached their national convention in San Francisco, a note that had been heard occasionally in Helms's earlier material started to gather volume.

In one mailing, he said, "My opponent is supported by the Old-Line 'Liberal Eastern Establishment' based in New York City. In fact, his campaign committee was able to collect $250,000 from special interest donors there, including many involved in the radical homosexual and militant feminist movements . . . Union bosses and homosexual militants and other liberal groups have also targeted me for incredibly harsh, personal attacks." In another, Helms devoted most of a five-page appeal to complaining that gay-rights advocates were raising big money and "pumping it into a vicious liberal 'hit-squad' to crush my campaign." "Incidentally," he asked in parentheses, "do you resent—as I do—the corrupting of the word 'gay'? These people are NOT 'gays'—they are HOMOSEXUALS." Later, Helms signed another letter saying he had just had a discouraging talk with his campaign treasurer, and that "unless a miracle happens, my whole re-election effort could be placed in danger." The liberal media were attacking him anew, he said, and their attacks "seem almost coordinated with my opponent's new drive to raise campaign funds. He's already . . . collected more than $100,000 from elitist financiers and 'gay rights' advocates . . . I desperately need to raise $209,600 in the next 16 days . . ."

That summer, Helms signed yet another fund-raising letter, saying, "As I write this letter it's early in the morning and my heart is heavy . . . For hours I've been trying to explain in just a few words why it's so important you send my re-election campaign an immediate contribution of $38 today." He had slipped behind in the polls again, he said, and his opponent had launched "a million dollar media blitz . . . a vicious smear campaign . . . One of his most repulsive ads shows the mutilated bodies of dead women and children in El Salvador—it's mud slinging at its worst—and it claims that I support the 'death squad' tactics being inflicted in that war-torn country . . . It's absolutely essential I immediately raise at least $410,500 to quickly defend myself from these lies and retake the ground I've lost," he said.

The commercial about which he complained was Hunt's effort to remind voters of Helms's ties with Roberto D'Aubuisson—the Salvadoran right-winger who had been invited by Helms to Washington, whose Nationalist Republican Alliance (ARENA) party was formed with the counsel of Helms's aides, and who was linked by diplomats with the "death squads." Thus it was based loosely on facts. But the consensus afterward was that it, more than any other Hunt commercial of the year, had overreached, and done the governor more harm than good.

Apparently many donors responded to Helms's transparent sales pitches about how "my heart is heavy" and only a miracle could save the campaign. Even public disclosure of their phoniness did not dissuade trusting contributors. Thousands of people got a letter mailed from Dallas during the Republican convention, signed by Helms. It was on paper resembling the stationery of the North Carolina delegation's hotel. Helms told donors that he had hardly arrived at the convention when he got news of "a major crisis in my campaign back home." He enclosed a copy of a telegram ostensibly from his treasurer, saying, "Deeply regret having to disturb you at convention. Have just discovered your opponent Jim Hunt has launched his fall media blitz early. Within the past few days, he's shelled out $373,000 for TV time. And this is only a down payment on what is coming." Helms's letter said, "These politicians are shrewdly taking advantage of my absence—launching a massive attack against me—hoping to bury my re-election chances in an avalanche of TV ads." The only thing that could foil that plot, of course, was an immediate injection of funds—starting with $150 from each recipient of the letter.

It seemed a standard, gimmicky fund-raising missive until the *Greensboro News & Record* discovered that the letters and telegrams had been printed in Raleigh well before the convention began and trucked to Texas to be mailed with the Dallas postmark. Helms tried to justify the pretense by saying he actually had phoned in his approval of the letter after he arrived at the convention. His campaign press secretary, Claude Allen, said there was nothing wrong with the fakery. "We did it in 1980 at the Detroit convention," he explained. "It's a very honest letter. It explains that the campaign . . . is needy." Hunt jumped on the incident and said, "The truth is Jesse Helms is far from broke. He has been collecting tens of thousands of dollars at private fund-raisers in Texas, some of it from people associated with the oil industry . . ."

He had indeed. At the Dallas Republican convention, Helms had nothing left to prove. What he had fought for at Kansas City in 1976 and Detroit in 1980 had all come true. Ronald Reagan, whom he had championed, would be renominated by acclamation. There would be no serious discussion of replacing George Bush as vice president. The principles Helms had striven to put into past platforms had been accepted as party writ. Although he was on the platform committee, his presence was unnecessary. His men Christopher Manion, lawyer John Carbaugh, and George Dunlop, staff director of the Agriculture Committee, were in on drafting the new one. Only a handful of GOP liberals resisted their ideas, and Helms left public defense of the platform to young House members, eager for the publicity. He was feted everywhere as a prophet triumphant, and free to pass his time as he would. He passed much of it courting Texas money and swapping compliments with political preachers.

During two weeks in Texas, he made five trips to fund-raisers in his honor. Two were in Dallas, one each in Houston, Abilene, and Lubbock. He also went to a NCPAC benefit at Bunker Hunt's ranch. Between events, Helms said of fund-raising, "I despise it. But it's necessary to run a campaign . . . The people in Texas have been very good to us." Just how good was a close secret, but all his benefactors were Texas high-rollers.

The Sunday before the convention opened, Helms went to services at the First Baptist Church in Dallas, biggest in the South, to hear guest preacher Jerry Falwell. Voter registration booths were set up around the church, in Lamarr Mooneyham style. Falwell pointed repeatedly to Helms, telling how the senator only ran again because "he felt in his heart that God wanted him to . . ." Then the church's pastor, A.C. Criswell, a leader of the right-wing faction that has deeply split the Southern Baptist Convention, called on Helms to speak the benediction. So impressed was Helms by all the attention, and perhaps by the progress of his fund-raising efforts, that he was seen to drop a fifty-dollar bill in the collection plate.

Later, the president himself endorsed the Helms-Falwell-Mooneyham crusade, speaking up for religion in politics at a mass prayer breakfast at the convention hall. (And Mooneyham said later that among Carolina fundamentalists, resentment of critical press handling of that prayer breakfast caused a big upturn in registrations.)

Since long before the campaign's official start, Helms had challenged Hunt to debate the issues with him. When finally they did confront each other, Helms must have wished briefly that he had never suggested it. He and Tom Ellis had tried to belittle Hunt as "a nice guy and a ribbon-cutter" but unequipped to handle the major issues of the U.S. Senate. Then in late July, the candidates squared off. Helms's strategy was to erase any public impression of him as a nasty gutfighter. He came on as friendly uncle instead. Hunt cut him up, taking the offensive and showing that he was fully briefed on the issues. Afterward, Helms responded with a salvo of TV commercials contending that Hunt had flip-flopped and dodged.

At about the same time, Democratic Congressman Charles Rose pushed for resolution of his anti-Helms case before the Federal Election Commission. He had charged in 1982 that Helms's election committee was subsidized by the Congressional Club's spinoff, Jefferson Marketing, Inc.—that by providing cut-rate services, JMI was illegally giving to Helms's campaign immensely more than the five-thousand-dollar maximum corporate contribution. Helms's people dragged their feet over every detail of the investigation. While Helms in Carolina said he hoped the FEC would issue its ruling before the election, in Washington his lawyers scrambled to repel a court order that it be ruled on by October 19. They succeeded not only in staving off the FEC decision beyond election day, but in blocking public access to papers filed in the case. More than a year after the election, the case was still mired in federal court.

As the candidates slugged through their four televised debates, Helms regained some of the initiative he had lost. He was heartened by commercials in which Reagan praised him for his "honesty . . . outspoken patriotism . . . courage." When Helms and Hunt met again, Helms foreshadowed the rest of his campaign by calling the governor a "Mondale liberal." In their third debate, Helms loosened up enough to cause some resentment by interrupting an exchange over veterans' benefits to ask Hunt, "Which war did you serve in?" (Hunt had been too young for Korea, and a married father during Vietnam.) Again, Helms made the telling link: "Walter Mondale, as [Hunt] has said, is Mr. Hunt's man. Ronald Reagan is my man. Now that's the measurement of your choice in November." Finally, in their fourth debate Helms mentioned Mondale no fewer than forty times. He had read the polls.

They showed that in North Carolina Mondale never reached

higher than 37 percent in Peter Hart's surveys, for example. He never got closer to Reagan than twenty-one points. As the election neared, it was clear to Helms that just as George McGovern on the other ticket had been his strongest advantage in 1972, Mondale was his best issue in 1984. Racial shifts already were working beautifully for him: white North Carolinians in 1980 had identified themselves as Democrats by a 52-31 margin over Republicans, but by October of 1984, they called themselves Republicans by 44 to 35 percent. Ninety percent of those Republicans said they were voting for Helms. (State Elections Board figures tallied the success of the registration contest. From 1981 to October 1984, more than 787,000 voters had been added to the rolls. Of them, 515,000 were Democrats, 221,000 Republicans. Almost 540,000 were whites, 247,000 non-whites. Overall, the drives together had succeeded: the registered percentage of those eligible had gone up from 59 to 77.) As the campaign went on, each man had worked at destroying the other, but Hunt had been dragged down much further than Helms. In 1983, Hunt's positive-negative rating was a strong 60-21, Helms's 55-29. In the end, Hunt was down to 45-45, and Helms was at 49-43.

Yet despite all those figures, softness was showing up in Helms's own standing. In early October, some polls found him from four to eleven points behind. Hunt said the race was dead even. Helms may have been helped when Geraldine Ferraro stumped in Greensboro and Raleigh, where she drew good crowds but mainly reminded voters of who they preferred at the top of the ticket. The senator definitely was helped when Reagan himself flew into Charlotte, where he pulled more than thirty thousand and made a strong Helms pitch. The president also assailed Democrats for allegedly favoring busing that turns "innocent children" into "pawns in a social experiment that nobody wants." Charlotte happened to be the site of one of the most successful, publicly accepted school busing programs in the country, and the city's school superintendent complained that Reagan was suggesting "resegregation." But the flap over the president's remarks did not hurt among Helms voters; it helped.

Less than a month before the voting, a letter sent to William C. Friday, University of North Carolina president, threatened to expose the identities of alleged homosexual faculty members at the university. It said its author would reveal more than thirty names in seven university departments if those persons did not resign immediately. This letter was signed by "Rev. M. Maynard Wilkes, Southern Christians for Helms." After Friday disclosed it, the State Bureau of Investigation could find no such Rev. Wilkes and no such organization. Neither did it find out the origin of another letter, this one anonymous, which accused Democratic gubernatorial candidate Rufus Edmisten and his associates of a variety of gamy conduct.

That these letters appeared in October simply confirmed that the election remained close enough for someone to think such scurrilous stunts could affect the outcome. Helms's camp was never linked to any of those tricks. But late in the month, he did pull out a surprise that broke election tradition. That was when twenty-two active U.S. ambassadors issued a statement publicly endorsing him for re-election. (One more, John Gavin in Mexico City, denied that he had done so. He said all he had done was send Helms a birthday telegram.) There were protests from Hunt and observers of diplomatic niceties, but the state department made clear that the ambassadors were political appointees not bound by the Hatch Act that forbids campaign activity by federal employees. Many of the endorsers were hard-liners appointed with Helms's backing, including David Funderburk in Bucharest, who would come back to North Carolina less than a year later and run as Helms's candidate to replace John East. All may have assumed that Helms would exercise his seniority to take over the Senate Foreign Relations Committee if the right conditions prevailed after the election.

It also was late October when Helms went down to Livingstone College, a black school where his speech was boycotted by some students who refused afterward to shake his hand. The resulting publicity could have cut either way. The Friday before election, he spoke to hundreds of members of the North Carolina Christian Educators Association, the people who run the private religious schools founded after desegregation of public schools, and assured them that Christianity was "the meaning of America as far as I'm concerned." It was part of a ritual touching of bases, of certain nerves, to remind anyone who might have forgotten where he stood on the most emotional issues of the campaign.

In a close election, it is possible to cite any number of factors that could have been decisive. It is doubtful that any one of those last-minute stunts made the difference between Helms and Hunt. But altogether, the campaign of attrition run by the Helms side, tearing Hunt's image down from clean-cut symbol of the New South to wishy-washy ambitious pol, had a major impact. It also is quite likely that if Jesse Jackson had never set foot in North Carolina for two years before the election, the white backlash and resulting heavy registration never would have taken place. (Jerry Falwell said he had been feeling a landslide coming for five months; Mooneyham claims in retrospect that the Moral Majority's drive put some 175,000 to 200,000 voters on the rolls.) Without Jackson and to a lesser extent Mondale as devil figures, Helms could not have raised another record amount of campaign money ($17.2 million, against Hunt's almost $11 million, itself a record for a Senate loser). All of those things together were necessary to bring Helms through. But in the end, based on the votes cast November 6, the one thing that counted most was Ronald Reagan.

The president carried the nation with 59 percent of the vote, and North Carolina with 62 percent. For him it was indeed a landslide, and in Carolina it had a more sweeping effect than anywhere else in the nation. It brought in a Republican governor, Jim Martin, who drew 54 percent of the vote. And it brought in Jesse Helms, who won fifty-two of a hundred counties and got 52 percent of the vote.

The effect of Reagan's strength on Helms's survival is clearly seen in the fact that the senator won no county where Reagan did not draw at least 60 percent. The biggest switch in his favor came in the small towns and countryside of the industrial Piedmont, where Hunt previously had run well but where this time the fundamentalist churches had car pools organized to drive members to the polls. Helms also carried the traditionally Republican mountainous west. Hunt came in with the sparsely populated, heavily black counties of the northeast and the major urban counties. But his margins were slim there. The governor won the women's vote, and got a solid majority among the poor. But Helms carried whites, males, and older voters.

Once again, he had combined an avalanche of money, exploitation of emotional issues including race and religion, merciless attacks on his opponent—and pure luck. Once again, when he returned to Washington he would seem less than grateful to the president whose coattails had pulled him to a narrow victory.

Chapter 13

The Long Spiritual
Struggle

*"There are values that are more basic to human dignity than democratic
values. Our democratic values are intended to support these more basic values,
and in that sense are subsidiary to the more fundamental human rights . . ."*
—JESSE HELMS, 1976

Jesse Helms has his own foreign policy.

He reliably seeks out the rightmost faction in any international
confrontation. He and his staff have blatantly interfered in the politics of other countries. He obstructs diplomatic appointments by the
president he labored so hard to elect. Often alone, he stands up for
foreign parties and personalities shunned even by other conservatives
in this country.

Though they may seem ad hoc, these egocentric actions are consistent in Helms's mind. They are based on a set of values that gives
them clear direction.

This Helms philosophy was laid down definitively a decade ago in
an obscure periodical edited by the same Roger Pearson who later
was chairman of the World Anti-Communist League. Pearson, who
had been a militant advocate of white racial supremacy, ran an
article from Helms in Vol. 1, no. 1 of his *Journal of Social and
Political Affairs.*

The article, "A New Policy for Latin America," was based primarily on what Helms found on his first trip to that part of the world.
But its broad strokes apply everywhere. They are indispensable to
understanding what drives Helms, at home and abroad.

To begin with, Helms wrote, we should be friends with our friends.
The Latin countries closest to basic U.S. values, he asserted, were
Argentina, Brazil, and Chile—all three then governed by military
dictatorships. To them, he added Uruguay and Paraguay. He praised

Brazil's economic development, saying Rio had cleaned up its notorious hillside slums. In Argentina, he said, there are "fantastic natural resources and an intelligent and industrious people." Augusto Pinochet's Chile, Helms said, "has rescued itself from the moral and economic bankruptcy of Marxism . . . it is also trying to restore its deep Christian traditions, and rebuild its priorities in favor of the cultivation of the home and the family and spiritual values."

Uruguay, he said, had pulled back from the edge of chaos by exterminating terrorists, but its economy was still burdened by "an extravagant social security and welfare system," which should be a warning to the United States. And Paraguay was achieving stability after turmoil over land reform.

There are some, he acknowledged, who maintain that Argentina, Brazil, and Chile do not share our democratic values.

"But," he said—and then he disclosed his thinking in a way that will chill anyone who subscribes to the Bill of Rights, and realizes that some day Helms could take part in a convention to amend the U.S. Constitution:

"There are values that are more basic to human dignity than democratic values. Our democratic values are intended to support these more basic values, and in that sense are subsidiary to the more fundamental human rights . . ."

The basic American values, Helms said, are "positive values—the worth of the individual, the importance of the family, the right to own and enjoy property, an orientation towards a spiritual outlook, and understanding of tradition . . .

"Human nature always consists of struggle between good and evil. In the end, only a spiritual reawakening can prevent man, or man in society, from being overwhelmed. That is why we should make common cause with men and nations who understand the dimensions of spiritual struggle . . .

"The right to property, for example, is one of the most fundamental of human values . . . [In those countries] such benefits have been restored, even though some lesser rights—that of a free press, or democratic processes, have been suspended in varying degrees."

Helms digressed to say that he, as a professional journalist first and senator second, was "acutely aware of such secondary rights as a free press and of a free ballot in buttressing our fundamental rights in the United States.

"But at the same time," he said, "my professional career in both has also made me acutely aware that even these secondary rights have been abused in the United States and have served to undermine the fundamental rights they were intended to support.

"When I look at a country to see how much freedom it has, I look first to the ordinary, workaday freedom that the average citizen has —his right to property, his freedom to make economic decisions, his ability to worship God . . . a state that throws off communism or socialism or anarchy already has taken the giant step towards restoring the most important freedoms to its citizens, even if all the secondary freedoms cannot be restored at once . . ."

The heart of this telling document is not Helms's misjudgment of the real situation in specific nations. It is the priority he assigns to "fundamental rights," beginning with the right to own property, over "secondary rights" like free ballot and free press.

It is the way he repeats the thesis, in case anyone could have misunderstood, that "there are values that are more basic to human dignity than democratic values," that democratic values are plainly "subsidiary" to those others.

It is his contention that the rights of free ballot and press have been abused in the United States to the detriment of property values, which he cites first again and again.

Questioners have asked many times whether Helms actually composes all the articles and statements to which his name is signed. His friend Tom Ellis insists that Helms does most of his own writing—"I think he's out of his mind," Ellis says, but Helms takes home stacks of mail at night and types out rough replies to turn over to his secretary the next morning. Ellis says it is partly habit, dating back to answering all the mail he got from his broadcast editorials.

Nevertheless, that Helms actually approves in advance every fundraising appeal, every newsletter to the homefolks that leaves his office, seems highly doubtful. That is not because he lacks the skill to grind them out. He simply could not originate or edit them all, because of their enormous quantity.

And whether the philosophy laid down in that remarkable 1976 article came out of his own old manual typewriter or was drafted by one of his highly ideological aides, it is his. If his staff puts him out on a limb, dangling very close to totalitarianism, he never lets on that he feels uncomfortable there.

Jesse Helms not only has his own foreign policy, he has his own state department.

It works in three widening, occasionally overlapping circles:

1. His Senate staff, and the aides he has appointed to jobs with the Foreign Relations Committee;

2. The nominally independent foundations set up by his staff and close associates, to raise money, research issues, pay for his and others' travel, and publish right-wing literature;

3. The appointees he has pushed into the Reagan state department and the foreign service—and perhaps more important, the ones he has intimidated by blocking or delaying their nominations to advance his own candidates and policies.

The senior idea man on Helms's Washington staff is James P. Lucier, always called "Dr. Lucier" by his juniors around the Senate. He comes closest in Washington to the role Tom Ellis plays for Helms in Raleigh. He takes the lead on issues and tactics. Clint Fuller, an ex-Democrat and ex-weekly newspaper editor from Louisburg, North Carolina, oversees administration of the Helms office. Lucier, like Fuller, is a former newspaperman. He joined Helms when the senator took his seat in 1973 and borrowed help from his friend and neighbor, South Carolina's Strom Thurmond. Lucier had worked for Thurmond six years, and before that had been an associate of James J. Kilpatrick, the *Richmond News Leader* editor. He and Helms got to know each other then, and exchanged notes admiring each other's opinions.

It was while working for Kilpatrick in the early sixties that Lucier contributed at least fourteen articles to *American Opinion,* the John Birch Society magazine. They were squarely in the Helms pattern, even a touch more aggressive, for example characterizing South Africa as "three and a half million civilized men surrounded by nine million aboriginal invaders and two million other citizens of color." Then in his mid-twenties, Lucier wrote that the separate development of the races "springs from the highest motives of Christian charity." Again, he commented on the spread of socialism in Africa by writing, "It is easy to convince cannibals and savages that socialism will supply abundance without necessitating the earning of it," and noted that some black African leaders "have learned to grasp only the concept that one eats one's enemies." Years later, Lucier told interviewers that he had been young then, publishing in the Birch Society's journal because it let him experiment with writing styles, and he probably would not write in the same "mode" any more—although he stood by the alleged factual accuracy of those pieces. But it is interesting how some of his youthful thinking resonates through the later works of Helms himself. In an essay foreshadowing Helms's statement of political philosophy cited above, Lucier wrote that voting is "not a basic right of a human being . . . majority rule is alien to American political tradition and ideals."

Lucier's title on the Helms staff is chief legislative assistant, but it is misleading. He deals with much more than legislation per se. He might also be called intellectual director. He is senior among the highly motivated staffers who have provided philosophical rationale and geographical specifics for Helms's general black-and-white judgments, his blanket anti-communism. No doubt he also has put words into Helms's mouth, and under Helms's byline.

Lucier would resent being told so, but in one respect his intellectual traits resemble Henry Kissinger's. It is his talent for imposing retrospective order, providing a theoretical base, for Helms's apparently reflexive actions. It may spring from the imaginative critical approach that goes into winning a Ph.D. in English literature; it is a bit like spinning out a thousand-page exegesis of one of Aesop's fables.

Lucier's favorite explanation of Helms's stands is that they are "pre-political"—simple choices between right and wrong, acts rather than discussions. Helms appeals to "people who stand outside the dialectic," who have no patience for the rationalization that goes into most policymaking. "The principles that we're espousing have been around for a thousand years," Lucier says: the family, faith in God and private property, loyalty to one's country. Only perhaps 15 percent of Americans are committed to the "rationalistic" approach, he maintains. The remainder are "looking at the world in terms of what's good or bad, and 'What's good for me?' "

This is not all theory. Those studying foreign affairs have seen that Helms is indeed pushing in the direction that Lucier suggests. In a thoughtful analysis in the *Foreign Service Journal,* Alan Tonelson, associate editor of the *Wilson Quarterly,* wrote that Helms's publicized attacks on policy and those who carry it out are not themselves the main point. "The real challenge—and danger—Helms presents has gone practically unnoticed," he maintained. "It is a challenge to the very idea of a professional diplomatic service, and to a foreign policy based on the systematic study of world affairs." Helms's campaign against Reagan's own appointees parallels the fundamentalist right's opposition to "secular humanism" and "evolutionism," Tonelson said. Helms "is explicitly attacking the very faith in rational analysis that spawned the creation of a professional diplomatic corps. And this rejection of reason in foreign policy-making is part and parcel of his broader, better publicized campaign to shift the ground upon which this country's politics is conducted, to hold up all of the debate, the posturing, maneuvering, and compromise of public life to the mirror of his medieval and unbending interpretation of Christianity . . ."

"A foreign policy bereft of or disdainful of reason and pragmatism is inconceivable for a democracy today," Tonelson argued. "A politics based on reason requires politicians to explain and justify their values, rather than simply to assert the superiority of their beliefs and attempt to impose them on non-believers. This pulls politicians and all citizens onto a common ground and makes political debate possible . . . Such debate is our last line of defense against the whims of policymakers whose values, intuitions and emotional judgments would otherwise go unchallenged . . . In the end, however, caprice and arbitrariness are all that Helms and his pre-political movement have to offer . . ." In the absence of American omnipotence in the world, Tonelson contended, "the tradeoffs, the compromise, the search for international cooperation and the concern demonstrated for other nations' interests which Helms so resents may be poorly executed, but they are neither treasonous nor amoral. They are simply unavoidable."

For most of Helms's first decade in the Senate, the contemplative Lucier had an eminently political collaborator in his efforts to carry out Helms's pre-political instincts. He was a highly visible, occasionally prankish man named John Carbaugh, whose main focus was foreign affairs, particularly Latin America. As a key figure on the Reagan administration's transition team between the 1980 election and the new president's inauguration, the assertive Carbaugh frightened both the outgoing Carter State Department and the more orthodox incoming Republicans. On some of their missions for Helms, Carbaugh and Lucier were variously called by the press his "gunslingers of the right" or again, "southern-fried Rosencrantz and Guildenstern." Except for their rightward ideology and their allegiance to Helms, they were drastically different men. Where Lucier is rumpled, reflective, and often seen shadowing Helms from office to hearing room and back, Carbaugh was a flamboyantly independent operator. He took reporters to lunch at expense-account restaurants where Helms would seem out of place, and tantalized them with leaks and hints, all on deep background. Carbaugh, a South Carolina veteran of the College Young Republicans with experience in Nixon's White House, was brought over by Lucier from Strom Thurmond's staff, and given the title of legislative assistant. It, too, was misleading.

In fact, there are no congressional staff titles imaginative enough to cover some of the assignments in which Carbaugh and Lucier involved themselves. Even before Helms switched from the Armed Services Committee to Foreign Relations after the 1978 election, he and his staffers were conducting free-lance diplomacy on at least four continents. In the Senate, the senator's most conspicuous foreign policy role before that had been in leading opposition to the Panama Canal treaties. But that was routine, above-board politics. His staff outriders were not bound by routine.

The most celebrated Carbaugh-Lucier adventure started out discreetly, though when its secrecy was blown it caused a memorable stir in Anglo-American relations.

Earlier Helms had involved himself deeply on the side of Ian Smith's white government of Rhodesia, and tried repeatedly to push the Carter administration to lift economic sanctions against Rhodesia as that country moved toward black majority rule. By the summer of 1979, Jimmy Carter wanted to talk with the newly installed black prime minister, Abel Muzorewa, but did not want to ask him officially to come to Washington, because the United States did not then recognize his government. Published accounts of this peculiar episode say Carter asked his arch-enemy Helms to invite Muzorewa as his guest—so the president could have a quiet talk with the African leader. But John Carbaugh told me he himself invited Muzorewa through Stephen Rosenfeld of the Washington Post—a scenario that would seem almost as unlikely but for the gregarious Carbaugh's contacts with journalists of all political stripes. After Helms's involvement was disclosed, the White House, annoyed, withheld comment on the Muzorewa visit. But the sanctions were still in place later that year when the Rhodesian parties were brought together in London to negotiate a new constitution.

Thus, off to London went Carbaugh and Lucier. Carbaugh now calls it "a fishing expedition." He says he and his colleague told Ian

Smith to "stay sick for a couple of weeks and wait them out"—not to be pressured by British demands and the economic sanctions. Back in Washington, passage of Helms's legislation to lift the sanctions seemed imminent. News reports said the British were furious, complaining to Washington about the conduct of Helms's agents. Helms was furious in return. He insisted that there never had been such a complaint, that the British were quietly circulating the story as a "dirty trick" and it was leaked by the State Department to embarrass him and sabotage his anti-sanctions amendment. Eventually, the British confirmed that there had been no formal, written complaint—their displeasure had been informal and verbal instead. The upshot was the same: Helms's "gunslingers of the right" had made a highly unorthodox raid on sensitive diplomatic negotiations in a foreign country, and come close to throwing those talks into chaos.

Questioned about the propriety of these excursions, Carbaugh would laugh and recall that he had done a law school thesis on the Logan Act, which forbids private diplomacy by U.S. citizens. The implication was that therefore he knew just how far he could go without breaking the law. He kept going—to Latin America, for example.

Carbaugh and Christopher Manion, Helms's man on the Foreign Relations Committee, have been the key contacts between the senator and Roberto D'Aubuisson of El Salvador. (Manion is the son of the late John Bircher and right-wing TV crusader, Dean Clarence Manion.) Out of those links, and with help from other interested parties in Washington, grew El Salvador's Nationalist Republican Alliance (ARENA). This gave political legitimacy to the ultra-right that had been linked so long with terrorist activities there, and directly defied the Carter administration's efforts to cut the violent right out of Salvadoran political life. ARENA's party creed was based on the U.S. Republican Party's 1980 platform, which was written to Helms's specifications, plus added language echoing the constitutions of foreign right-wing parties like the Nazis. Helms's people reportedly functioned as liaison between ARENA and important money sources in this country. Helms thus put all his prestige behind D'Aubuisson, giving the right-wing candidate the implied backing of the Foreign Relations Committee. That added to the senator's frustration when the people chose the moderate José Napoleon Duarte instead.

Helms effectively has functioned as Washington public relations man for an array of Latin American dictatorships. A specialist familiar with the workings of the Senate Foreign Relations Committee says these independent ventures often have misled the right wing in Latin America to believe it has powerful backing from the U.S. government. This was the case specifically in Argentina. There, the military regime got the impression from Helms and his aides as well as other outspoken Reagan administration figures that it could do whatever it wanted in the Falkland Islands showdown because the United States would not interfere. When the military dictatorship tried to take the islands from Britain by force, Helms turned out to be the only person in the United States Senate willing to stand up for Argentina against the British. At the same time, Helms's encouragement to the Latin American right has made this country seem even more unfriendly than it is to politicians on the left. This can make them more radical, turn them toward Cuba for help. The result is that finding a moderate balance, the traditional U.S. objective, becomes even harder to achieve. Of course this does not disappoint Helms's pre-political, anti-traditional, "either-or" attitude—and it tends to prove Tonelson's thesis, that pre-politics frustrates rational progress toward stable relationships.

Helms proudly claims that he never spends government funds for expenses on his independent missions. That is appropriate, because so much of what he and his staff do is defiant of government policy. Notwithstanding his voluminous commentary on foreign affairs, Helms himself was a novice who had traveled little until he had been in the Senate at least a year. His first trip abroad then, to speak to the World Anti-Communist League convention in Taipei, was paid for by the Asian Peoples' Anti-Communist League. Since then, he has averaged about one excursion a year. Only those to funerals, inaugurations, and conferences, undertaken at the president's request, have been paid for by the government. None was financed from his Senate funds. The anti-union National Right-to-Work Committee flew him to London for four days in 1981, the Panama Canal Company picked up the check for a day's stay there in 1977 as the Senate approached its showdown on the canal treaties, and the Freedom Federation of Brazil paid for his trip to that country for another World Anti-Communist League meeting in 1975.

Helms told me that his first trip to Israel, in 1985, was by courtesy of the brother of Nevada Senator Chic Hecht, who had financed building of a synagogue there. That trip marked a turnabout in Helms's position toward Israel, a shift he has solidified in speeches and articles since then. He had been strongly critical during the 1982 Israeli invasion of Lebanon, calling then for an end to U.S. arms sales to Israel and suggesting that Prime Minister Menachem Begin resign. But after Jewish voters overwhelmingly backed Jim Hunt against him in the 1984 election, Helms started shifting his attitudes. He conferred with conservative Israeli politicians, and in early 1985 led six other conservative Republican senators in urging U.S. support of continued Israeli occupation of disputed border areas.

Helms's and his staff's most ambitious excursions abroad have been financed by the Institute of American Relations, one of the tax-free foundations that are an integral part of his personal foreign policy establishment. For instance, the IAR paid for Helms's tour of Argentina, Uruguay, and Chile in 1976.

(As he left Chile, *El Mercurio* of Santiago, typical of the controlled press there, delightedly quoted him as saying U.S. criticism of the Augusto Pinochet dictatorship was "exaggerated" and "malicious." Helms reportedly said he had been "impressed beyond measure" to see an open Bible on Pinochet's work table, and concluded that Chile clearly had chosen Christianity over atheism. "A country that believes in God will always be ready to sacrifice in order to build a great and powerful nation," he said.

(On the same trip, Helms upset the U.S. embassy in Buenos Aires when he met with high Argentine officers just before the military coup there. The embassy had been trying to avoid any suggestion that Washington approved of what the military plotters were doing. Helms disputed the word of an American diplomat who later told Joel Brinkley of the *New York Times* how military leaders "gave the impression that Senator Helms was on their side and that with an important United States senator on their side, the military had won the battle of bringing the U.S. government around.")

The Institute of American Relations also paid for Helms's flight to Panama in 1977, for a three-day trip to London to meet with Prime Minister Margaret Thatcher during the Rhodesian nervousness in 1979, and for his outing to Seoul at the time of the Korean Air Lines shootdown in 1983.

Apparently due to misunderstanding the rules, Helms did not report all these trips on his financial disclosure statements filed with the Senate until they were brought up by his opponent in his 1984 re-election campaign. His explanatory letter to the secretary of the Senate then read like a campaign news release. Helms reiterated that "I have never taken a so-called 'junket' at taxpayers' expense. When I have felt it important or essential to travel, I have always used private funds . . . Whenever I have traveled on Air Force One with the president, I have always sent the White House my personal check equivalent to first-class airfare. I have returned more than $1.6 million allocated to me for the operation of my office during my tenure as a senator . . ."

Strictly speaking, his claim seemed correct. Quibblers noted that usually when he was not traveling on government funds at the president's request, or accepting expenses from groups that had a high interest in his positions as a senator (the Panama Canal Company, the National Right-to-Work Committee), his tours were financed by the tax-deductible contributions of those who gave money to the Institute of American Relations. Thus indirectly the taxpayers were picking up an important part of his expenses. The expense dollars spent by Carbaugh, Lucier, Manion, and Helms's other representatives were many times over what was put out for the senator himself. But that quibble about travel expenses was a minor note among the many questions raised by the Helms network.

Carbaugh, Lucier, and Howard Segermark, another former Helms aide, were instrumental in setting up the string of Washington groups that Helms calls "the institutes."

Victor Fediay, another alumnus of Strom Thurmond's staff, was president of the Institute of American Relations while Carbaugh was vice president and Lucier secretary-treasurer. (A related group called the IAR Foreign Affairs Council was created to do outright lobbying, which was legally forbidden for the tax-free IAR itself.)

Carl Anderson, a former Helms legislative assistant, was president of the American Family Institute.

Carbaugh was secretary-treasurer of the Centre for a Free Society (and he insists that was its only relationship to Helms).

Segermark was executive director, Lucier president, and Carbaugh vice president of the Institute on Money and Inflation.

Helms liked to say that he had merely "authorized" creation of this network by his aides. But his early explanation that its function was to provide him timely research for Senate debates against the liberals was swiftly overtaken by events—by what the groups actually did with the hundreds of thousands, eventually millions of dollars they raised.

In 1980, for example, the Centre for a Free Society paid for two trips by Utah's Senator Orrin Hatch to interview fugitive financier Robert Vesco in Nassau. This was said to be part of the Judiciary Committee's investigation of the Justice Department's Office of Public Integrity. *Congressional Quarterly,* which published a thorough study of "the institutes," discovered that the Centre also paid expenses for Hatch's wife on the first trip. Although other committee personnel joined him at Senate expense, Hatch refused government reimbursement, to keep up his reputation of not traveling on taxpayer funds.

That same year, the American Family Institute paid Supreme Court Justice William Rehnquist for a lecture on the family and the law, and the following year it financed a trip to this country by Mother Teresa. The Nobel Peace Prize-winning nun spent much of her time in America speaking against abortion, in addition to meeting with Ronald Reagan and attending conferences with right-wing groups.

The Institute on American Relations paid for public opinion polls on the Panama Canal controversy and raised money to oppose the SALT II treaties. It published a foreign affairs newsletter to spread the rightist version of impending issues.

It also enlisted Admiral Thomas H. Moorer, former chairman of the Joint Chiefs of Staff, and General Lewis W. Walt, former commander of the marines in Vietnam, to sign fund-raising letters against the arms treaty and for an intensified U.S. arms buildup. Their letters were full of the hyperbole that typifies other Helms fund-raising literature: "The grim facts are that the U.S. has been unilaterally disarming for a decade . . . Right now, within the next ten days, the Institute of American Relations needs $13,000 to pay for printing, postage and telephones," said the general. The SALT II treaty "could guarantee the permanent nuclear superiority of the Soviet Union and, in fact, put this nation at the mercy of that totalitarian regime . . . I need your help today . . . The Institute of American Relations budget for this project is $147,200," said the admiral.

But while the literature was standard, the relationship of Helms's aides to this network was anything but. There was no precedent for the way they drifted back and forth from Senate office to foundation, from country to country on institute funds.

Always sure of himself, strutting with a smile instead of humbly whispering advice to his elders, Carbaugh became so expansive for a while after Ronald Reagan's victory in 1980 that he threw the State Department into a state of alarm. The Reagan transition teams that moved into every department as soon as the election was over included some who considered it an honorary appointment, some who were specialists, and some who were into everything. Carbaugh epitomized the last group. John Goshko of the *Washington Post* likened his striding down the corridors at State to "a Vandal running loose inside the walls of Rome." In the past, Carbaugh had been an active practitioner of "the guerrilla warfare waged by neoconservatives against the Carter administration's most cherished goals." Now he led the charge as the right prepared to take over. His omnipresence persuaded many that he was due for a major appointment, at least as assistant secretary for congressional relations, or for Latin America or Africa. When Secretary of State Alexander M. Haig, Jr., offered him the ambassadorship to Paraguay later that winter, Carbaugh disdained it. He stayed outside the administration, helping Helms carry on his style of irregular warfare even after the transition. In that role, said another writer, Carbaugh "might just as well be called a senator, for his influence rivals many of that institution's elected members."

But by mid-1982, House Democrats had started an investigation into whether the Institute of American Relations' campaign against SALT II and for the B-1 bomber constituted lobbying that was illegal for a tax-exempt foundation. The *Congressional Quarterly* study of the Helms institutes, following earlier reports in the *Raleigh News & Observer,* raised questions about whether Carbaugh and Lucier had spent too much of their time with, or drawn too much money from, the foundations.

Carbaugh, though nominally a full-time Senate employee, was putting in about half his time at the IAR. For his efforts, he was drawing funds from the Institute's tax-exempt treasury, created by people like oilman Nelson Bunker Hunt, Jr., its biggest contributor. Helms, keenly aware that he faced a re-election campaign soon, became nervous that his aides were stretching or perhaps breaking Senate rules by their crossing back and forth. A query reportedly was made to the Senate Ethics Committee. Under the rules, what the Ethics panel found was not publicly disclosed. Carbaugh told me, "We conformed with the Ethics Committee. The Ethics Committee basically left us alone."

But in late June, Carbaugh announced that he was leaving the Helms staff to upgrade his finances by joining a Pennsylvania Avenue law firm, where he could continue to be on call for Helms. Potential embarrassment for Helms was headed off. But before Carbaugh departed, he and Helms had their impact on the new administration. It was not precisely the kind of impact they and their ideological allies had foreseen.

It seemed unlikely, in November of 1980, that Helms would have to continue his role as critic, obstructionist, third force against this new administration. Ronald Reagan was his man. Helms's Congressional Club had spent $4.6 million helping to get the new president elected. Like his ebullient aide Carbaugh, the senior senator from North Carolina felt that he had earned—perhaps bought and paid for—the right to swing major influence on what happened in the Reagan White House, in foreign and domestic policy, on key appointments. But that illusion did not last long.

The week before Reagan's inauguration, Helms met with seventeen other hard-line Republican senators and they agreed that the Reagan revolution was not looking revolutionary enough. Already, it was clear that too many pragmatic professionals and not enough right-wing faithful were being picked to conduct foreign affairs in the new administration. Helms, as leader of this "conservative steering committee" and the man who had campaigned earlier to save the nomination of Secretary of State-designate Alexander M. Haig, Jr., wrote to Haig to complain.

But Haig was more courteous than obedient. He kept releasing the hard-line transition staff largely recruited by the Helms faction, replacing it mainly with people who had served earlier presidents—the very people about whom Helms and his allies had complained for so long. Thus by late March, Helms started using his traditional Senate right to put a "hold" on first one, then a growing list of foreign policy nominees who were not approved beforehand by him and his ideological aides. Chairman Charles H. Percy of the Foreign Relations Committee felt personally challenged, as indeed he was. Haig and others in the administration seemed surprised, but they should not have been.

Anyone watching Helms since his arrival in the Senate recalled that he had been challenging nominees for years. In fact, he began the habit when he was on the Raleigh City Council, many years earlier. He had objected to Richard Nixon's elevation of Henry Kissinger to Secretary of State. He had held out against a series of Gerald Ford's nominees, including Nelson Rockefeller for vice president and later Donald Rumsfeld for Secretary of Defense. He had resisted many of Jimmy Carter's choices. But of course those were presidents he did not elect. Ronald Reagan thought he deserved better from Helms—and vice versa. But on the very day of Reagan's inauguration, Helms and his newly sworn colleague John East were the only two senators to vote against confirming the president's old friend Caspar Weinberger as secretary of defense.

Then Helms held up the nominations of a flock of assistant secretaries of state: Chester Crocker, for Africa; Lawrence S. Eagleburger, for Europe; Robert Hormats, for economics; Thomas Enders, for Latin America; and Myer Rashish, as undersecretary for economic affairs. In time, Eagleburger, Hormats, and Enders persuaded Helms that they were sufficiently anti-communist. But Crocker, one of the nation's acknowledged experts on Africa, resisted. Helms tried unsuccessfully to bargain the appointment of a right-wing Boston researcher, Clifford Kiracofe, Jr., as Crocker's deputy in exchange for lifting the hold on Crocker. Eventually those nominees were cleared by the Foreign Relations Committee with Helms not voting, and then by lopsided margins in the Senate itself.

Some maintained that Helms's blocking efforts thus had been in vain. On the contrary, they were almost a no-lose tactic for him. Although Helms could not dictate the list of appointees, he could raise unshirted hell if his wishes were ignored. He could make it clear that he intended to cash in on his exertions on Reagan's behalf; the noise he made about appointments carried over into policy. For example, while Helms was wrestling with Haig over that first list of nominees, the State Department sought to pacify him by sending a cable to U.S. allies saying the new administration had made no decision on whether to observe the terms of the SALT agreements with the Soviet Union—which was a matter of high concern to Helms. And Chester Crocker, while resisting Helms's deal on taking Kiracofe as his assistant, noticeably shaded his own rhetoric on South Africa while his nomination was hanging. South Africa is making "a serious and honest effort to move away from apartheid," he said late that spring.

These developments provoked Gerald J. Bender, a southern Africa specialist at the University of Southern California, to write that the

Reagan administration already was doing what it had criticized Jimmy Carter for: "continually changing its foreign policy to placate domestic political constituencies." Nowhere, he wrote in the *New York Times,* "is this more evident than in the growth of Senator Jesse Helms's power and the influence he has been able to exercise in foreign policy." Bender said that "for the president, who knows virtually nothing about Africa, to take his cues from Mr. Helms—who knows even less about it—is not only absurd but highly dangerous." And, ironically foreshadowing Helms's own warnings in the later debate over U.S. economic sanctions against South Africa, Bender said, "History will undoubtedly show that at present no American is advocating policies toward Africa that would further the Soviet Union's interest more than Senator Helms. If Jesse Helms, Republican of North Carolina, didn't exist, surely the Russians would have had to invent him."

But that summer, Helms served notice that he was still unsatisfied. He wrote in the conservative newspaper *Human Events* that a clear picture of the new administration's foreign policy was yet to emerge. Objecting to plans to go ahead with sale of American-made pipeline equipment to the Soviet Union, he said, "Decisions of that sort are being made in the State Department by the very policy-making officials whose nominations I have been questioning . . . These officials include several officials from the Carter administration; others are described in Washington terminology as 'Kissinger retreads.' There are signs, in other words, that the more things change, the more they remain the same." But he hinted that on some matters, the administration was getting his point: "There are occasional indications that the U.S. will be more attentive to our friends than heretofore, especially in Latin America. But the liberal politicians and news media are screaming to high heaven—they are resisting better relations with anti-Communist countries which want to be friendly with us."

Helms obviously judged the tactic of holding up nominations submitted by a friendly administration to be politically productive, because he kept it up. Some were reminded again of Senator Joe McCarthy, who had led a knot of right-wing senators in blocking a list of Eisenhower appointees shortly after that Republican administration began in 1953, because the general's selections were allegedly soft on communism. Eisenhower was angry: those GOP senators were "the most stubborn and essentially small-minded examples of the extreme isolationist group in the party." Their leader, Ike went on, "is ambitious. He wants to be president. He's the last guy in the whole world who'll ever get there." Significantly, however, Eisenhower was saying all that only to his diary—just as Reagan, whatever he might be saying to his wife in privacy, did not risk offending Helms and his ideological friends in public.

So Helms kept delaying, obstructing, extracting concessions. He kept agitating on behalf of the right-wing dictatorships in Latin America, welcoming a stream of their henchmen to his office, dispatching his staff troubleshooters to meet them abroad. When Chile's foreign minister came to Washington in 1981, Helms met with him. Because the Chilean government was charged with killing and torturing political opponents, the administration restrained its comments about the visit. But Helms was hospitable: "We have an obligation to give Chile equal treatment. The Chilean system is not much different from what we have here."

It was comparable to Helms's earlier ostentatious get-together with Colonel Luis Arce Gomez, the Bolivian interior minister who was rebuffed by the Carter administration, and later indicted on dope-smuggling charges. "I'll meet with anyone," Helms said after taking him to lunch in the Senate dining room.

The Reagan administration and the Senate Intelligence Committee were infuriated when word leaked that the Central Intelligence Agency was secretly supporting José Napoleon Duarte in the El Salvador election of 1983. They suspected Helms had put out this word to benefit his protégé, Duarte's opponent D'Aubuisson. Helms angrily denied that he was the leaker. But the following week, the following month, he was in controversy again, as often as not in defiance of Reagan, who had disappointed him so.

There were payoffs. Flailed so often, the administration thought twice before taking policy steps that would offend Helms. Frustrated so often by him, it found ways to accommodate his stubbornness in policy spots in the foreign policy establishment.

Helms's unremitting opposition to strategic agreements with the Soviet Union was a factor finally in pushing out arms control director Eugene Rostow, himself a tough negotiator. Rostow was replaced by Kenneth Adelman, a novice in the field but one bearing the right ideological stamp of approval. For another example, although Myer Rashish had been confirmed at the Senate Department after long delay by Helms, he was replaced less than a year later—and in the shuffle, one of Helms's former aides, Richard T. McCormack, moved into the position of assistant secretary for economics. But the most interesting Helms placement, in terms of future politics, drew few headlines when he was nominated. He was David B. Funderburk, a young history professor at North Carolina's Campbell University, where Helms served on the board of trustees.

Funderburk, only thirty-seven when nominated, first came to political notice in 1978, when he wrote a tract for the Helms re-election campaign entitled, "If the Blind Lead the Blind: the Scandal Regarding the Mis-Teaching of Communism in American Universities." The sixty-seven-page book's theme was that "It is time more Americans were cognizant of the myth-making whitewash of communism dished out in universities in the United States."

It was just the sort of thing Helms liked to hear, and when a friendly administration came to power he sought a place for Funderburk. The ideal spot was the Bucharest embassy, since Funderburk had specialized in Romania and spoke the language. His nomination sped through the Foreign Relations Committee until Paul Tsongas of Massachusetts called him back to ask further questions, and requested another hearing. Although many assumed at first that Tsongas was playing games with Helms's protégé to retaliate for the many delays imposed on others by Helms, Tsongas let the nomination go after detailed questioning on the Funderburk book.

After serving four years, Funderburk quit his ambassadorship with a publicity-grabbing statement about the State Department's inadequate toughness toward human rights violations by Eastern European communist governments. Then he returned to Campbell, at Buies Creek, North Carolina—but he had ambitions beyond the campus. A few months later he was tapped by Helms's Congressional Club as its candidate to take over from Helms's earlier protégé, John East, who was ill and would not run again.

In a way, each time anybody connected with Helms and his Congressional Club ran for office, the controversy put Helms himself before the voters again. But no surrogate election, no electoral campaign of his own had ever so tested Helms as the one he faced in 1984. His record seemed know-nothing obstructionism to some, and reckless zealotry to others. But that was not a unanimous impression: each time he offered that record to the voters, they supported him. Journalists, scholars, other politicians spent a lot of time trying to figure out why.

Charles William Maynes, for one, editor of *Foreign Policy* magazine, discerned that with Helms and his followers, the nation was seeing a successor to the prairie populism of the late nineteenth century. This time, Maynes said with a certain pin-striped condescension, it is more like "polyester populism." (Although they would reject much of what Maynes said, some philosophers of the New Right would cheer his broad thesis, because they are spending millions trying to usurp the populist brand as their own—to persuade the world that they stand for public indignation rather than for private greed.)

In the 1890s, the nation witnessed left-wing populism, anger at the Eastern banks, Wall Street, the railroads. This time, Maynes said, it is right-wing, anger at the government and what it seems to have wrought.

Now as then, the adherents have "a deep sense of personal inferiority . . . a hatred for the cultural trends emanating from our major cities . . . a conviction that the plain people of the country are losing their ancient heritage of economic independence and equal opportunity because the God-fearing are no longer being given their rightful place." Now as then, the populists are "likely to lose most of the battles yet still influence the course of the war, perhaps significantly . . . Whenever millions of Americans are as angry and as frightened as are the supporters of Helms—even though they remain a distinct minority—there will be an impact on policy."

The United States cannot go it alone today, Maynes said. Most international problems in our time demand a reasoned international strategy. But, he concluded, that is hard to achieve as long as national leaders exaggerate foreign threats and thus feed popular fears. As long as that goes on, "the frightened and angry minority represented by Helms will not diminish . . . Nor should we be surprised if on occasion it becomes a majority."

In North Carolina, "polyester populism" has never become a majority by itself. But again in 1984, it had provided the decisive difference between Helms's survival and defeat. And again in that campaign, the most corrosive element in the new populism was the old factor of race.

Chapter 14

Jesse and "Fred"

When Jesse Helms was a boy in Monroe, he sometimes sat in front of his house in the morning, watching the older children pass by on their way to school. Often, a group of black girls walked past, going to their segregated school a few blocks away. Jesse would watch them solemnly. One of them remembers that they made faces at him, imitated his bug-eyed look, laughed at and teased him, giggling until they were out of earshot. It may have been their mischievous, second-hand way of taking a dig at Jesse's father, the policeman at whom they would never have dared make a face, to whom they would never have said a sassy word. In all the times they passed by and made fun of young Jesse, he never jeered back, never retaliated. He just sat there and took it.

"He looked like he was scared," one of those girls recalled more than half a century later. By then she had moved away from Monroe. So had young Jesse. Shortly before she reminisced about her childhood in Monroe, Helms was standing in the United States Senate, fighting bitterly against a national holiday to honor the black civil rights leader, Martin Luther King, Jr. Soon afterward, he was leading congressional defenders of the South African government, opposing U.S. sanctions against apartheid—a system devised to keep sassy black people in their place.

It is tempting to assume a direct link between Helms's boyhood experiences and the philosophy he has embraced through his adult life. But it is a delicate matter to discuss racism as a motivating factor in a political career. The word is thrown about much too freely.

Too often it is used to paint anyone who disagrees with a particular policy favored by some black leaders, whatever the reason, however remotely it concerns race as such. It was tossed at young and ignorant southerners who reacted violently against school desegregation, who were too young to know better. In fact, it is a term that should be used sparingly, because it carries strong emotional impact. Therefore it is worthwhile to consider carefully what it is, and is not.

Anyone born in Monroe, North Carolina, in the 1920s grew up in a segregated environment. Even educated whites, even political liberals by the standards of the time and place accepted legal separation of the races. It was the same in a thousand towns of that size—on tobacco and cotton farms, in steel and cotton mills, in congregations of Bible-believing churchgoers. Children in that environment heard adults saying "nigger" and in the same breath swearing undying affection for the people they thus addressed. They took many wrongs for granted, like White and Colored signs on public drinking fountains and washrooms. Life was segregated from birth in black and white hospitals to burial in black and white cemeteries. And because they were children, they unthinkingly assumed that was the way things were supposed to be.

Some never learned any better. Others had the luck to learn, from parents, teachers, or preachers. Some left home and saw how life was lived in the world beyond. To those who stayed, radio and television later brought the world vividly into their lives. They had the chance to see the difference between their own and the world's view of what they had always thought was right.

Considered against this background, perhaps racism is a trait that can be attributed properly only to the educated, sophisticated mind. A child, even an ignorant man or woman may viciously offend another race, without being guilty of racism so defined.

Yet the reverse of that premise is not automatically true. An educated adult may take a position opposite that of the best interests of the black minority, he may indeed make what is clearly a racist remark, without being down deep a racist. Generously defined, racism requires a clear and steady pattern of thought and conduct. An occasional blunder does not qualify, offensive though it may be.

But if a person is mature, sophisticated, and world-traveled, and his words and actions recur time and again, they probably are not accidental. If he is a veteran of public affairs whose consciousness has been raised by years of political dialogue, a plea of ignorance rings hollow. If he joins in common cause with people and groups whose reason for being is to advocate racial supremacy, that is powerful evidence. If, after decades of exposure to polite, cultured company, he still falls back on jokes and code words like those of his benighted youth, he can hardly be unaware of how they sound. And if he cites dozens of different reasons but always, without exception, arrives at the anti-black position in interracial controversy, it is reasonable to look past the reasons cited to what may lie beneath.

Among all the descriptive terms used about Jesse Helms by his political enemies, "racist" is one he objects to strongly and always. He has seldom sat down to discuss at length why he is so sensitive on the subject. But on the public record, he has talked about race and issues with racial connotation literally thousands of times. That record is consistent.

When young Helms left Monroe to go to Raleigh just before World War II, he was not leaving segregated society behind. The races were separated in the state capital as strictly as in the county seat. Wake Forest College then was as segregated as the public schools of Monroe, and little Wingate College. Jonathan Daniels's *Raleigh News & Observer* where young Helms found a job was capital-D Democratic and liberal, for its time, on the editorial page. But its city room was all-white and remained so for years to come. So was that of the *Times,* to which he switched. The U.S. Navy was still segregated in World War II, and so were the towns to which it sent Helms.

The first political campaign in which he took part was thick with racial charges, doctored photographs, scare tactics. Influentially for Helms's later political career, those tactics succeeded in electing Willis Smith. Then Helms went with Smith to Washington, a city almost as segregated in 1951 as Raleigh or Monroe. There he met and idolized Richard Russell, the pre-eminent leader of the anti-civil rights southerners in the Senate. He volunteered to work for Russell, to handle his broadcast publicity in his states' rights candidacy for the Democratic presidential nomination.

But in those years, on past his thirty-first birthday, Helms was in an environment others had created before him. He was associated with questionable campaign tactics, he was on one segregationist senator's payroll and strove to get another nominated for president. But essentially he was an underling, dealing in other men's opinions, boosting their ambitions. It was not till he returned to Raleigh in 1953 to become executive director of the North Carolina Bankers Association, to write editorials and columns under his own name, that he began creating the public record of his own opinions, in his own words, in his own behalf.

The great national awakening now known as the civil rights movement was barely stirring in the early fifties. When Helms did his first signed commentaries in the *Tarheel Banker,* the monthly magazine of the bankers association, the Supreme Court had not yet handed down the May 1954 decision that underlay it all, *Brown v. Board of Education.* "Separate but equal" was still the theory under which southern school systems operated. Southern political protests against federal intervention were not yet focused on the Warren court, and the later leaders of the freedom rides and non-violent marches were still to emerge. There was not yet a sense of crisis in the South.

Yet, strikingly, although his predecessors at the bankers association had stuck to comment on banking and related matters, Helms had hardly read the news of the court's historic decision when he raised the alarm about mixing of the races. Long before Orval Faubus of Arkansas, George Wallace of Alabama, or Lester Maddox of Georgia arrived in the national consciousness, he manned the ramparts in North Carolina. He made it clear that public education was less important than segregated education—asserting, "Unless our Negro citizens submit more easily than we predict they will, North Carolina does not have the simple choice between segregated schools and integrated schools. Our only choice is between integrated public schools and free-choice private schools . . . The decision will have been made by a very small minority of people who are hell-bent on forced integration."

Long before it occurred to most other guardians of segregation to tell the people that the civil rights movement was part of a world communist conspiracy, it occurred to Helms. He came across that theory early, and has never abandoned it.

During Arkansas Governor Orval Faubus's confrontation with federal troops when the courts ordered desegregation of Little Rock's Central High School in 1957, Helms wrote that "what is happening in America is exactly in tune with the forecasts of Karl Marx. The America which should be concerned by the curtain of Communism falling throughout the world is, instead, ripping itself to shreds over a false and completely phony issue called 'integration.' The cackles you hear have a Russian accent . . .

"Today's Southerner is a citizen who recognizes that government cannot successfully tamper with the emotions of human beings, regardless of where they live," Helms went on. Asserting that many more "race riots" and other such troubles occur in the North, he declared, "These slanders upon the South, these assaults upon the Constitutional sovereignty of the States, this pious sweeping around the other fellow's doorstep should cease . . . Perhaps, as some contend, integration is inevitable . . . But if these are, indeed, messages of truth, it is also true that the South cannot read them imprinted upon the points of bayonets. Nor will the South read them between the lines of slander and abuse."

As the fifties moved on into the high-tension sixties, Helms preached against the black student sit-ins attempting to desegregate luncheon counters in downtown Raleigh. "There will be the pious semantics about human dignity, inalienable rights, and all that. But that is a poor argument," he insisted. "The young Negroes cannot escape the fact that in their quest for *their* 'rights,' they are trampling underfoot the 'rights' of others, namely the luncheon counter operators who have a 'right' to serve or refuse to serve whom they please."

Later, Dean Clarence Manion, that elder statesman of the Old Right, turned up on his program an elderly, conservative black Pittsburgh editor named George Schuyler, who said just what Manion and Helms wanted to hear about black protests. Within a Viewpoint editorial, Helms rebroadcast a filmed Manion interview with Schuyler, in which the black editor "traced the origin of today's racial demonstrations and violence back to a master plan drafted by communists in the early 1920s," as Helms said. Asked by Manion whether there was any truth in suggestions that "cries of 'police brutality' are communist-inspired," Schuyler said: "Oh, definitely. One thing we must remember is that the police brutality charge is a long-time Communist project . . ." Later, Helms liked to reach back to that communist "master plan" when he needed a citation to back up his own assertions. "Two barrels full of documented proof of the communist conspiracy" were found when police raided a Communist Party convention at Bridgman, Michigan, in 1922, he said, quoting a book titled *Reds in America,* published in 1924 by Richard Whitney. "Nobody took seriously the carefully detailed format for provoking a Negro rebellion," Helms maintained, "but that was the first step, Richard Whitney wrote, to be used by the communists."

Helms heralded each report of the House Un-American Activities Committee and the Senate Internal Security subcommittee. In 1964, while the FBI was looking in Mississippi for the bodies of three slain civil rights workers, the Senate unit issued what Helms called a "frightening" document laying out "numerous examples of communist infiltration of the civil rights movement in every section of the country." "Much of the turmoil . . . is being promoted by second-generation agitators," he said. "Children of men and women clearly identified with the communist movement in America one and two decades ago are now in the forefront of the disorder that is spreading across the face of America." Graciously, he conceded that the report "does not purport to show that everyone connected with the civil rights movement is a communist, or sympathetic to communism. Nor do we." But, he said, it does provide clear warning that "many of those who chant about 'freedom' while advocating violence and disregard for the law are not really friends of the Negro, but agents for a conspiracy to destroy America."

When the 1964 Civil Rights Act was moving toward passage, Representative (former Senator) Alton Lennon asked Attorney General Robert Kennedy to confirm his suspicions that the movement was infiltrated by communists. Kennedy said he had no such evidence. Helms countered with quotations from Kennedy's own nominal subordinate, FBI Director J. Edgar Hoover. The pending bill is "extremely dangerous," Helms said, and should be defeated on its lack of merit, rather than merely because the communists would be delighted by its passage. Still, he said, "It is important that Negro citizens recognize the perils of their being exploited by those who would destroy the freedom of all Americans, including Negroes. Disobedience of the law, which unfortunately has become such a part of Negro demonstrations, is precisely what the communists seek to hasten their divide-and-conquer technique."

Helms found ready ammunition for his conspiracy theory in the Robert Williams case, in which the discredited NAACP president in his home town of Monroe broke with the national organization's policy of non-violence and then, after being charged with kidnaping two whites, fled to Cuba. Helms told his broadcast audience of the reported communist ties of the outside attorneys who came in to support Williams. "Negroes and whites alike should examine the nature as well as the source of unsolicited assistance," he said. "Otherwise, Trojan horses will continue to roll into our midst, which will please nobody in the long run—except, possibly, Mr. Khrushchev and other Communists who hope to defeat us by dividing us."

This technique of discrediting leaders of the movement with communist or criminal allegations, often old or irrelevant, was used repeatedly by Helms.

When black civil rights lawyer Constance Baker Motley was nominated for the federal bench by Lyndon Johnson, Helms said proceedings should have been held up because the Senate possessed "sworn evidence . . . that Mrs. Motley was a communist." He never mentioned Bayard Rustin, the organizer of the great, peaceful 1963 march on Washington, without some reference to Rustin's arrest on morals charges many years before. "Oddly enough," he said, the press had been "strangely silent" about this incident. "We will not go into the sordid details," he added, and then offered some suggestive hints. He added that Rustin, a veteran civil rights and anti-war activist, not only was a "moral degenerate" but had been arrested eleven times, had served thirty days on the road gang at Roxboro, North Carolina, had refused service in World War II, and had been a Young Communist.

But no single American, or Russian for that matter, has been so thoroughly flayed by Helms, over so long a time, as Martin Luther King, Jr. Helms began his opposition soon after King came to public notice in the fifties, and was still attacking King's memory more than fifteen years after he was slain in Memphis.

As city councilman, he warned Raleigh officials that appearances by the likes of King threatened to stir violence. When King came and went and there was none, Helm's alarms were seen to have been unnecessary. That embarrassment may help explain his particular, seemingly permanent enmity toward the principal leader of the civil rights movement.

In the first week of his broadcast editorials for WRAL, when the lunch-counter sit-ins were in the news, Helms took on King, warning him that "when anarchy exists, nobody has any rights of any kind." As he grew more confident in his role, Helms's broadcast criticisms became more openly bitter. At one point, he was delighted to have help from the *Atlanta Constitution,* whose editor, he noted, was "Ralph McGill, regarded as extremely liberal and a longtime advocate of forced integration . . ." Those who knew McGill would be surprised that he was that extreme, but Helms said so to strengthen the credibility of a *Constitution* story about King's alleged communist ties. The paper pushed an inquiry into the background of Jack O'Dell, a King associate whom Helms called "a Communist, clearly identified . . . an organizer for the Communist Party." That called for yet another Helms warning, this time quoting J. Edgar Hoover again, about how "the Negro situation is being exploited fully and continuously by Communists on a national scale . . ."

Ten days before John Kennedy was killed, Helms voiced resentment that King had become "a cherished item of political property. His every word is well nigh a command. The federal boys bow and scrape . . . Dr. King can incite his followers to riot, and President Kennedy hails it as a great adventure of freedom. Some of Dr. King's important associates can be labeled and proved as communists and sex perverts," yet, Helms said, Attorney General Robert Kennedy goes before a congressional committee to say he knows nothing about it. Referring to President Kennedy's ties with King, he said, "No election, the political career of no man, is worth the discord being created by efforts to weld together the votes of Negro Americans into a solid bloc . . . This is a sorry ladder which Negroes are trying to climb . . ." When riots scarred American cities in 1967, Helms said, "America is being transformed into a fiery jungle of violent lawlessness." He blamed King and Robert Kennedy for offering "the antidote of more gasoline on the fire, more surrender to the mobs . . . What is happening in America is precisely what our enemies from without have been counting on. We have been carefully following the communist blueprint, with scarcely a deviation. There are chuckles in the Kremlin these days . . . What is needed most is enough law enforcement, whatever the cost, to put down any further rebellion."

Helms predictably was angered by each step in the world's recognition of King's success. In 1965 he said, "King can wave his Nobel Peace Prize to his heart's content, and it may be impressive to misguided clergymen and others who cluster in pious knots around him." But, he said, King's "non-violent" movement "is about as non-violent as the Marines landing on Iwo Jima, and it is a 'movement' only in the sense that mob action is moving and spreading throughout the land." Examining the Selma march for voting rights led by King in the spring of 1965, Helms focused on reports of "shocking sexual activities and general depravity" along the march route. Yet, he complained, the press still "portrays this monstrous violation of human decency as a gallant bid for freedom."

Shortly after King himself was killed, Helms cited with approval columnist Drew Pearson's comments about King's "associations with communists," and "King's love life with another man's wife." He eagerly picked up similar allegations about King's successor as head of the Southern Christian Leadership Conference, Ralph Abernathy, which were placed in the *Congressional Record* by segregationist Representative John Rarick of Louisiana. Most such allegations spread about civil rights leaders were fed to antipathetic congressmen by J. Edgar Hoover.

During the Poor People's March on Washington led by Abernathy in the spring of 1968, Helms declared that " 'the civil rights movement,' so-called . . . has been largely a political charade from the outset. The wonder is that so many Americans, white and black alike, have found it so difficult to see the humbug in the cry of 'Freedom Now!' . . . Negro militants have taken over . . . Bus drivers are being murdered, shopkeepers are being shot and robbed, newsmen are being assaulted, stores are being burned, women are being raped. It is, all in all, a splendid demonstration of 'non-violence.' "

Often Helms's indignation toward King, Abernathy, or some other individual turned loose broader anti-black rhetoric. In 1966, he said a march King had just led in Mississippi "surely can have nothing to do with voting rights . . . There is an incredible federal law on the books giving every Negro of voting age the right to register and vote . . . Like too many other Americans, Mississippi Negroes already have more freedoms than they care about exercising or preserving . . . An unlawfully pitched tent by Negroes in Mississippi is no less an affront to society than, say, efforts by the Ku Klux Klan to set up camp on the lawn of Broughton High School in Raleigh. What America needs, more than anything else, is for its loafers and loud-mouths to go to work, to earn their livelihood instead of parading to the welfare office for it . . ."

Helms was not alone in those years when he put questions like, "Is survival possible when civilization reverts to the law of the jungle?" and declared that "the hour approaches when we must decide whether we will be ruled by sanity or ruined by savagery."

He had companions in the Congress, in the Thurmonds and Eastlands. He had backing in some southern and non-southern newspapers. The most forceful journalistic voice resisting the march of civil rights in the fifties and into the sixties was a man Helms respected, frequently quoted, and obviously sought to emulate: James J. Kilpatrick, editor of the *Richmond News Leader*. For years before he moved to Washington as a syndicated columnist, Kilpatrick provided the constitutional and intellectual justification for less sophisticated bitter-enders. He filled his editorial pages with historical documents supporting his campaign for states to interpose their sovereignty to nullify the Supreme Court's desegregation decisions. He was deeply involved with old Senator Harry Byrd in Virginia's policy of "massive resistance" to federal authority. That the limits to states' authority in such matters had been settled by the Civil War did not deter him. Hardheaded as it was, it is likely that his and his state's verbal resistance, keeping the fight going in the press, the legislature, and courts, helped minimize physical violence in Virginia. In North Carolina, the state administration took a similar course, with something called the Pearsall plan, which would allow closing of public schools faced with integration. Under it, only 203 black children were in school with whites there by mid-1962. Yet it got less national attention than Virginia's dramatically titled policy.

At the outset, Helms himself was not in a spot conspicuous enough for his *Tarheel Banker* opinions to function as a safety valve for the public. And by 1960, when he began his widely noticed television editorials, Carolina had picked a new, progressive governor who was ready to move on. It was a transition point, when Helms too could have moved gracefully with the times, could have seemed to be in line with the voting majority. Instead his opinions hardened, and his audience widened.

Jackson, Mississippi, was not only the capital of the state considered most viciously resistant to desegregation. It was headquarters of the White Citizens Councils, an organization with chapters throughout the South, devoted to fighting civil rights progress and federal encroachment in general. It published a monthly magazine, the *Citizen,* which printed original essays as well as collecting the most provocative work being done elsewhere in its cause. Kilpatrick was a favorite there, and Helms became one. The tone of the *Citizen* is suggested by its choice of a 1962 Kilpatrick dissertation, "The Lunatic Thesis of Human Equality." "Without meaning to be altogether facetious about it, the very finest deed that Assistant Secretary of State for African Affairs G. Mennen (Soapy) Williams could do for his country would be to get eaten up by African cannibals," Kilpatrick wrote. "Then maybe a sufficient number of Americans would stand up and consent to the self-evident truth that people are not the same the whole world over."

One of the first Helms pieces reprinted by the *Citizen* was headed "The Supreme Court Has Gone Too Far!" This might have been a handy title for everything the magazine printed, but in this case Helms was exercised about the court's decision against school prayer, rather than anything racial. Later, his works became a frequent feature, complete with cover blurbs and a thumbnail portrait beside his byline, as if he were a regular columnist. "Nation Needs to Know of Red Involvement in Race Agitation!" shouted another headline.

In the *Citizen,* Helms was surrounded not only by Kilpatrick and other journalistic contributors, but by a stable of those who preached the "scientific" case for white supremacy. Names like Carleton Putnam and Henry E. Garrett were there alongside others like Robert B. Patterson, John Synon, and William J. Simmons, the magazine's editor and head of the Citizens Councils' national propaganda effort.

While Helms did not gain a personal reputation as an advocate of "scientific" racism, he upheld that view. In 1967, when statistics showed a high percentage of North Carolina draftees rejected for mental reasons, he emphasized that most of those rejected were blacks. "No intelligent Negro citizen should be insulted by a reference to this very plain fact of life . . . ," he said on the air. "It is time to face, honestly and sincerely, the purely scientific statistical evidence of natural racial distinctions in group intellect . . . There is no bigotry either implicit or intended in such a realistic confrontation with the facts of life . . . Those who would undertake to solve the problem by merely spending more money, and by massive forced integration, may be doing the greatest injustice of all to the Negro . . . The only way to solve a problem is to admit it exists, identify it honestly, and then do what is necessary to correct it."

Helms seemed quite comfortable there among the white supremacists at the *Citizen,* since his contributions began appearing soon after he started his broadcast editorials and continued till after he had announced as a Senate candidate more than a decade later.

In the era of McCarthyism, where Helms has his political roots, liberals used to cry out against "guilt by association." It was wrong, they objected, to cast doubt on a person's loyalty, or his cause, because one of his associates once was a communist—or because that associate in turn had shared a taxi with someone who was accused of being linked to an alleged member of a communist front organization. Helms, however, voiced no qualms about this practice. He was in the midst of a campaign based on it, in the 1950 election of Willis Smith over Frank Graham. And he himself rejoiced in the practice, through the years, as when he persistently belabored Martin Luther King with what the FBI or Senate investigators said about King's associates' one-time connections. Perhaps Helms's assertions of guilt by association make it fair to look at his own eagerly indiscriminate associations through the years.

His frequent publication in the *Citizen* is one. Obviously he was flattered at distribution of his thoughts nationally, regardless of the vehicle. Vanity can get public figures into embarrassing situations. Sometimes they refuse to blush at what others would consider embarrassing.

Soon after election to the Senate, Helms began getting speaking invitations from groups that admired his right-wing zealotry. The 1974 Dean Manion tribute at which he called for conservatives to consider abandoning the Republican Party was one of those. Another was something called the World Anti-Communist League, which was started in 1966 by Nationalist Chinese and South Korean political figures. Its main function originally was to propagandize against Communist China. Later it grew into an international anti-communist forum with far-right member groups from Europe, Latin America, and the Middle East. As it accepted those groups, it took on conspicuous tinges of anti-Semitism and neo-fascism, and some of its leading figures were well-known prophets of racial superiority. Those connections caused its British chapter to withdraw in 1973. Even Sun Myung Moon's aggressively anti-communist political organization, the Freedom Leadership Foundation, pulled out in 1975, calling its move a "repudiation of fascism." The John Birch Society stepped back, too, with one of its spokesmen explaining that some of the European member groups tended to equate conservatism with nationalism, with resulting overtones of racism. Yet Helms flew to Taipei as an honored speaker at the World Anti-Communist League's rally in 1974, and was featured again at its convention in Washington in 1977.

Helms's association with the Ku Klux Klan has been rather coy—not wanting to put himself on the record as a fan, but not wanting to alienate Klansmen or their many quiet admirers, either.

In the sixties, the Klan flared up in Carolina during the height of civil rights activism. An investigator for the House Un-American Activities Committee testified that the state had 112 local Klan "klaverns." Although Helms in his TV editorials was careful to state his disapproval for "vigilante law," his main concern was for the constitutional rights of the Klan. He was particularly upset by Malcolm Seawell, who as an Eastern Carolina solicitor earlier had prosecuted Klansmen rounded up for floggings and cross-burnings. Seawell chaired Governor Dan Moore's law-and-order committee, which pressed for action against the Klan's resurgence. Helms insisted he was only asking for even-handed law enforcement, instead of "one-eyed justice squinting at any group that happens to be unpopular or even presumptuous." He maintained that "the pros and cons of the race question are not really relevant to the discussion— though it could legitimately be asked why many editors are so hostile to the Klan but so apologetic for racial extremists on the other side."

He reduced the issue, in other words, to a simple political debate between two sides, one the KKK, the other the civil rights movement. To him, the Klan was equally legitimate ("no court has declared that the Klan is in violation of any statute law on the books").

With his long, conspicuous record as editorialist and then senator, Helms has understood there was no chance that he would ever get a significant number of black votes. Genuine Klan voters were not that many, either, but they had a very different view of Helms. When Helms ran the first time, in 1972, State Grand Dragon J. Robert Jones told a Klan rally outside Winston-Salem that while officially he could not support either Helms or Nick Galifianakis, he did like Helms. "Jesse is a Christian and a great American. He started as an ultraconservative and he hasn't changed a bit," the state Klan leader said. Pressed for response, Helms told reporters he had not talked with Jones or his representatives, so he would not comment on such a "nebulous" report. But he added, "I appreciate anybody saying complimentary things about me. I'll welcome all the votes I can get in the boxes in November."

Twelve years later, when Helms ran for his third term, the Klan in the state put on an intensive voter registration drive in response to black registration efforts against the senator. There was no evidence that Helms either encouraged or discouraged this Klan activity, or the votes it brought in.

If Helms's associations with the Klan have been remote and apparently involuntary, his choice of close associates has been intentional and highly personal. And the one who has been beside him longest, to whom he turned over his full confidence and authority to act in his name, is Tom Ellis.

When the senator tried to do Ellis a minor favor in 1983 by getting him named to help oversee the anti-communist direction of U.S.

foreign broadcasting operations, it turned out to be an embarrassment. In fact, the whole exercise was an important demonstration
of where Helms stands in the eyes of his Senate colleagues, and of
both his and Ellis's position on the most fundamental of human
questions.

At Helms's instigation, President Reagan nominated Ellis to membership on the Board for International Broadcasting. The board
broadly oversees the management and policies of Radio Free Europe
and Radio Liberty, which beam to communist Eastern Europe and
the Soviet Union. At the Senate Foreign Relations Committee's
formal hearing, Ellis and his five fellow nominees (including authors
James Michener and Michael Novak and publisher Malcolm Forbes,
Jr.) started out smoothly. Helms's friend Ellis said the right things
about truth as "the most powerful weapon we have." Helms himself
questioned Catholic layman Novak about "what role you think religion should play in the programming which BIB oversees," and
added, "I was interested to hear that in Europe and even in the Soviet
Union the most often heard request is for more religious programming on the Voice of America."

Then, niceties over, Senator Paul Tsongas of Massachusetts
homed in on Ellis. That colloquy and what followed it are interesting
not only because of Helms's continuing absolute reliance on Ellis to
run the political end of his affairs, but because Ellis occasionally
suggests himself as a candidate for high office.

Tsongas said he was concerned about Ellis's being a director of the
Pioneer Fund, which had sponsored studies in the genetics of race
by such men as William Shockley and Arthur Jensen. He traced the
fund back to a textile millionaire named Wycliffe Draper, whom he
said also was active for many years in "genetics research." Then he
asked Ellis just what his involvement had been with the fund. The
savvy lawyer said, "I probably should have known more than I did,"
and that all he had done was sign blank authorizations for money
to this or that university. Tsongas asked, "You had no idea what the
fund was about and who was getting the grants?" and Ellis answered,
"No, sir." He said he did not know the fund was set up to look into
racial betterment and genetics, and said he had served on the board
merely as a favor to a friend.

Tsongas read him a quotation from Shockley, who had said, "My
research leads me inescapably to the opinion that the major cause for
the American Negro's intellectual and social deficit is hereditary and
racially genetic in origin and thus not remediable to any major degree

by practical improvements in environment." Tsongas asked Ellis, "Do you agree with that?"

Ellis: "No."

Tsongas: "Do you denounce it?"

Ellis: "I have no way to know—I know no more about genetics than I do about Einstein's theory of relativity. I have never studied it. I have no opinion."

When Tsongas asked whether Ellis felt the need to divorce himself from the Shockley research, the Carolinian said he did—because an earlier *New York Times* article about it threatened to embarrass Helms.

Tsongas also brought up the handbill produced by Ellis in the 1976 presidential primary, when he tried to help Reagan by spreading the word that Gerald Ford favored a black for vice president. After Tsongas finished his turn, Senator Joseph Biden pursued the issue with Ellis. The aggressive Delaware Democrat said he was concerned that some of Ellis's past statements about race could be used by America's adversaries to attack the credibility of U.S. broadcasting services.

He quoted a memorandum from Ellis's time as counsel to the North Carolina Advisory Commission on Education, in the mid-fifties. "The eventual goal of this movement to integrate public schools," Ellis wrote, "is racial intermarriage and disappearance of the Negro race by fusing into the white."

Biden: "Do you still believe that?"

Ellis: "I don't believe so, sir."

Biden: "You don't know whether you do?"

Ellis: "No, I don't believe that I do believe that. I think at the time there were a lot of statements where people felt like things were going to happen. I attribute a lot of that to youth and not really understanding as much as I should have." (Ellis was in his mid-thirties at the time.)

Biden noted that Ellis had suggested preserving segregation by repealing North Carolina's compulsory school attendance laws and providing grants for tuition in private segregated schools. Did he still favor that approach? Ellis said no, and Biden cracked, "You may have to bump him off the board, Jess, if he keeps answering this way."

But Biden and Tsongas were not through, and that sentence was as light as their conversation got. Biden brought up the Citizens for the Preservation of Constitutional Government group in which both Ellis and Helms had been active during the sixties.

Ellis: ". . . I had even forgotten that I was a member . . . it was basically a states' rights organization. It believed that the states should be able to adopt constitutional amendments without having to go through a convention. It believed in having a fifty-state supreme court over the Supreme Court . . ."

When Tsongas took over again, he switched to South Africa, and Ellis conceded that he had taken a twelve-day trip there paid for by that country's government but "sponsored" by the Council on National Policy. That, Ellis explained later, is a group he himself chaired, organized by such New Rightists as television preachers Jerry Falwell and Pat Robertson plus Paul Weyrich of the Committee for the Survival of a Free Congress and Edwin Feulner of the Heritage Foundation. Pressed, Ellis disclosed that he held substantial personal investments in South Africa because "I have felt the federal government was spending so much money and creating so many deficits that sooner or later we were going to have such extraordinary inflation that I felt some gold mining stocks would be a hedge against inflation . . ." But he said that even after his visit, he still was not sure he understood South Africa's system of apartheid. "I think they are doing the best that they can with their problem . . . I do think they are moving," Ellis said—in mid-1983.

Helms defended Ellis by recalling Citizens for the Preservation of Constitutional Government, which he had plugged in his broadcasts, and on whose board both men had served. Not much came of it, he said, "except meetings at which citizens discussed the means of handling a very difficult problem in the South. At the time . . . I favored freedom of choice for the schools . . . that everybody ought to be fed out of the same spoon and ought to have the opportunity to attend whatever school he or she wished. But there has been an evolvement of attitudes. As you yourself, Senator Biden, have indicated, I doubt that any of us would relish having everything we have ever written or said examined with a fine-tooth comb."

Biden's frustration burst through. "The real question," he said to Ellis, "to be very blunt . . . is whether or not you are a racist. Your past statements are those of a racist, in my view . . .

"A racist would be very damaging to have in a position of public exposure . . . exposed and able to become a pawn of the Soviet Union in an effort to discredit a legitimate American effort . . . If you said what you said and meant what you said, that is my definition of a racist . . . [If so], I would do everything in my power . . . to stop you because I think it would be outrageous for a racist to hold such a position."

Ellis said, ". . . I do not believe in my own heart that I am a racist."

Ellis's answers, his memory lapses, his professed ignorance about apartheid, the stubborn way he resisted so Tsongas and Biden had to dig their answers out of him may have been a skillful performance by his own standards as a lawyer. It was more of a third degree than Helms has ever submitted to publicly about his own views on racism. Helms's intercession about how he used to believe in freedom of choice, "but there has been an evolvement of attitudes," came close to saying that he had changed his stand on such matters. But it did not quite say it. In effect Helms was left dangling there with Ellis, who denied that he was a racist while surrounded by what his questioners clearly considered evidence to the contrary.

After the hearing, Tsongas put out a press release predicting that all the committee's Democrats and some of its Republicans would vote against confirming Ellis. Taking him at his word, Ellis withdrew. In a bitter letter to Tsongas, he asserted that the hearing had "turned into a personal attack on me totally unrelated to my views of the Communist world." He said he was willing to take personal heat, but when they used the hearing "to distort facts in an effort to hurt President Reagan and Jesse Helms, you seriously damage American foreign policy. I feel sure that the countries behind the Iron Curtain will be pleased that you have so succeeded in distorting the issues that I have withdrawn my name . . .

"Finally and personally, I believe you have overreached the bounds of propriety and fair play for purely partisan politics," Ellis said.

The next day, he sent a letter to Reagan, saying the Democrats' attack at the hearing "was an obvious partisan political effort to drive a wedge between you and the black community using me as the instrumentality." He told Reagan that he was "most anxious to serve as I believe our only hope to survive the spread of Soviet slavery across the free world and to free the hostage people of the USSR is to broadcast the tenets of Christian belief through mass communication . . ." In expressing that hope, Ellis touched another subject, religion, on which his and Helms's views alarm some of their critics.

Ellis went back to Raleigh madder than ever at liberal Democrats like those who had done in his nomination. He put that anger to work the following year in another of the election campaigns for which he and Helms have made North Carolina famous.

The tactics of those campaigns vary with the closeness of the contest, the vulnerability of the opponent. One constant throughout is warnings about the "bloc vote" that supports Helms's or his friends' opponent. It was used in the 1950 Willis Smith campaign, and Helms has fallen back on it in all his own Senate campaigns. The "bloc" is of course the black vote, and it inevitably does support the other side.

As commentator and candidate, Helms has been particularly adroit in making big news of who blacks supported in primaries— knowing that his own contender would benefit from that news in the next round of voting. In talking about those primary results, he hammered at them until nobody with ears could miss his point.

Helms as editorialist was criticized for this practice after the first 1964 gubernatorial primary, in which his and A.J. Fletcher's friend, the segregationist I. Beverly Lake, was beaten out by Judge Richardson Preyer. Delightedly, Helms used that criticism for another editorial, which only served to raise his listeners' consciousness still higher. He said innocently that he was "astonished" by his critics, that "insofar as we know, Candidate Preyer and his campaign associates have accepted with grace and gratitude the loyal Negro support given Mr. Preyer on Saturday. This is as it should be, for if knowledgeable political observers are accurate, Mr. Preyer owes his success at the polls to the marvelous Negro vote which he received." Then he proceeded to tick off once again the returns from selected black precincts where Preyer had won with lopsided margins. Breaking down statistics and projecting what might have happened if the black vote had been split evenly, he then said, "Such calculations are, of course, beside the point and we introduced them simply to illustrate the importance of the Negro vote in North Carolina, particularly when cast in a bloc . . . the measurable sentiments of all minority groups constitute news of significance . . ." Anyone familiar with Helms's vendetta against the press in later years will grin at the way he brushed off those who complained to the station. "They may not be entirely familiar with the news business," he said "—or the obligations of news reporters."

In that runoff, Preyer lost. Four years later, on cue, the subject arose again. Again, Helms as commentator was only reacting to complaints he had heard. Supporters of conservative Melville

Broughton ran an advertisement pointing out that last time, his opponent Bob Scott had become lieutenant governor by the margin of "bloc votes in six North Carolina counties," Helms said. "It ought to be a trifle insulting to Negro voters for there to be such resentment about disclosures of their voting habits," he commented ingenuously. "There is no law against bloc voting . . . A lot of folks other than Negroes participate in bloc voting. So there's nothing 'bigoted' or 'racist' about the distribution of any relevant truth."

The Helms campaign pattern goes on, election to election. And in office between elections, Helms as senator and committee chairman has many more varied ways to uphold his beliefs and make a further record appealing to his hard-core backers. He has stood against virtually every economic and social program favored by the black community. He has used the filibuster and other obstructive tactics to that end. He has opposed extension of the Voting Rights Act, repeatedly pushed anti-busing legislation, favored tax breaks for segregated private schools, led the opposition to a federal holiday to honor Martin Luther King, Jr. He has imaginatively used his chairmanship of the Agriculture Committee to get around the fact that he is not on the Judiciary Committee where most civil rights matters are handled.

As his 1984 re-election campaign warmed up, he called hearings of the Agriculture Committee to hear testimony on legislation that would reverse the federal courts' Grove City College decision. He supported the decision, which limited the use of federal fund cutoffs to enforce anti-discrimination laws. (Coincidentally, he had made a speech and gotten a $1,050 honorarium five years earlier at Grove City College, the Pennsylvania school involved.) Helms maintained that his Agriculture hearing was justified because the bill he opposed would be an unwarranted burden on farmers. No witnesses who disagreed with him were asked to appear. Helms "acknowledged" to reporters that questioning a civil rights bill in an election year was not popular among his colleagues, most of whom supported the bill. He was not seen to chuckle as he spoke.

George Wallace and Strom Thurmond are two of the most noticeable practitioners of racial politics who changed drastically after the Voting Rights Act cleared the way for massive black registration in the South. Wallace so shifted ground that he actually won decisive black support in his last run for governor in Alabama. Thurmond, holder of the filibuster record for his resistance to 1957 civil rights

legislation, is recognized now for the way he has brought South
Carolina blacks onto his Senate staff, pushed for black federal judges,
and helped blacks seeking federal aid. Old Senator John C. Stennis
of Mississippi is another who has survived in politics by changing
with the times, supporting Voting Rights Act extension and getting
black backing for re-election in 1982. But Helms has not given
ground.

He has been in the Senate for more than thirteen years, but at this
writing has never had a black on his thirty-nine-person staff there.
After this fact was remarked on repeatedly, he hired a young black
named Claude Allen as his campaign press secretary in 1984. Allen,
a religious conservative just out of the University of North Carolina
at Chapel Hill, said he asked about the absence of other blacks on
the Helms staff when he was interviewed for the job. "It was explained to me simply that they have had very few blacks apply," he
said. He also acknowledged that the shortage of black conservatives
and Helms's image among blacks might have had something to do
with that.

Allen got into politics by serving as press secretary in 1982 for
William W. (Bill) Cobey, Jr., a Helms protégé who ran for Congress
and lost before trying again and winning in 1984. He and Cobey met
at church, Allen said. After that election, he said, he was offered a
low-level job on Helms's Washington staff but turned it down. Then
he took the campaign press job. He told reporters he supported
Helms's stand against abortion and on most other issues. But, he
conceded, "It was kind of rough" during debate on the Martin
Luther King holiday bill. After repeated questioning about how he
could work for Helms, Allen recalled, "I said I'd had enough of this
for one day and I am just going to go home." That night, Helms
telephoned him "to just talk to me about it and tell me where he was
coming from on that holiday. He had very serious reservations
. . . and I took his word for it." When that campaign was over, Helms
sponsored young Allen as press aide with the Foreign Relations
Committee.

Those are official manifestations of Helms's private feelings. Unofficial incidents through the years suggest more about the inner
man.

During the period when he was publicly denying any bigoted
motive in discussing "bloc voting," for example, Helms made no
apparent effort to shield his feelings in private. One weekend when

WRAL executive Fred Fletcher's son, another white youth, and three black students were using a studio at the TV station to rehearse their band, Helms came in the office on Sunday afternoon. Young Fletcher remembered that when Helms saw the group, he was furious, and ordered the boy to get the blacks out immediately. Embarrassed, the boy did.

Even in the decades since discrimination was outlawed, there has been less integration of churches than of any other southern institution. Gradually, however, blacks have been accepted into many previously all-white churches, including Southern Baptist congregations. The issue arose in the early sixties when Helms was a key figure in blocking acceptance of the first black applicant, Charles Earl, into Raleigh's First Baptist Church.

Helms told reporters years later that he merely stood up in a congregational meeting to "move the previous question," to cut off debate and vote on Earl's admission. The pastor, John M. Lewis, gave me a slightly different version. He said that before the congregation cast its final vote, Helms had been strongly opposed to Earl's acceptance. One objection was that Earl was student council president at black Shaw University, and during the same period was leading anti-segregation demonstrations downtown. He also had applied to several other white churches. When some members said, "He's just testing us," the Rev. Lewis said, "Right—let's pass the test." But when the congregation voted, Earl was rejected by 367 to 147.

Several years later, Helms and his family left First Baptist to join Hayes Barton Baptist Church, where A. J. Fletcher and a number of other well-to-do citizens were members. Backers of Nick Galifianakis in the 1972 Senate campaign charged that Helms had moved because of integration at First Baptist. Helms fired back, complaining of a "whispering campaign" against him. He insisted that he had transferred simply because Hayes Barton was nearer his home, and it was easier for his adopted son Charles to get to the Boy Scout and Sunday school programs there. Since Helms departed, First Baptist has accepted several black members without controversy.

Some of Helms's public effusions about blacks as individuals, rather than as civil rights marchers or voting blocs, could be considered paternalism, old-fashioned but well meant. Some suggest a sense of humor that has not outgrown Monroe in the twenties. The way in which some of Helms's ostensibly private feelings slip into public knowledge provokes a suspicion that sometimes it is not accidental.

In the mid-fifties, when Helms was in his mid-thirties, he com-plained indignantly about a "severe restriction" placed on speakers at a certain Raleigh civic club—"each speaker is advised in advance that he is not to tell a joke or anecdote which makes reference to a particular race or a particular religion. That's a mistake, I think," Helms wrote in the *Tarheel Banker.* He suspected it was just the result of concern about "the so-called race issue," and added, "I just don't think there's a race issue in North Carolina except the phony one that is kept alive by a few outside rabble rousers." All the stories he had heard about Negroes, he said, "emphasize down-to-earth philosophy," rather than insulting them. As an example, he offered a tale told by his minister. It was about an old black who bought a ticket for a sixty-minute railroad trip that started in the Eastern time zone and ended in the Central. When he asked what time it left and what time "de train gets there," the agent told him. "Whereupon the Negro scratched his head, thought a moment, then handed back the ticket. 'Boss,' he said, 'I don't believe I wants to make dat trip—but if you don't mind, I'd like to stand here and watch de train take off.' "

Helms insisted "there's nothing in that story intended to ridicule the old Negro; in fact, it indicates pretty good judgment . . ." And for a certain level of sensitivity at that time in America, he was right. After all, Amos 'n' Andy were still a big hit on national television. There was no obvious malice intended in the story; indeed, it was told by a respectable preacher. And so Helms implied that other things he heard and told also were harmless, and meant that way.

Two years later, about the time Martin Luther King was making that first visit to Raleigh, Helms counseled his banker friends that in a time of racial tension, "The worst mistake we can make is to lose our sense of humor." He said he had no trouble discussing the question with his Negro friends around town, and that oddly most of them said they wished the Supreme Court never had handed down the 1954 decision that stirred things up. (It was a discovery much like that by Helms's friend Jerry Falwell more than a quarter-century later, when the Moral Majority leader came back after five and a half days in South Africa and announced that he knew more about what blacks there wanted than did their own Bishop Desmond Tutu.) To illustrate his point, Helms passed on to his readers a letter he had picked up at City Hall, ostensibly written by an Arkansas farmer to members of the Supreme Court. It was a list of questions about whether the farmer would be allowed to put his black and white peas in the same row, his black and white cattle in the same field, and so on. Helms said, "I thought it was quite clever, but I honestly believe the Negro elevator operator in our building enjoyed it more than I did. See what I mean? The Negroes aren't taking this thing *nearly* so seriously as the Supreme Court thinks they are."

That was in the fifties. By the mid-sixties, when racial consciousness was heightened pro and con, when Helms himself was battling against civil rights advances, he retained his talent for finding black friends who shared his perspective on events. He told his television audience about some of them. One was a young mechanic who drove him to the office one day, who recalled his childhood, when "we lived on this white man's place. We helped them pick their cotton and they helped us pick ours. When some of us were sick, they come down and looked after us . . ." The young man's memories, Helms said, "were a contradiction of the evil image of the South which the agitators of today constantly seek to build."

Soon afterward, Helms spoke of another black friend, a man of "unshakable faith and fundamental wisdom." On the way to work he passed the old man, mowing someone's lawn. His shirt was wet with perspiration, his shoulders stooped. Helms stopped to chat with him, and later reflected on their friendship.

"He possesses a nobility which all mankind would do well to try to emulate," Helms said. "He has made his life count for something . . . On that summer day, many another younger and stronger man was sitting idle, complaining that there is no opportunity. Yet here was a man, certainly in his middle seventies, cutting grass and clipping hedges . . . He has never relied on a welfare office; he has had faith in himself. 'I don't want the government looking after me,' he said. 'I might get used to it.' "

In the seventies, Helms was a widely known U.S. senator and may have heard some broader ideas about racial philosophy than those he heard before leaving Carolina. Early in 1978, as he approached his first try for re-election, he sat for breakfast with reporters. One asked whether he thought segregation had been wrong. Helms answered, "Not for its time."

Later that election year, he used a one-liner that was well received by many of his stump audiences. Soon after getting back into the campaign from his back operation, he reported receiving a get-well card from Andrew Young, then Jimmy Carter's ambassador to the United Nations. "He [Young] said some of his African friends wanted to have me for dinner," Helms joked.

After angry complaints from some Democrats, Helms stopped telling the joke in public. In fact, he insisted it was not a joke at all —"It was the truth. I got a get-well card from a senator in a northeastern state and that was on it." He added that he saw no reason why anyone should be offended by it. "Someone's going to get a hernia straining to make something out of it," he predicted, and he was about right. At the White House, Young presided over a gathering of southern black leaders talking last-minute campaign strategy. Democratic chairman John White read a News & Observer editorial condemning the postcard joke, and that "really stirred up the people in the room against Helms."

That session was reported in Carolina papers eleven days before the election. Helms won easily.

Helms's rise to national prominence attracted reporters, and despite his misgivings about "the media," he occasionally invited one to visit him at home. Bill Arthur of the Charlotte Observer wrote about how a photographer started to take Helms's picture in his study when the senator pulled an illustration off the wall. "That'll get me in trouble," he said. The picture showed a black man in a rocking chair on the verandah of a plantation, sipping a mint julep and saying, "This is what me and Martin Luther had in mind!"

Earlier, the Wall Street Journal reported that Helms had a generic nickname for blacks: "Fred." He told the paper that actually that was not his usage, but perhaps that of two of his former Senate staffers. But an aide said the senator had a habit of saying, in response to a black request, "What does this Fred want?" or "Take care of that Fred." The aide said Helms thought it was funny.

Race was an important factor, perhaps the decisive one, in Helms's hardest Senate race, in 1984. His overall record may have been enough to mobilize the anti-black vote, but Helms and associates did not leave that to chance. He wrangled in the Senate for days against the Martin Luther King holiday bill. He complained early and often of the "bloc vote extremists" aligned against him. He benefited from a huge, organized white backlash against a publicized effort by Jesse

Jackson to register black voters. Late in the campaign, he visited the campus of Livingstone College, a black school in Salisbury. There, his speech was boycotted by many students, and he was photographed extending his hand to young blacks who refused to shake it. As he left, Helms suggested the whole thing had been "orchestrated," although he did not say by whom. Asked whether his opponent's camp might be responsible, he said, "I wouldn't be surprised." For him, it was as good as a series of the costly commercials he was broadcasting every night.

Nineteen days later, he won again.

This examination of Helms's official record and known private utterances on race establishes a clear pattern: All his public life, he has done and said things offensive to blacks, and to anyone sensitive to racial nuance. He does them, says them, and eventually people complain. He either denies his action or its racial intent. But he never says he is sorry. Instead, he turns around and does it again, and again. Then he is called on it again, and the process is repeated, over and over. Its effect is to assure those whose base motive is race that while he has to be polite and deny those accusations in public, down deep he is one of them. It is one reason why Helms has won every election he has ever run.

It is hard to believe this consistent, politically profitable pattern is an accident. But only Helms himself can say whether it is calculated. I asked him directly how he responded to the many charges that he is a racist.

"People make that charge, they say look at the record," he told me in his Senate office. "Then they're not willing to look at the record. What are they talking about, the Martin Luther King holiday?" Of course he was opposed, he said, because "I think we ought to reduce the number of holidays. But if we're going to close down the government for another day, I've got my own hero, named Thomas Jefferson . . . On top of that, I may not be around, I probably won't, but when those [FBI] records are finally opened—if a man is so worthy, what's your reluctance about opening the records on it? They certainly would open them on me, on you . . .

"You know, [in 1984] I was the only candidate in North Carolina who had a black press secretary. He's over at Foreign Relations now, one of the greatest young men I ever saw. You'll be impressed with him. He speaks four languages."

Later, outside on the Capitol steps, Helms had an afterthought, and offered what seemed to be his clincher: "All I can say is, ask the blacks that know me. There will be some professional blacks who don't know me who might say different, but I doubt you'll find anybody who knows me who says that. We've got a lot of blacks working here around the Senate, security officers and others. Ask them."

I asked Claude Allen, the one black who had ever been on the Helms payroll. He conceded that Helms's broadcast editorials of the sixties had been "pretty harsh," but said, "That's far different from the man I know."

The twenty-five-year-old Allen said he believed Helms's personal "born-again experience," when he saw the light while traveling on a plane during his 1972 campaign, had changed the senator's attitude on race. But what about his voting record since then? "I looked into it," Allen said, "and if he harbored racism, he cloaked it very well with his reasons for voting as he did, on voting rights, Martin Luther King and so on. One person he trusted a lot was Sam Ervin, and all his arguments were based on constitutional reasons. So why should he change, then?"

Black former sports stars Roosevelt Grier, Meadowlark Lemon, and Lenny Moore have become Helms's friends because of their shared support of school prayer, Allen said, and he thinks Grier also has had an impact on Helms's thinking.

Allen's own memories of Carolina racism include the first time he went to the beach after moving to the state from Washington, D.C., at the age of fifteen. Not far east of Raleigh, he and his family shuddered when they encountered a road sign saying, "The KKK Welcomes You to Johnston County."

He also recalls the night, early in Helms's 1984 campaign, when a man approached the senator after a barbecue rally in an eastern Carolina town and said, "Senator, you're wrong on abortion." Helms said, "What do you mean? I don't believe in taking the lives of the unborn." The man replied, "That's not what I mean. Abortion is the way we can get rid of all the niggers." Allen said Helms "got mad, red in the face," and brushed the man off. Flying back to Raleigh, Helms talked about the incident with his young aide.

"He's not the ogre people make him out to be," Allen said. "He's not the Jim Crow type."

Chapter 15

The Red, White, and Blue Bible

Hayes Barton Baptist Church is an imposing brick building with tan columns. It dominates the north Raleigh intersection it shares with two service stations, a branch of the First-Citizens Bank, an Apple Computer franchise, a Winn-Dixie supermarket, and the Hayes Barton Pharmacy.

It is a friendly church, in a businesslike way. Deacons and ushers greet worshipers in the vestibule, and invite visitors to sign the guest book. Members speak to each other in near-whispers as they file in. In the Baptist tradition, the church has no conspicuous crosses or other ornaments in its plain white auditorium. On the Sunday before July 4, the blinds at its tall windows were open and the congregation could see the crepe myrtle bushes just beginning to bloom outside in the rain.

As I sat in a pew near the back, I looked around the congregation. Everyone was neat and attentive. There was one black, a teen-age girl in a prim white dress. The first hymn of the day was "America the Beautiful." We stood and sang it with feeling.

Dr. Malcolm Tolbert, the preacher that Sunday, is not Hayes Barton's permanent pastor. He was there as an interim pastor, filling in after the retirement of the church's regular minister. He is a gray-haired man of barely medium height, who teaches the New Testament at the Southeastern Baptist Seminary at Wake Forest. He wore a gray suit that Sunday. He is a quiet but forceful speaker.

Independence Day being so near, he spoke on church and state. The subject was bubbling beneath the polite surface of Hayes Barton, week in and week out. Tolbert brought it into the open.

In Old Testament times, he said, the ideal state was a theocracy —its modern counterpart is probably Iran under the present ayatollah. He doubted that we would want that—"the only way I'd be in favor of religion taking over the state is if I could be in charge." He remembered that his grandmother was for prayer in schools as long as she wrote the prayer—in southern Louisiana schools where he grew up, they had a school prayer, and it was the Hail Mary. "Most of us would prefer to stay here where we can say prayers, or not say prayers," Tolbert said. "I don't think anybody does God an honor if he tries to coerce others" to believe this or that.

His text was Mark 12, "Render to Caesar the things that are Caesar's . . ." But, Tolbert said, "don't give him what doesn't belong to him—worship, ultimate loyalty." "In our relationship with the state, certain loyalty and responsibility are demanded. But it's easy for the state to get mixed up with the church. That's what happened under Hitler . . ."

This, he said, "is a danger in this country today, though here it's more subtle. I've heard people say, for example, 'My country, right or wrong.' That's an idolatrous statement. The issue of right and wrong has to be settled at a higher level . . ." There is a danger "of identifying nationalism with Christianity, of getting patriotism and love of God all mixed up. I've never liked a political platform of God and country. You can't make God a plank in a political platform . . ."

Tires whined on the wet street outside. The congregation listened in silence as Tolbert sharpened his point.

"The idea that if you're a Christian you're a Democrat or Republican—we sort of had that come up in the last election . . . God is not a Republican, not a Democrat, not an Independent . . . Christians voted for all the candidates.

"When we make that test, my friends, we have introduced politics into our relations with God," Tolbert said. "I have never felt I was capable to tell anybody who to vote for . . .

"People say we need to get back to God, but they don't realize that at the beginning of this country, only 10 percent of the people in the colonies were members of any church. No nation is Christian . . ."

In the Southern Baptist Convention, he said, "we're having a revival convention-wide next spring—to 'win America for Christ.' That disturbs me." The Bible for that occasion will be in the colors of the American flag, he said: "That's about as idolatrous as you can get. It comes awfully close to putting church and state together. A red, white, and blue Bible? I wouldn't have one in my house. The Bible, like God, belongs to everybody . . ."

As he closed his sermon, he said emotionally, "I'm so grateful to be an American. Children in America can dream dreams, can hope to be president . . . I didn't do anything to deserve this."

As we stood to sing "Amazing Grace," I inspected the back of every head in the auditorium, hoping to find Jesse Helms there in his home church during the congressional holiday. He had been there Easter, and he came Labor Day weekend. But he was elsewhere that Sunday. I was disappointed. Tolbert was, too. Helms would have been interested in his sermon.

The senator might have been provoked by it, in fact, because the idea of a red, white, and blue Bible perfectly symbolizes his thinking about church and state. His public record is rich with testimonials to that effect. He has asserted many times that "the historic values and mission of the United States have always been profoundly Christian."

In his pocket, Helms has carried a silver cross, given to him by his church's retired pastor. He not only goes to church, he sometimes preaches.

But his most noticed attendance has been at moments of high political tension, and in recent years his speaking has been mostly at high-growth, off-brand fundamentalist churches rather than at his own neighborhood Hayes Barton or other churches in the mainstream of Southern Baptist tradition.

There was the time, less than three weeks before his first re-election campaign ended, when Helms appeared on Jim Bakker's PTL Network religious call-in program. That day, over a widespread TV hookup, he gave his "Christian witness," suggesting that God had intervened at a timely moment to assure him about his political career: Although he had joined the church as a child, he had his first religious experience during his first senatorial campaign, on a flight from Raleigh to Asheville.

He has repeated the story since. "I got so depressed," he said. As he watched the lights pass below, he realized that in each house there was an individual human story unfolding. Suddenly, he said to himself, " 'Jesse, what in the world are you doing in this plane flying to Asheville in a campaign you didn't even want to be in?' I didn't even want to be in politics. I was running myself to death. And for the first time, I really prayed. Not 'Lord, let me win'—I didn't think I was going to win anyhow— but 'Lord, don't let me embarrass my family. Help me to do what's right in this thing. Help me live through it somehow' . . . I don't know how long I prayed. But all of a sudden, I looked out the window and the sun was shining. I felt a sense of serenity I'd never felt before . . . I've got it today . . . Up until that point, I think my religion was sort of rote . . . But I don't think it was until that very morning that it really dawned on me what this was all about."

On the PTL show, he went on to criticize Jimmy Carter's foreign policy and to restate his belief that private schools should be tax-exempt. "Private schools are more efficient," he said. "They have a higher quality of education than can be found in public schools." Helms did not mention his campaign opponent, John Ingram. Somehow Jim Bakker had not invited Ingram to join Helms in testimony.

On other occasions, in the closing weeks of the 1984 campaign, when Helms stood in the pulpit of Charlotte's Northside Baptist Church, with Lamarr Mooneyham of the Moral Majority beside him. Waving his arms, he declared, "There is an infestation of compromisers. How many times have you heard public figures say, 'I am personally opposed to so-and-so, but . . . ?' " Such people are responsible for "the deliberate destruction of the lives of one and a half million of the most innocent, most helpless human beings imaginable, the unborn . . . These are the people who do nothing to restore the most basic human right of all—the right of little children to engage in school prayer . . . who contend that pornography and homosexuality are private matters . . . They talk about freedom of religion when what they mean is freedom from religion . . . They are running full tilt against the very meaning of America!"

Again, Helms did not mention his opponent. And of course he did not need to: the pastor reminded the crowd of 3,500 that Brother Mooneyham had voter registration tables set up on the picnic grounds, and Mooneyham himself spoke out for Helms's blend of religion and politics. "We're in somewhat of a war . . ." he reminded them.

There were many other times, for example four days before that same close election, when Helms told the North Carolina Christian Educators Association, the people who run the state's private, mostly segregated Christian academies, that Christianity was "the meaning of America as far as I'm concerned." There was the time he spoke at "Old Fashioned Day" services at Midway Baptist Church, an independent congregation south of Raleigh. He told the congregation, "What we need is a Christian nation, with people unafraid to say they love the Lord."

"Amen!" they shouted.

Helms's habit of appearing in the pulpit at opportune political moments, his insistence on blending political issues with religion may make these seem attitudes of convenience—adopted for the home stretch of a campaign, then put away until the autumn of another even-numbered year. Not so. The broad consistency of his opinions on social and moral issues is one of the striking things about his long broadcasting and political career. He was in the public eye on these issues long before Falwell and most of the TV preachers, long before Viguerie invented his New Right mailing machine. He also was rousing the righteous to apply religious judgments to public affairs long before journalists and academics realized the growing political activism of fundamentalist churchmen.

For many years after the decline of the anti-evolution and anti-liquor crusades of the twenties, even as other prominent churchmen campaigned for social justice, the evangelical and fundamentalist movement had stayed out of politics. Even as it grew, its followers were largely non-voters, its preachers venting their wrath into a political vacuum. They were outsiders, out of the mainline churches, out of secular society, out of party politics. But both their numbers and their anger were growing.

Theologians have found ingenious ways to explain fundamentalist beliefs. Kenneth T. Langston, in a political science thesis at the University of North Carolina, offered this: "In many ways, the fundamentalist world view was a unique combination of both Enlightenment liberalism and Evangelicalism . . . Such theoretical combination resulted in a metaphysical system of thought based on (1) radical Biblical empiricism, (2) ontological dualism, (3) epistemological monism, and (4) an eschatological imperative." Not only that, but "premillennial dispensationalism" also became a part of fundamentalist thinking.

All those terms do mean something, but few of the millions of fundamentalist churchgoers and the thousands of their ministers have studied or even heard of them. Their theology could be boiled down to two principal beliefs: the word of the Bible is literally true, and anyone who does not believe it, who does not agree with them on what is right and wrong, cannot be "a Christian." Theirs is a polarized world: true believers and nonbelievers, good and evil. No shades of gray, no hints that man himself might be capable of making independent moral judgments, are acceptable. And the more rational the rest of mankind became, the angrier the fundamentalists grew, until at last, the long-time outsiders' pent-up fury burst into political activism.

Calculatedly or not, Jesse Helms anticipated and helped inspire this outburst. He began at least thirty-five years ago, back when he was by title a radio reporter rather than commentator, almost a decade before he became a television editorialist.

In February 1951, only days before he went to Washington as a senatorial aide, Helms used his WRAL microphone to chastise the pastor of a liberal Raleigh church as "a man who tries to mix religion and politics, or considers them inseparable." The minister of the United Church, Fred Eutsler, presided over a lecture series called the Institute of Religion. It had brought to Raleigh such speakers as Ralph Bunche, the United Nations ambassador who was the first black public speaker to address an unsegregated audience in the city. On the night yet another controversial speaker was to appear, Helms took the air to say that Eutsler was "perhaps as liberal as an individual can become without completely denouncing the capitalistic form of government . . . The Rev. Eutsler finds segregation incompatible with his views on religion, politics or government . . ." Eutsler's church had become a haven for liberal intellectuals, Helms charged. He noted critically that the month before, thirty United Church members including the minister had signed a newspaper ad opposing resisting communism by force.

After he had been to Washington and come back to be executive director of the North Carolina Bankers Association and a Raleigh city councilman, Helms still was agitated by the Institute on Religion's often controversial lecture series. In 1958, he wrote his provocative letter to Raleigh's city manager warning that police reinforcements should stand by for trouble when people like Martin Luther King, Jr., spoke. In it, Helms said that while he respected the forum's right of free expression, he felt that "religion" was the wrong word for a lecture series that "appears to be more political than religious." In the sixties, he repeatedly criticized ministers' involvement in the civil rights movement.

What this discloses, of course, is that his principles on mixing religion and politics have turned 180 degrees as the main direction of politico-religious activity has reversed itself in a generation.

As with his strictly political beliefs, Helms's developing thoughts on religion were revealed most extensively in the hundreds of editorials he wrote and broadcast during the turbulent sixties. I can testify that nothing brings out a commentator's innermost concerns so reliably as a recurring deadline, day after day, year after year. Under that pressure, a writer falls back repeatedly on what is gnawing at him from inside. In Helms's case, only race excited as much public passion as religion.

One of his favorite targets was "situational ethics"; by attacking it he reminded listeners of his own unyielding consistency. But there were points on which his own stand changed with the situation. In 1962, for example, before desegregation had inspired creation of the extensive system of private white academies across the South, he applauded Sam Ervin for opposing federal funding for church-run colleges. Speaking up for separation of church and state, Helms said "a principle that has endured throughout the history of this republic is being ground under legislative heels." Those backing private school funding "should now do some soul searching and ask themselves if expediency is worth the price," he said. In the eighties, when tax exemption for segregated schools and tuition tax credits for church school students became issues, Helms was conspicuous on the other side.

But at the first hints of a constitutional showdown over prayer in public schools, he leaped into a defensive stance that did not shift over the decades. When a Yale professor addressed a Charlotte PTA meeting and suggested that religious observances be banned from schools, Helms responded angrily, "The fact that some people in this country do not believe in God is of no consequence in this matter. The fact remains that this nation was founded upon a belief in God . . . Those who possess no such faith or trust are to be more pitied than scorned, but their superficial protests are hardly worthy of consideration." In this early assertion, Helms displayed positions he still shares with the fundamentalists: anyone who disagrees with him on a politico-religious matter is ipso facto a non-believer, and the Founding Fathers were motivated primarily by religion.

When the Supreme Court issued its school prayer decision later in 1962, Helms professed himself delighted by public reaction against it. "The judges apparently yielded to the notion once again that in the name of a frivolous assertion of 'civil liberty' the minority tail has the right to wag the majority dog. But encouragingly enough, this time the Supreme Court overstepped the limits of the patience of the American people," he said, adding confidently that the court should reverse itself promptly. "Most citizens understand that the founders of this Republic sought to guarantee freedom of religion, but not freedom from religion."

But as months went by and no court reversal seemed imminent, Helms's confidence changed to angry frustration. Jeering at a New York group that pushed the school prayer issue, made up of five Protestants, two Unitarians, a Catholic, and a Jew, he said, "These people are not a cross-section of anything but insanity. They have indicated no demonstrable knowledge of either religion or faith . . . The best that can be said for them is that they are legal lint-pickers." As the court approached its verdict in the school-religion suit brought by Madalyn Murray (O'Hair), Helms expressed fear that if prayers, then Christmas observances were forbidden in public schools, Easter might be next.

In his warning he made a leap of reasoning that has become familiar in the marathon school prayer debate: that forbidding religious observances in public schools equals forbidding them, period. "Every man is free to decide for himself whether he believes the story of the Resurrection. But if he chooses not to believe, is it within his rights to deny the observance to those who do? . . . If the decision is against God, then the whole keystone of our nation is blown apart and buried beneath the rubbish of so-called 'minority rights.' "

The high court ignored Helms's warnings. When it ruled in the Madalyn Murray case, he called it "an indelible blot upon the history of a proud nation . . . the court is giving atheism equality with religious faith in America." From the beginning, he insisted, the U.S. government "has been anything but neutral on the question of religion. It has been neutral only as to denomination or variety of faith in God . . . The court is in the process of converting America into a Godless state . . . It is more important today than ever before because freedom is locked in a death struggle with communism."

Of course the Supreme Court was not literally ignoring Helms, because it never heard him: his range then was limited to one region, and one fringe of politics. But in Carolina, his voice was booming—and it stirred response. Much of the disagreement with him came from the religious community, specifically from the Baptist tradition in which Helms himself had been brought up.

Contrary to the assumption of many Americans, the Baptist denomination is not synonymous with fundamentalism. Superficially, what has distinguished Baptists from other Protestant movements is their belief in baptism by total immersion. Much more important is their ancient belief that infant baptism is wrong because a decision to follow Christ must be a conscious, voluntary act. Beyond that, very few generalities could be stated about Baptists, for the very reason that they cherished independent thought. For many generations, they emphasized that it was up to the minister, the congregation, indeed the individual worshiper to decide for himself just how he interpreted the Bible. There was no Baptist hierarchy, no extensive dogma. Before the Civil War, the Baptist movement split over the issue of slavery. But the Southern Baptist Convention (SBC), which became by far the biggest Protestant denomination, was more an administrative convenience than a central authority. Yet even it was too confining for many of the independent-minded believers who called themselves Baptists. Thus there was a proliferation of Baptist churches, some growing into sub-denominations of their own, some consisting of no more than one lonely congregation up a hollow in the southern mountains. As a century passed, the Southern Baptist Convention itself became the main keeper of tradition. Just as the original Baptists had been rebels against the established church, many of the fundamentalist and evangelical offshoots of latter days were defiant of the SBC establishment. As states like North Carolina industrialized, many rural fundamentalists, wearing Baptist and dozens of other labels, converged on the textile towns and mercantile cities. They clustered into churches there, often recruited by golden-tongued broadcast preachers. As social change accelerated, their resentment swelled, and increasingly they were at odds with the federal government, the liberal northern churches, and often with the mainstream churches in their own towns.

In Carolina, the official voice of the Baptist State Convention is the *Biblical Recorder*. Its editors have been outspoken in defense of church traditions. When the *Recorder* spoke out in support of the Supreme Court's prayer decision, Helms called it a "curious position," and insisted again that "separation of church and state is not at stake here." When the *Biblical Recorder*'s then editor, Marse Grant, wrote to object, Helms took three days' broadcasts to read his letter, paragraph by paragraph, stopping in between to dissect each of Grant's points. The short of it, he concluded, is that "atheists have a right to be atheists, but they do not have a right to deprive their religious fellow men of their right to continue the heritage of a land founded on religious concepts." He did not say that Grant, a lifelong Baptist layman, was an atheist, of course. He merely said he was taking the atheist position.

No one who had followed Helms's thoughts in this area was surprised in 1984 when Ronald Reagan, at a mass prayer breakfast at the Dallas Republican Convention, suggested that whoever opposed prayer in schools was "intolerant of religion." Neither Reagan nor whoever wrote his speech paid attention to the fact that the most knowledgeable opponents of school prayer are themselves serious churchmen. The entire Reagan talk, which provoked excited reaction, was but a far milder version of dozens of Helms statements over a whole political generation.

Nothing stirred Helms's endorsement of church-state separation so surely as the involvement of churchmen in the civil rights movement, and none of them so provoked Helms as Martin Luther King. The week after King was slain, Helms was upset by the resulting "effort to deify some public figure who has managed to capture the imagination or seized upon the emotions of great masses of people." Without mentioning King's name, he used his Easter editorial to say that "it is perfectly possible . . . for any man to contend, or pretend, that his conduct parallels the methods of Christ. But . . . Jesus never advocated a governmental program . . . It is hypocrisy to suggest that if Jesus were among us today in mortal form, He would support this movement or that . . ." As Helms rode into politics atop the burgeoning fundamentalist movement, of course, he himself maintained that in his moral crusades, he was doing God's will.

Others who believed they were doing the same thing simply did not qualify as true Christians to Helms. When Ralph Abernathy was trying to fill the place of the recently assassinated King, Helms said, "There is a very grave danger in the careless identification of the church with various political schemes . . . They voice threats. They curse their country, and they give unblushing support and encouragement to the atheistic forces of communism. They encourage people not to work, but to congregate and move about in angry hatred and bitterness, and under circumstances that have bred violence, immorality, thievery and destruction . . . Jesus was mindful of injustices, and He did not condone them. But He carefully separated earthly politics and His heavenly kingdom."

The World Council of Churches and its national affiliate aroused Helms almost as often as King and civil rights leaders. He was proud of his antagonism toward it. "When this station and other media revealed the extent to which the National Council of Churches was dabbling in subversion, rioting, and racial tensions—even to the extent of training young people to circumvent the law—we were chastised by both laymen and clergy," he said. "The organization is on record, for all to see, in favor of violence and revolution. It is for recognition of Red China. It is for draft evasion. It is, in fact, in favor of almost everything this nation is committed against." Lashing at the Council and militant ministers again, he cited for contrast a California pastor of a huge Baptist church who had said, "We will observe the separation of church and state. It is time that we returned to our calling as ministers, not as politicians. I will use the voting booth, not the pulpit, for my political views."

Just before he left broadcasting to go national with his own unique blend of voting booth and pulpit (and TV camera and computer), Helms commented on the "Jesus movement" among American youth by saying, "A true Christian cannot accept the philosophy that his government owes him a living; to the contrary, he believes that he must be a workman worthy of his hire. He cannot accept the theory that he should support a political philosophy based on an invasion upon his neighbor's right to choose."

In view of Helms's unending effort since then to extend government into the private lives of American citizens, the right to choose seemed a peculiar point for him to emphasize. But at that time the Supreme Court had not yet handed down its decision legalizing abortion. That verdict came soon after Helms arrived in the Senate, and energized his career. More than any other single issue, abortion brought him together with a variety of electronic preachers, single-issue lobbyists, and political entrepreneurs to form what is called the New Right.

Helms's stubborn crusade on the issues of abortion, school busing, school prayer, and communism is the first thing anyone learns about him, the thing that keeps him constantly in controversy with his Senate colleagues—and in headlines across the nation. We have seen how, though knowing he will lose, he forces senators to vote on emotional issues and then uses that record against them in their own home states. (One of the sharpest exchanges he provoked on the Senate floor was with Arkansas' Dale Bumpers, whose temper flared after Helms had spent a month attaching school prayer and anti-abortion riders to a pending debt ceiling bill. Pointing toward Helms, Bumpers said, "His presses are running, his letters are going out. He is going after all the troglodytes in the Senate who are opposed to school prayer. But how many times do we have to vote on this? What advantage is there to being on record ten times instead of nine?" And Helms, quietly, as if taking notes, replied, "I understand the senator is against prayer in the schools.")

Helms helped push through the legislation that forbade federal magnet-school funds to schools that teach "secular humanism"— and left it up to local complainants everywhere to define that vague menace invented by the religious right. (There was the time, too, when he voted against Jimmy Carter's nomination of Judge Shirley Hufstedler as secretary of education, because she had been on the board of the Aspen Institute for Humanistic Studies. "I don't know what the purpose of the Aspen Institute is," he said. "But the implication of its name bothers me." He added that anyhow, he didn't like the idea of a Department of Education in the first place.)

Again and again, before religious audiences, Helms has suggested that his favorite issues are bound together by a common thread, that they are all what God would have him do. Almost as starkly as his allies like Jerry Falwell, he has sought to turn every worldly political issue, from tax reform to aiding the Nicaraguan contras, into a test of religious faith. And although he complains unceasingly about mistreatment by "the media," he has gotten all the best of the publicity battle over these deeds. There has been nothing like equal time for churchmen who challenge him and his cobelievers on these assertions.

Carolina's own Billy Graham, for example, himself a world-famous television moralizer, got little notice when he said, "I'm for morality. But morality goes beyond sex to human freedom and social justice. We as clergy know so very little to speak out with such authority on the Panama Canal or superiority of armaments. Evangelists can't be closely identified with any particular party or person . . . Liberals organized in the sixties, and conservatives certainly have a right to organize in the eighties, but it would disturb me if there was a wedding between religious fundamentalists and the political right. The hard right has no interest in religion except to manipulate it." In fact, Graham must already have been disturbed: when he spoke, that marriage already had been consummated.

The nation's best-known historian of Protestantism, Martin E. Marty, took more scholarly issue with the repeated assertion by Helms and his friends that religion motivated the Founding Fathers. "The impression they give is that we were once a specifically Christian nation from which we've fallen, and that is just plain not true in their sense of the term," Marty said. Of the nation's Founders, "not more than one or two could have been members of any of their [fundamentalist] churches. Most were Episcopalians or Congregationalists, whom the fundamentalists today would call humanists, Unitarians, or even secular humanists," he added. "In effect, the fundamentalist political movement is trying to make second-class citizens of everyone who isn't a part of it, and the Founders deliberately set out not to do that." The fundamentalists are in line with a worldwide trend toward retribalization, in which sects justify their hopes and power "by making a unique, divine claim," Marty said, citing the Shi'ite Moslems in Iran as the best example. He also questioned the fundamentalists' claim to promote a Biblical program. "It seems to me that if you will simply compute the Biblical mandates and injunctions to human society, you will find that nine out of ten would have to do with eliminating poverty, bringing a better measure of justice, equalizing the conditions of the people . . ." he said. "I'm certainly not socializing the Bible. But its concern is for the poor. One never hears a trace of that in the fundamentalist political program."

W. W. Finlator, before his retirement as pastor of Raleigh's Pullen Memorial Baptist Church, noted that as used in fundamentalist politics, the very word "humanism" has "become a no-no word, as if it were subversive or communistic . . . I think some people are using the word 'humanism'—and this is all the more upsetting—as a means of defeating humanitarian causes. This seems to be little short of perversity."

In each election year, Helms and his friends on the fundamentalist right prove again that they provide each other much more than mutually supportive rhetoric. The massive Moral Majority registration drive that boosted Helms in 1984 is only one example.

In 1980, when Helms's friends John East and I. Beverly Lake, Jr., were running for senator and governor, an organization called Churches for Life and Liberty just happened to occupy office space in Helms's Congressional Club's building. That group of fundamentalist preachers put out a "Biblical Position Rating," grading state candidates on eleven controversial public issues. And it just happened to find that Lake scored 90 percent, while his prospective Democratic opponent, Governor Jim Hunt, only got 10 percent. The ratings were distributed to churches from one end of the state to the other. Many of those churches published the lists in their Sunday bulletins. Jim Hunt's protest that the "inaccurate and scurrilous" ratings distorted his positions on capital punishment, liberalized divorce, and marijuana laws never caught up with the initial distribution. Neither did the acknowledgment, by one of the group's own lobbyists, that the ratings were based on "shoddy research."

A few days later, a companion group named Friends of Life and Liberty, this one a registered political action committee, conducted a voter canvass with questions loaded to steer voters away from Hunt. Like Churches for Life and Liberty, Friends of Life and Liberty was based in Congressional Club headquarters. But the groups' leaders predictably denied Hunt's charge that they were merely an arm of Helms's political machine. Their idea for rating the Carolina candidates apparently came from the Washington-based Christian Voice organization, which gave a "morality rating" to members of the Senate, based on issues from school prayer to creating an Education department. Not surprisingly, it rated Helms at 100 percent, and Ted Kennedy at zero. But Senator Robert Morgan, an active Southern Baptist layman who was challenged by Helms's protégé John East, scored only 50 percent. Morgan protested that there was no moral or immoral position on issues like creating an Education department. But nobody heard him.

That summer, Helms was a hero at the Republican convention in Detroit. It was there that he said Ronald Reagan should have a running mate with "strong appeal to Christian people." What that meant to some political strategists was that Reagan should pick someone who could attract many of the southern fundamentalist voters who were first attracted and then disappointed by Jimmy Carter. But many Americans heard something else in that phrase, and in the religious right's repeated declarations that this is and should be "a Christian nation." Helms has preached that "as Christians we need to work with missionary zeal to reinstate the rule of Christ in our sadly demoralized country."

That sounded innocent enough to those who have heard the word "Christian" used at church all their lives to mean good, moral, upright. But it reminded many Jews, for example, of Europe only a long generation ago, when such talk preceded the horrors of Hitler and the Holocaust. To them it sounded as if "Christian nation" meant one exclusively Christian, in which there would be no place for anyone not fitting the narrow definition of Christianity expounded by the fundamentalists. This legitimate objection was voiced often enough to have been heard by Helms and other spokesmen of the religious right. If originally the phrase "Christian nation" had been used in all innocence, its continued repetition after those protests had to raise questions about whether it was so innocent after all. Many Jews who did not like Helms and his politics found in it a scarcely veiled anti-Semitism.

As Helms looked ahead to his most difficult election, against the same Jim Hunt who got a failing grade from the North Carolina arbiters of biblical standards, he saw correctly that he would need all the help he could get. After the Moral Majority got into voter registration in 1980, he saw its potential in Carolina. Thus he found it wise to tighten his bonds with Falwell. He sent out a typical direct-mail appeal crying that "there are forces in this country who would silence Jerry Falwell . . . They reject his reminders that the words, IN GOD WE TRUST, are the most vital part of America's very meaning." Falwell's Liberty Baptist College in Lynchburg must keep building, Helms said. The Moral Majority must keep campaigning. "It is important that we make certain that Jerry remains a dominant voice on the American scene. He must not be silenced!" Thus, of course, the letter's recipient should send in twenty-five dollars, fifty dollars, or even a hundred dollars quickly. "I will be looking for your gift every day," Helms said.

Falwell, whose smooth, highly professional pitches for donations seem everywhere on television, may not have been all that desperate. But he was appreciative. He cemented the alliance a couple of months later by appearing at a Raleigh press conference wearing a "Jesus First" pin, to anoint Helms as new leader of the conservative movement. Then as Helms's electoral test approached, the senator went to Lynchburg to visit Falwell's Thomas Road Baptist Church.

His host said, "If we had a hundred Jesse Helms up there [in Congress], praise God, we'd have a spiritual awakening . . . I wonder how many Tarheels know how privileged they are to have Jesse Helms representing them in Washington." In return, Helms praised Falwell, the church, and Liberty Baptist College, and said, "I've reached the conclusion there's nothing this crowd of people can't do." As they admired each other publicly, the Moral Majority's political hands were meeting privately in Washington to plan their highly effective Carolina voter registration drive, kicked off by Falwell on Helms's behalf that summer.

That drive had been running for more than a year when the election turned into the home stretch just before Labor Day of 1984. About that time, Carolina Baptists realized their denomination was being split by the intrusion of Helms's political friends. Eighteen thousand state Baptist preachers and other church workers received a letter urging them to support Helms and hold church voter registration drives to help him. It said "every ultra-liberal organization," including the National Organization for Women and the homosexual community, was fighting to defeat Helms. Some Baptist leaders were outraged: the mailing used the Baptist State Convention's computerized "Key Leadership List," without permission from the state board. It turned out that a copy had been sold to the Rev. Coy Privette, one of the letter's four signers, ostensibly for fund-raising. Privette was executive director of a lobbying group called the Christian Action League. R.G. Puckett, editor of the *Biblical Recorder,* said use of the list was "an abuse of the Baptist denomination . . . That list should not have been made available to anybody for political purposes." But such protests were in vain; the letter was an accomplished fact.

Following up that year's success, the Republican National Committee tried in 1985 to persuade 100,000 Democrats in four selected states to switch parties. One of its agents sent letters to fundamentalist ministers in North Carolina, asking for their church membership lists. That agent was Robert Touchton, an employee of Jefferson Marketing, Inc., the corporate arm of Helms's Congressional Club. Touchton's letter, enclosing a photograph of Helms, said conservative victories in 1984 were "due in large part to the efforts of thousands of evangelical Christians, not just here in North Carolina, but also nationwide . . . It is for this reason that we are trying to involve the evangelical Christian community in our Operation Open Door."

And Jerry Falwell, addressing a political how-to workshop for the American Coalition of Traditional Values in Washington, said, "Six or seven years ago we got past the psychological barrier, 'It's a sin to vote.' Now, it's a sin not to be registering voters."

The political contest within the Baptist church was not confined to North Carolina. The contention there was a particularly heated flare-up of a struggle that still troubles the entire Southern Baptist Convention. When delegates of the almost fifteen million-member SBC convened for a showdown in Dallas in 1985, Helms's lieutenants were deeply involved in maneuvering to tighten the grip of the TV evangelist-fundamentalist-political wing on the top leadership. That faction took over the presidency in 1979 from the traditionalists who had dominated the SBC's boards, seminaries, and other offices for decades. Although "messengers" from Helms's home church, Hayes Barton, voted about 8 to 2 for the traditionalist, moderate challenger, Carolinians were in the thick of the successful fight to re-elect right-wing SBC president Charles Stanley of Atlanta. Among them were Samuel T. Currin, a Hayes Barton member and former Helms Senate staffer picked by the senator to be U.S. attorney for eastern North Carolina, and considered since then to become a federal judge.

The right wing was so well financed and organized for the Dallas confrontation that some on the opposing side suspected money from one of the Helms foundations helped pay for the long trip to Texas. But no one offered proof of this, and there was plenty of Texas money flowing into the power struggle. Hundreds of buses rounded up "messengers" to support the fundamentalists in each critical vote. The prevailing side also was accused of strong-arm tactics, such as crowding its rivals away from floor microphones, and of ignoring SBC rules and bylaws. The moderates have filed suit over these tactics.

Whatever their role in Dallas, Helms's people are conspicuous among the right-wingers campaigning to control the organizational machinery of the SBC and to dominate the Baptist State Convention in North Carolina. The most remarkable exhibit of this was in the U.S. attorney's office occupied by Helms's young former Senate assistant, Sam Currin.

Currin, though a member of Hayes Barton, was never widely known for his church activities until he returned to Carolina from duty with Helms's staff in Washington. After that, he was so zealous that his nomination by Helms for a federal judgeship was delayed by controversy for many months. Currin drafted and lobbied for a constitutionally questionable North Carolina anti-pornography law that allows arrest of vendors on the complaint of a policeman, before proof that the offending merchandise is indeed pornographic. His opponents charged him with racial discrimination and political use of his office. Helms asserted that all opposition to his nomination was merely political. But one of the most telling objections came from Helms's old friend, Judge Pou Bailey, who wrote to the Senate Judiciary Committee that "I personally believe Sam Currin would use any method for any purpose he thought was right. I can conceive of no more dangerous person than a fanatic with power. If he is appointed a judge, that's what we would have." The issue eventually could be resolved in the Judiciary Committee, chaired by Helms's ally, Strom Thurmond.

Currin was picked by Charles Stanley, the Atlanta TV evangelist who heads the SBC, to be chairman of the Baptist Joint Committee on Public Affairs. That body, whose working office is in Washington, is the lobbying and publicity arm of the SBC. Joseph T. Knott III, who was an assistant U.S. attorney under Currin, was named to the SBC's Sunday School Board. (And his father, the chairman of Democrats for Helms in the 1984 election, was appointed to the church's powerful Committee on Boards, which chooses members of the other boards and committees.) Currin's other assistant, William Delahoyde, was named to the board of the SBC's Southeastern Seminary, one of the surviving outposts of older Baptist tradition that the right wing is trying to bring under its control.

This cluster of Helms patronage in the U.S. attorney's office was only the most conspicuous example of how his political allies moved into key church positions. Coy Privette, the minister and Republican state representative who provoked outcries from the Baptist State Convention when he put its closely guarded leadership list to use in the 1984 Helms campaign, was named to the SBC's Christian Life Commission. Henderson Belk, a wealthy Charlotte retailer who signed that pro-Helms letter along with Privette, was put on the influential Committee on Boards. Anne Frazier of North Carolina Conservatives United, an aggressive lobbyist against "secular humanism" and pornography, was chosen for the Committee on Committees. Many more Helms loyalists have appeared in such important Baptist positions since the right wing took over the SBC presidency. And Helms's ties with other prominent Baptists like Norman Wiggins, immediate past president of the Baptist State Convention and president of Campbell University, long predate this flurry of activity in the eighties.

In delayed reaction to the right-wing thrust for power, delegates to the Baptist State Convention in late 1985 elected traditional churchmen to replace Wiggins and fill the top statewide offices. Coy Privette nominated Sam Currin as second vice president, praising him for his "leadership in applied Christianity." Currin was defeated in a runoff there, but remained chairman of the much bigger Southern Baptist Convention's Joint Committee on Public Affairs. The backlash against the right wing in Carolina did not reverse the fundamentalist drive for control. It was a momentary turn in the ongoing contest, proof of how deeply the Baptists are riven by ideological struggle, there and across the nation.

The names and specific assignments of all these men and women may be of interest mainly to Carolina Baptists. But the political potential of this move to dominate the Baptist church is hard to exaggerate. In North Carolina alone, there are more than 1.2 million members of the Southern Baptist Convention, plus the many Baptists who are not affiliated with the SBC. In another state, in another time, those who believe in keeping religion and politics apart could say confidently that these developments were not their concern. But in Carolina in Jesse Helms's time, the Moral Majority, the fundamentalist churches, the Christian Action League, Churches for Life and Liberty, Friends of Life and Liberty, and a still-multiplying host of other religious groups already have done their basic training in one or more statewide elections. Their companion groups have shown their strength nationally.

The politicization of the Baptist convention points in a straight line to the next election, and the one after that—in which all those elements will be arrayed behind Helms's latest protégé, or behind Helms himself.

Chapter 16

The Media Conspiracy

Long after he left broadcasting to become a United States senator, Jesse Helms still called himself "a professional journalist."

That is legitimate; in our country, all a person must do to be a journalist is write, edit, photograph—or today, merely read into a microphone—material that relates somehow to current events. All he has to do to be a professional is get paid for it. Journalism is a trade, a business, a profession that has high standards. But they are unofficial; the government may impose no test, and no specific degree is required. Disagreement over who does and does not meet those standards is a staple of both professional and political debate. Along with the protection of the First Amendment comes the certainty of criticism, from within and without the business.

Helms spent almost twenty years as newspaperman and broadcaster, and seven more when he made editorializing part of his job as a banking lobbyist. Thus as former journalist and especially as current politician, he has standing to criticize what are now called "the media," and he uses his license to the fullest. He was at it when he himself was an editorialist, and as a senator he is at it very nearly every day. Tomorrow he may be inspired by yet another way to tar his erstwhile colleagues, but till now the height of his vindictiveness was in the winter of 1985. That was when he began his hullaballooed campaign for a conservative takeover of the CBS network, and when he made the most scathing speech against "the media" since the heyday of former Vice President Spiro T. Agnew.

In three decades of covering politics, I have watched and heard many different demagogues taunt the press—sometimes the liberal press, sometimes the fascist, capitalist, Eastern, effete, elite, establishment, or captive press. When I was reporting from Moscow, I used to watch Nikita Khrushchev do it before a factory yard full of

proletarians or a Kremlin hall full of Communist Youth. George
Wallace in his segregationist prime loved to do it, for a courthouse
square full of believers on a hot summer afternoon. I remember the
snarling roar of the Goldwater convention at San Francisco's Cow
Palace when Dwight Eisenhower took a surprising swing at "sensa-
tion-seeking columnists [he pronounced it colyumnists] and commentators," and how so many in the crowd rose and shook their fists
toward the press deck.

Ike touched a chord that has been plucked constantly by the right
wing since then, resoundingly in the alliterative excesses of Agnew,
who tried to damage the credibility of "the media" as they turned
toward Watergate and his own bush-league graft. Some anti-war
demonstrators of the sixties chanted and carried signs parroting old
communist slogans about the press's role as "running dogs of capitalism," even as they exploited the certainty that their words and
pictures would get prime-time attention on the capitalist networks.
It is a tactic used by communists and anti-communists, Republicans
and Democrats, left-wing kooks and right-wing kooks. Sometimes it
is done with a half-grin, and afterwards the politician laughs about
it and offers you a Coke. Sometimes it is done with cold, calculated
anger, and the politician wouldn't offer you a handshake if you
wanted one.

Never, East or West, hot or cold, have I sat through an attack
more mean-spirited, surrounded by an audience more silently hostile, than when Jesse Helms spoke to the annual meeting of the
Conservative Political Action Conference in late February, 1985.

He had just won a close re-election contest. Ronald Reagan had
just carried forty-nine states against Walter Mondale. Helms and his
audience—spokesmen, organizers, technicians, contributors representing all the overlapping interests of the New Right—were riding
high. But rather than exulting together, he spoke and they reacted
as if they were joined in combat against a treacherous enemy.

"There are forces around the world eager to see America swept
into the dustbin," Helms warned. "What we have today is a confrontation between tyranny and freedom, between spirituality and atheism, between justice and brutality. And I find myself wondering, as
I know sometimes you do, why the opinion-makers in our own land
—the major news media—so often attempt to lead us to believe that
communism is just another philosophy, just another political
system."

That was his thesis. He elaborated it through his whole long speech. He cited communist offenses around the world. As we confront them, he said, "there is a cacophony of exhortations by cunningly false prophets . . . overwhelming efforts to dictate what our people shall think, and say, and do . . . When I read the *Washington Post,* I sometimes wonder whether I'm on the same planet as the reporters and editors who put that paper together . . .

"How can the major media be so wrong so often? The answer is obvious: They are profoundly out of sympathy with the ideals and goals of the American people."

Of course, Helms said, there are sound and honest journalists all over the country. "But," he cautioned, "the elite media—and you know who they are—are overwhelmingly produced by men and women who, if they do not hate America first, they certainly have a smug contempt for American ideals and principles."

These men and women "reject the goals and aspirations of ordinary Americans . . . the moral and ethical values of ordinary Americans . . . the success which America has achieved and the political and economic institutions which are the foundation of that success . . ." Helms asserted.

For support, he quoted a 1980 survey by two people named Stanley Rothman and Robert Lichter, which has been manna for press critics from the right since its publication. Sampling "hundreds of journalists from the elite media," Helms said, it found that most of them thought government should reduce the gap between rich and poor and guarantee jobs; that most saw no wrong in adultery, homosexuality, or abortion on demand, and some 45 percent believed the United States caused Third World poverty.

Such people attack "the foundations of the American political and economic system," he declared. We all recognize the menace of communism, "but the real threat to freedom, the threat to freedom of speech, and the threat to our constitutional system, is on our TV screens every evening, and on the front pages of some of the nation's most powerful newspapers every day. If we ever lost our freedom in this country, can the elite news media be absolved of a large share of the blame?"

About there Helms looked up toward reporters near the back of the hall. "I don't want to offend any of you fellows back there," he said. "Good luck to you, and I hope your dog comes out and wags its tail when you come home tonight." His audience tittered; the reporters did not.

The press has the power of character assassination, Helms declared—the power to set the national agenda, and of "psychological warfare against the American people . . . Have we reached the point that the elite media in the United States are no longer defenders of democracy; are they not a threat to democracy?"

As he wound down, Helms almost apologized for "taking advantage of my hosts" by mentioning his Fairness in Media project to take over CBS. He believed it important, he said, and apparently "our liberal brethren in the major news media" do, too. "Otherwise, why are they living on a diet of fingernails at the prospect of a board of directors at CBS that would insist on objectivity and fairness?"

When he was done, when the audience of right-wing activists had applauded him, Helms made a point of offering two reporters a ride downtown from the Washington Sheraton.

To understand the content and motivation of that merciless attack, it is useful to start with Helms's own initiation into "the media" as a boy sportswriter on a country paper. His own working experiences and his political excursions through the decades disclose much about the standards he brings to judging others in journalism.

He was captivated by the romance of small-town newspapering. He decided correctly that he did not need to study journalism, or finish college at all, to get started in that direction. From the beginning, he had the knack of writing fast and brightly. It was an advantage in breaking in, but in a way a disadvantage. If he had gone on to study journalism, or completed a liberal arts degree, or even read widely, he would have been grounded in the ethics of the business, exposed to the historical and cultural traditions on which Americans make political judgments. He would have gotten used to the questioning of common assumptions and established authority that is the very fundament of higher education. Instead, his quickness took him through his newspaper apprenticeship so fast that he learned the techniques but missed the deeper values. His mind was wide open to the hard-line conservatism he learned from his father-in-law and the commentators he admired, but unequipped with the skepticism to help him assess it. When he shifted into radio and came under the wing of A.J. Fletcher at WRAL after World War II, he was well trained but not well educated.

As Helms approached his first important political experience, he was on the payroll of a man of hard conservative ideology, and the contest was a clear choice—between liberal Frank P. Graham and conservative Willis Smith. The Democratic voice of Carolina, his old employer the *News & Observer,* was all out for Graham. There is no question that its commitment to one side helped push A.J. Fletcher, Helms, and other Smith backers to over-react in opposition. Not that this was the whole explanation; 1950 was a year when the smear tactics of Joe McCarthy were used and passed around from state to state, and figured importantly in California, Florida, and Maryland in addition to Carolina. But to conservatives, the *N & O*'s role as Democratic stalwart was a galling state tradition. Until a decade ago, the paper always celebrated Democratic victories by printing the southern party's old ballot symbol, a crowing red rooster, atop its editorial page. Not only that, but its proprietors, Josephus Daniels and his son Jonathan, were openly and proudly involved in Democratic politics at state and national levels.

The right wing in North Carolina was deeply resentful that the state's dominant political paper was thus committed. Whatever the conservatives did in response seemed only fitting. Therefore Helms, with Fletcher's enthusiastic blessing, was deeply committed to the Smith campaign, cheering him on to enter the runoff primary. After Willis Smith showed his appreciation by inviting him to join his staff in Washington, Helms was offended again by the partisanship of the *News & Observer* in opposing the senator.

These thirty-five years later, he cites that period as the origin of his continuing vendetta against the press. In his Senate office, he told me that "because [Willis Smith] dared oppose Dr. Frank [Graham] —and he never said a word against Dr. Frank personally—he was pilloried by various newspapers, misrepresented to the point that I was almost nauseated. I came up here and watched the *News & Observer* attack Mr. Smith day after day. I was here and knew what he was doing, and was astonished at what they said he was doing, and I resented it. That was the beginning . . ."

Helms's title was administrative assistant, but he functioned as Smith's press secretary as well. Then in the summer of 1952, he took leave to handle radio and TV publicity for Richard Russell's abortive presidential campaign. When he returned to Raleigh, he was executive director of the North Carolina Bankers Association, which meant lobbying, publicizing, editing the bankers' house organ. He laid out his own political opinions under the masthead of the *Tarheel Banker,* as if he were the opposition newspaper voice he believed the capital needed so badly.

Helms says now that he was personally friendly with old Josephus Daniels, who until his death in 1948 lived in a mansion across the street from the Cobles. "He had the cannon off the USS. *North Carolina* over there, almost pointed at our home," Helms told me. "Dot and I used to go Sunday afternoons and visit him. He was lonely. I've got twelve or fifteen books he gave me . . . Old Josephus was a firebrand Democrat, but he would at least publish the other side. It's not that way any more."

Hardly had the old man died when Helms started his running feud with the *N & O,* and he kept it up through the fifties. Not only did he find it overly critical of banking. He also suspected it of softness toward the agitators he saw coming in to change the southern way of life. The argument over Helms's warning about possible trouble when Martin Luther King, Jr., came to speak in Raleigh in 1958 also heightened their mutual dislike. The *N & O's* editorial chastising Helms said he had "made the organ of the North Carolina bankers the journal of his personal prejudices." It characterized his warning as "Bosh and nausea!" Two years later, when A.J. Fletcher offered Helms the chance to editorialize full-time on WRAL-TV, the two believed they had a mission to bring rightward balance to political opinion in the capital.

Helms had barely introduced himself on the air when in his second editorial he attacked the state's press. It sounded much like the scathing speech quoted above, against the national press, twenty-five years later. "There is substantial evidence to indicate that many North Carolinians are becoming increasingly distrustful of the major daily newspapers they read, and that respect for the integrity of the newspaper profession may be on the wane," he began. He said Carolina's daily press virtually ignored "the Southern, conservative viewpoint . . . while headlining the liberal views of almost any spokesman who happens to come along." He concluded, "The surest death for freedom of the press lies down the road of unfairness, partiality, and bias. America's free press should ponder the possibility that it may one day be its own executioner."

Helms's five-a-week commentaries had not been on the air long when the station heard a rising chorus of complaints that its own efforts were unfair, partial, and biased. Helms responded that WRAL's policy was adopted in full awareness that some would be offended, but that it filled the local need for "an editorial expression different from that to which they previously had access." Soon after-

ward, Helms hailed FCC Chairman Newton Minow's encouragement of broadcast editorializing, nothing that "there is not a city in
North Carolina with competing daily newspapers." He charged that
the "monopolistic editor" of Raleigh's morning daily had expressed
"sneers and sarcasm [for] the free enterprise system." And soon after
that, WRAL-TV was contesting the first of the public challenges that
brought its editorial one-sidedness before the Federal Communications Commission.

As we have seen, the FCC renewed the station's license, but with
a warning that it should invite and broadcast contrary opinion.
When Baptist editor Marse Grant wrote a response, Helms demonstrated just how he would handle those who differed with him. As
Grant told Katherine Fulton of the *North Carolina Independent,* "I
was naive enough to think my letter would be treated like most
letters to the media—aired or printed without comment. Instead,
Helms devoted two or three programs to it, even though it was not
worth that much attention. The strategy was clear: A weak, effemi-
nate voice off camera quoted from my letter as it appeared on the
screen. Then Helms took it apart sentence by sentence, sarcastically
ridiculing every point I was trying to make. I was made to look like
a fool for daring to question one of his editorials, although viewer
response was encouraged. To say the least, the program was stacked
against those who disagreed."

The tone of Helms's attacks on the Carolina press made it seem
that all the state's papers were outright liberal, integrationist crusaders. In fact, many of the county weeklies and smaller dailies were just
as adamantly resistant to change as Helms. But it is true that North
Carolina has a tradition of high-quality journalism that contributed
mightily to its pre-Helms reputation as the South's most progressive
state. In the early fifties, when not many southern editors were
standing tall against racism, a country editor named Willard Cole
won a Pulitzer Prize for taking on the Ku Klux Klan in Columbus
County, down in the state's southeastern corner. The *News & Observer,* joined by papers in Charlotte, Greensboro, Winston-Salem,
and Asheville, spoke out editorially for moderation and obedience to
the law of the land. But back then they were indeed moderate voices,
by national standards and by comparison with the positions they take
today. Their strongest language was mobilized not so much for racial
change as against the Klan, McCarthyism, know-nothingism,
Republicans—and pseudo-Democrats like Helms.

Helms, however, even then liked to point his criticism at the "major media" and "liberal newspapers." When he had been at it through the sixties, his friend Gene Price, editor of the *Goldsboro News-Argus,* lamented the "public inclination to lump all newspapers, indeed all news media, under the tent of political 'liberalism.' " Helms sympathized. "To be sure," he said, "newspapers published in metropolitan areas are, with only rare exception, controlled by editors who goose-step automatically to the tune of socialist doctrine. The same is true of the major radio and television networks." But of course, he said, that did not include editors like Gene Price.

In that 1970 editorial, after his warning ten years earlier that the liberal press might be its own executioner, Helms laid out the same line he would elaborate in 1985 about the "elite major media." He has done it hundreds of times between those examples. It is a broadside that his listeners cheer, and one that even newsmen seldom challenge. Let us examine it:

When Helms uses surveys like the one that found most "elite" newspeople to support liberal political positions, he gets knowing nods from his audiences, but he adds nothing to the common knowledge. Journalism, like teaching, historically has been a low-paying business for most of its practitioners, but it offers a chance to be socially useful. People whose main drive is for financial success do not set out to become working journalists. So it is true now and always has been true that many of those who come into the news business are supportive of civil rights, civil liberties, and the poor—not communists or socialists, but dedicated believers in the American system, interested in their fellow man. But that does not automatically translate into liberally biased journalism. That fact is hard to understand—and inconvenient—for Helms, whose journalism and politics were intermixed throughout his broadcast career. He never made any apparent effort to separate them.

As for the editors of metropolitan papers "goose-stepping to the tune of socialist doctrine": In the 1984 election, 381 U.S. newspapers answering a survey by the trade magazine *Editor & Publisher* editorially supported Ronald Reagan, against sixty-two for Walter Mondale. The biggest newspaper in the country is the *Wall Street Journal,* the biggest magazine is *Reader's Digest.* Both are unapologetically conservative. In Sacramento, Phoenix, Salt Lake City, Omaha, Oklahoma City, Dallas, Houston, New Orleans, Chicago, Detroit, Indianapolis, Columbus, Nashville, Tampa, Columbia, Richmond,

Charleston, Manchester, indeed New York and Washington and dozens of other cities, one or more of the leading papers is uniformly conservative. Columnists like William Safire, James J. Kilpatrick, and George Will provide conspicuous conservative balance on the opposite-editorial pages of most of the papers that lean the other way.

On radio, the most widely broadcast opinionator is that rip-roaring rightist, Paul Harvey. On television, Pat Robertson, Jimmy Swaggart, Jerry Falwell, and their brethren reach more than thirty-three million households, ranking with the top-rated prime-time network shows that rile Helms so. A channel-switcher is likely to find one or a host of them on the air morning, afternoon, and evening.

Helms knows all this, yet persists. To the string of adjectives he affixes to the media he dislikes, he routinely adds "elite," for reasons that are not totally clear. Coming out of Monroe, he retains an instinctive feel for the populist anger of county seats and farmers against the cities, the universities, the new. He has expertly fanned that fire although he himself spent years as spokesman for the banks, the arch-enemy of the turn-of-century capital-P Populists. The very word "elite," of course, is ideal for the demagogue. It carries negative connotations for many of Helms's fans, implying wealth and snootiness, the opposite of populism. Sometimes Helms likes to leave his specific targets to his listeners' imagination by saying, "You know who they are," or "I'm talking about the people who think they're smart enough to do the thinking for the American people." But often he names the papers he is talking about—especially the *New York Times* and *Washington Post,* omitting for national audiences his original arch-enemy, the *News & Observer.* Based on that pair, what he means by "elite" may be "influential." The *Times* and *Post* are big but not the biggest papers in the country, although their influence is extended by their news services, subscribed to by many other papers. But it unquestionably is true that these are "elite" media if by that Helms means those reaching the decision-makers, the economic and political leaders of America. He is entitled to resent that, but both papers have won their status in the open market, in competition with conservative rivals. They have done it more by the strength and comprehensiveness of their news coverage than by liberalism on their editorial pages.

Increasingly, as he turned toward national themes and personal political ambitions, Helms's pique reached beyond Raleigh and beyond the newspapers to the television networks. Along with many non-ideologues, he was upset by the networks' coverage of the 1968 Democratic convention in Chicago. He decried "the unbridled eagerness of television commentators to use the event as a vehicle for their self-righteous condemnation of police officers and others charged with the responsibility of keeping order . . ." He cited an unnamed CBS reporter (Dan Rather) who tangled with security officers when he failed to clear an aisle, and then joined "a pious tirade about 'brutality.' " This, Helms asserted, "is not news reporting. It is dangerous nonsense. Somewhere along the line reporters must learn— or be taught—that they are not privileged characters . . . The civil disorders throughout the country have too often been inflamed and exaggerated—and, say it like it is, distorted—by newsmen who have wantonly tossed aside their professional integrity."

When Spiro Agnew began the Nixon administration's anti-press vendetta, Helms cheered: "At last, there has emerged an outspoken leader who identifies with millions of Americans who have long been fed up with the daily diet of left-wing propaganda flowing under the disguise of 'news' . . ." Then when Walter Cronkite objected to the administration's offensive, Helms called him a "hysterical crybaby." For years, he charged, Cronkite had taken part in "a vast ultra-liberal mechanism tirelessly dedicated to brainwashing the American public." The networks, he advised, should "review the vicious subtlety of the major news media's attacks upon the South, the exaggeration of racial matters, the inflaming of hostilities, the encouragement given militants, the agitation, the false portrayal of all those with whom the major news media disagreed." For years, Helms asserted, the "free press" had "been asking for public distrust. Now they're getting it."

In focusing on television, Helms and other complainants got immense public feedback. TV is an omnipresence in the life of Americans; when its newsmen are imperious, their bad manners intrude into everybody's living rooms. (Many in the writing press resent their occasional bad manners, too, and resent the way critics and laymen so often lump all newsmen together indiscriminately as "the press" or "the media.") Helms, Agnew, and other politicians played on this public feeling to damage the credibility of the press that criticized them. Once in the Senate, Helms seemed eager to go beyond that.

Within a month of being sworn in, he endorsed White House proposals to act against "deliberate bias" in network news unless the broadcasters did it on their own. He said that in his twelve years as a TV executive, he "must have filed five hundred protests with the networks" in vain, especially about coverage of civil rights activism in the South. Predictably, the *News & Observer* responded with an editorial about Helms's own broadcasts. Suppose, it said, that the Johnson and Kennedy administrations had decided to move against biased stations during their time in office. Suppose they had objected to "the completely conservative—some even felt they were reactionary—editorials that Senator Helms read over WRAL for so many years . . . Helms should remember that when a liberal loses his freedom, all conservatives lose a part of their freedom," and vice versa.

Helms did not blink. Anti-press tirades were his stock in trade, red meat to be thrown to hungry audiences on the growing right-wing convention circuit. When he and Tom Ellis got into the direct-mail fund-raising business after his first election, they cultivated those many thousands who imagine that the newspapers, magazines, wire services, and networks are in an immense conspiracy to do in the nation, and that the only reliable news comes through certified right-wing sources. As they solicited for money, they and their colleagues whetted their donors' appetite for more inside information like that in the next fund-raising letter, the confidential newsletter obtainable by contributions to this or that cause, the revealed truth as laid out by broadcast preachers. And in this lucrative campaign by the New Right, the networks and their stars were productive "devil figures" ranking up near Ted Kennedy and Jesse Jackson.

Thus when Helms signed thousands of letters early in 1985 urging conservatives everywhere to pitch in and buy CBS stock, it first amused, then shook up Madison Avenue, Wall Street, and the corporate offices of the network. But Helms-watchers found it right in character for him. If necessary, he said, conservatives could vote their stock to take control of the network and elect a new board of directors "committed to ending liberal media bias." Helms said the group for which he spoke, Fairness in Media (FIM), was addressing almost a million conservatives in something "very much like a presidential campaign," to "end liberal bias at CBS."

Asserting that "the liberal news media are the voice of the liberal movement in America," he added, "CBS is the most liberal network." To prove that, he cited a study by *TV Guide* magazine. Helms reminded recipients that businesses, pension funds, and IRAs could buy into CBS—and his punch line, of course, was that Fairness in Media needed money to carry on its national buy-CBS campaign. Even if conservatives were unable to buy network stock, he said, surely they could send $15, or maybe $25, or $50, or $100, or $250, or even $500 to "help us urge thousands of conservatives to become CBS stockholders."

Helms himself was not the head of, or even an official part of, Fairness in Media. He was just the front man. The campaign was another brainchild of his political partner, Tom Ellis, who cast about immediately after the 1984 election for some new project to keep the Congressional Club and its sister organizations busy. Carter Wrenn, executive director of the Congressional Club, was co-founder, and its staff essentially was one man, James P. Cain, serving as lawyer and consultant. FIM was quartered in a room in the offices of Jefferson Marketing, the corporate arm of the Helms-Ellis network. And the same receptionist answered the phone for all three—Congressional Club, JMI, and FIM. As has been said of many of the New Right's vaunted clubs and foundations, FIM was little more than a glorified mailing list. But at first, the very nerve of it puzzled onlookers.

Many brushed it off as just another fund-raising and publicity venture, which it surely was. Even some of Helms's friends doubted its wisdom. William F. Buckley, Jr., wrote in *National Review* that it was a quixotic venture whose main effect would be to "make the existing 24,000 stockholders of CBS a little richer than they are now by building up the price of the stock." Even if FIM should succeed, there is not enough right-wing journalistic talent available to run CBS News, he said. "Jesse Helms should be told . . . that without Dan Rather (and others like him), CBS loses its lead in the industry. And if it loses its lead . . . before long all those shares his friends bought will not be worth anything because nobody will be viewing the new conservative broadcasts."

Another spokesman of the right, the Moral Majority's Cal Thomas, wrote that it was too bad Helms as a government official led this crusade, because "the specter of government entanglement with a free press is far worse than the frequent ideological liberties the press takes . . ." It would be better for conservatives to "test market" their idea for media involvement by buying a local TV station and newspaper and committing themselves to fair and balanced coverage. "Conservatives, who so often champion free enterprise when it comes to economics, ought to adopt an ideological free enterprise system when it comes to ideas," Thomas said.

CBS itself took the matter seriously. It treated it with dead-pan objectivity on its news programs. Then the network's chairman, Thomas H. Wyman, traveled down to Helms country, to Duke University, to respond at a communications colloquium. The public should support journalists against any group trying to subject their work to political influence, Wyman said. "Whatever the proclaimed goal of such groups may be, their actual agenda is usually . . . to manage the news according to standards other than those of journalism . . . The government is not comfortable with us, but it was not meant to be . . . The absolutely polite, respectful, and error-free press does exist—in countries where it is totally controlled."

While the newscasters and corporate officers were responding publicly with mere words, behind the scenes CBS was preparing a massive legal counterattack. CBS employees "are asking themselves . . . whether Helms is a character out of 'Seven Days in May' or a character out of 'Li'l' Abner'—a dangerous loony or a colorful loony," TV critic Tom Shales wrote in the *Washington Post*. The network's lawyers saw him as dangerous. When Helms's old friend Hoover Adams sued CBS for its list of stockholders in anticipation of their annual meeting, the network hit FIM with a countersuit asserting that it was merely a project of the Congressional Club, Jefferson Marketing, and the rest of the Helms-Ellis combine. "Although styled a proxy contest, FIM's efforts are in fact a vehicle to raise funds and publicize partisan political views and individual candidates," CBS charged.

It went beyond that. It brought up Tom Ellis's old connection with the Pioneer Fund, the research foundation focused on proving that blacks are genetically less intelligent than whites. And it noted that FIM's lawyer in the case, Harry F. Weyher of New York, had been president of the Pioneer Fund for at least twelve years. When Ellis explained to Senate questioners two years earlier that he had taken a place on Pioneer's board just as a favor to a friend, Weyher was that friend. A native North Carolinian, Weyher had become a partner in a Park Avenue law firm. Carter Wrenn told reporters Weyher was retained in the FIM case because he was Ellis's old acquaintance, a competent lawyer, and "even more importantly, understood what our concerns were philosophically." A *Washington Post* investigation discovered that in addition to giving hundreds of thousands of dollars in grants to genetic research each year, the Pioneer Fund had contributed ten thousand dollars in 1983 to the Coalition for Freedom, another offshoot of the Helms-Ellis conglomerate. The CBS move also recalled to public attention Ellis's 1955 role in fighting school desegregation in North Carolina ("The eventual goal of this movement is racial intermarriage and the disappearance of the Negro race by fusing into the white," his committee report asserted, and therefore state funds should be cut off to any locality where a school was integrated.)

CBS's blast was intended to discredit the people trying to organize the takeover, and to delay a court ruling on giving its stockholder list to FIM. But of course the First Amendment disallows any political test for involvement in the news business, and in that respect all the network's research on Ellis and his allies was moot. Eventually CBS gave FIM the stockholder list, on being promised it would not be used for any political or fund-raising purpose. Nevertheless, the CBS countersuit did stall FIM's effort long enough to prevent an effective proxy fight at the April 1985 stockholders' meeting. CBS's strong reaction had given Helms, Ellis, and their colleagues a kind of publicity they did not seek. The delay also gave analysts of the takeover campaign an opportunity to inspect the merits of FIM's allegations, and become acquainted with some of the players in the drama.

Helms's initial letter said a *TV Guide* study had shown CBS to be the "most liberal" network, and therefore the clear target for conservative takeover. After that, there was much talk about how "Jesse Helms wants to be Dan Rather's boss"—Rather, as anchorman, being the most visible symbol of the network's alleged sins. FIM solicited support in an ad that ran Rather's photo and name, and directly beneath them in bold type a quotation: "The lower people and the middle class and poor people are just going down the tubes while he's [President Reagan] living fat . . ." Obviously the ad was quoting Rather—but wait, in fine print below that it said, "—Interview on Dan Rather's CBS Evening News 10/26/82. An example of how Dan Rather cleverly uses selective interviews ('talking heads') to carry CBS negative attacks on President Reagan." The quote was not from Rather at all, but from some citizen interviewed by someone on the CBS Evening News during the mid-term elections twenty months earlier. This was Fairness in Media's version of fairness in media.

It turned out that the 1983 *TV Guide* study cited by Helms was an unscientific, one-man, one-week venture. At George Washington University, Michael J. Robinson, a scholar affiliated with the conservative American Enterprise Institute, ran a carefully organized study. He had four researchers cover hundreds of network evening news programs through 1983. Separately, he had six researchers (mostly Reagan voters) analyze more than eight hundred network reports on the presidential campaign. To each report, more than twenty different tests were applied to rate its bias or objectivity. The result, Robinson wrote, is that "Senator Helms is mostly wrong if he thinks taking over the CBS Evening News will give him control of the most liberal network news program. And he is definitely wrong if he believes that Dan Rather practices much liberal bias on the Evening News." Laying out a vast stack of data, he said that quantitatively and qualitatively, "the evidence is that in some important respects, CBS is slightly more 'conservative' than the other two network evening shows." He acknowledged, however, that anyone looking beyond the 365-day annual output of the Evening News and judging by the occasional specials from CBS's documentary division might conclude that it is the most liberally biased network. As for Rather, "whatever his personal feelings about policy or politics, on the air [he] rarely talks like a liberal. Actually, in the eighties, Rather more often sounds a tad right of center."

(Anyone who knows Rather needs no extensive study to be able to laugh at Helms's suggestions that Rather is a wild-eyed left-winger. I have shared foxholes and various other accommodations with him all over the world, and know his personal and political attitudes to be typical for a man who worked his way up from Houston after a poor Texas boyhood and a brief football career at Sam Houston State College.)

Another figure in the takeover attempt, Helms's old supporter Hoover Adams, had brought suit on FIM's behalf because he was owner of 111 shares of CBS stock, so had a legitimate claim on the stockholder list. After he, Helms, and Ellis became friends in the Willis Smith campaign headquarters in 1950, Adams had considered Smith's offer to work for him in Washington, but stayed in Carolina to start the first daily paper in Dunn, a small town south of Raleigh. Through the years, Adams and the *Dunn Daily Record* have been adamant backers of Helms and hard-line conservatism.

As the CBS case hit the headlines, the man and the paper got more widespread attention than ever before. Adams ran long stories about the suit, quoting himself copiously. Out-of-town reporters looked into back issues to assess the fairness and balance of the 8,700-circulation paper run by this vigorous critic of other media. They were not surprised to find that the *Dunn Daily Record* was heavily weighted with right-wing opinion, and that its political coverage shed kindly light on Adams's favorites. Roy Parker, Jr., editor of the *Fayetteville Times,* who has known Adams most of his lifetime, said, "He's made a career of being biased in favor of things he wants. He's got this wonderful attitude that 'everybody else is biased and I'm not.'" (Later in the year, Adams's paper led a campaign against cancellation of long-running religious classes in the Dunn public schools. The frightened family whose objections had halted the classes left town.)

Although CBS's stalling tactics put off a proxy showdown, the FIM campaign did have results. The controversy brought attention to the fact that CBS in all its parts was worth much more than its stock market valuation. Thus while it seemed unlikely that FIM could inspire conservatives to come up with the $1.5 billion originally thought necessary to buy control of the network, the campaign raised the chance that some Wall Street corporate raider might do just that. Ted Turner, the proprietor of the Cable News Network and Atlanta's TV superstation, mounted one major bid. In a deposition before CBS attorneys, Turner admitted that he had held extensive discussions with Helms and FIM about how they might cooperate in their efforts. The prices of shares shot up as speculative sharks surrounded the network. One rundown of CBS properties, which included five major-market TV and thirteen radio stations plus publishing and recording subsidiaries plus the network itself, estimated the fair market value at from $6.68 billion to $7.21 billion. To defend against the sharks attracted by such values, CBS management worked out a scheme for the corporation to buy back an important fraction of its own stock.

Although FIM's first offensive against the network had not succeeded, it kept up its war. It filed a complaint against Dan Rather, alleging that without naming FIM, he had commented unfairly on the takeover effort. The Federal Communications Commission threw out the complaint. FIM filed another, alleging that CBS promotion spots praising Rather's fairness were themselves unfair. As its direct-mail campaign to enlist private stock purchasers lost momentum,

FIM redirected its appeal toward potential corporate buyers. "We have been focusing on the liberal political bias, but have not been focusing on the anti-business, anti-free enterprise bias, so we're starting that campaign," James Cain said. That a $6- to $7-billion corporate colossus was habitually anti-business and anti-free enterprise was as laughable as the suggestion that Dan Rather was a liberal zealot. But the continuing barrage of suits, complaints, and direct-mail ideas kept FIM in the news, kept hacking at the network's credibility, and kept providing new angles from which the Helms-Ellis combine could appeal for funds.

Indeed, while the underlying premise of FIM's campaign may have been laughable, many directly involved were not laughing. They included CBS's top management and Helms himself.

Sitting in Helms's office as the year wound down, I realized I had touched a nerve when I asked him just what incident in the past had made him so angry at "the media." He went through a series of incidents beginning more than thirty-five years before, and then summed up: "I have no obsession about the media, and I'm not talking about all the media. But I do contend that it's demonstrable that many in the media have ceased to report the news. They want to make the news, they're going to cut the cloth to whatever pattern they decide is appropriate.

"Let me put it this way," he said. "I have never asked, nor do I want, any editor or TV or radio commentator to be a Chamber of Commerce for Jesse Helms or any conservative, including Ronald Reagan. All I want is for our point of view to be given respectful consideration, and I don't think that has happened, don't think it is happening. It has gotten a little better since the CBS project, though . . ."

Even if the FIM takeover campaign completely fizzled, Helms could and obviously did take pleasure in what it had done to CBS. The network's protective buyback of its own stock had cost it close to $1 billion, temporarily driving its profits down. And most satisfying to critics of the network's news policy, the campaign would put about 125 CBS News employees out of work—their positions eliminated in a cost-cutting drive to help finance the buyback.

These direct victims of Helms's anti-CBS offensive were not million-dollar performers, but working people—a few correspondents, but mostly writers, assistant producers, and other inside staffers unknown to the watching public. The big-name stars like Rather and

Mike Wallace, and the arbiters of corporate policy like Tom Wyman, rode out the unpleasantness untouched. If Helms's aim was indeed to become "Dan Rather's boss," it failed, and of course it was never realistic to start with. It is hard to imagine any circumstances under which Rather would work for Jesse Helms, whatever the salary. But if Helms's intention was to make trouble for CBS, he succeeded. If it was to raise the consciousness of all network newsmen to the idea that someone is watching and judging every word they say, he succeeded. If it was merely to provide a fund-raising gimmick for the Helms-Ellis political machine in the electoral off-season, he succeeded in that, too.

More broadly, Helms's vindictive anti-media crusade has served notice on the nation that he and the hard right have the nerve and now the means to take on any institution that they perceive as their enemy, be it large or small, public or private. Looking back at his personal record as hybrid journalist-politician makes clear what Americans could expect if he and his allies ever did gain control, and set the standards, of a major news organization.

Chapter 17

The Truth Next Time

The winter of 1984–85 was jubilee for the right. Jack Kemp told the Conservative Political Action Conference early in 1985 that America was in the midst of a new and fundamental political realignment like those presided over by Jefferson, Lincoln, and Franklin Roosevelt. It has many names, he said—the Reagan Populist Realignment, the Populist Conservative Movement, the Second American Revolution, the Conservative Opportunity Society. Whatever it is called, he told his bright-eyed listeners, they were part of it.

At the same time Democratic congressmen were attending an aptly named "retreat" in West Virginia, listening to Reagan's ex-media adviser, a cosmetics firm's psychologist, and Ted Kennedy tell them what was wrong with their party. Kennedy pointed them toward moderation. Other liberals said well, yes, maybe so—because they had no better suggestions. The Democrats were demoralized, confused, and leaderless.

Helms and his companions on the right laid new strategies to put through their familiar social agenda. They were more optimistic than before, with Bob Dole of Kansas as new Senate majority leader in place of Howard Baker of Tennessee. Dole said he would "set a different agenda." That meant to Helms and friends that in exchange for their cooperation on high-priority administration items, Dole would be more willing to schedule the emotional votes that Baker had tried to keep on the back burner as he expedited Reagan's economic program.

They lunched at the Capitol with Pat Robertson, the engaging TV host whose 700 Club out of Virginia Beach had encouraged him in his own political ambitions. There they talked about school prayer, and Helms renewed his plans to legitimize it again by pushing a bill to strip the Supreme Court of authority to rule on that subject, rather than going for a constitutional amendment that would require an apparently unattainable two-thirds of the Senate. In other sessions, they talked of moving again against abortion, of keeping the pressure on those "hot-button" issues that energized their followers. But early in the Ninety-ninth Congress, it was clear that much of the opportunity to exploit new territory would be in foreign affairs.

That fact heightened a dilemma Helms faced as the new Congress organized itself. Moderate Republican Charles H. Percy of Illinois had been defeated in the fall (after Helms's Congressional Club had helped tear him down, with contributions to his primary opponent). Percy's loss opened up the chairmanship of the Foreign Relations Committee. It was a spot the vocal right lusted after, the chair in which a senator could operate the stop-and-go signals for policy hearings, nominations, investigations. And at last the right's champion, Helms, had a chance at it. Few among them could imagine he would turn it down. He clearly wanted it, badly. But—in a rash moment during his close re-election campaign, Helms had told the folks down home that if they sent him back to Washington, they would not have to worry about the welfare of their tobacco, peanuts, and soybeans. He personally would see that their farm interests were well protected.

Helms pledged to keep his Agriculture Committee chairmanship, and after the election he was not allowed to forget it. Under Senate rules, he could chair only one committee. Despite heavy pressure from his ideological supporters, he honored his promise to stick with Agriculture. "If I can't keep my word, I don't belong here," he said to reporters. "If there's one job I'd like to have, it's Foreign Relations. There it was. All I had to do was bend a principle." Later, speaking to disappointed fans at a dinner of Howard Phillips's Conservative Caucus, he laid off some of the blame on the press. "The liberal news media have been salivating at the very possibility that I might be enticed into breaking a commitment that I clearly made," he said after Phillips complained that Senate Republicans did not do better for the New Right in choosing committee chairmen. Had he gone back on his promise, Helms said, he would have been painted "day after day, forevermore, as a man whose word is worthless."

That was probably true, but the situation was more complicated than that. The key chairmanships turned on the GOP senatorial leadership election, in which the strongest contenders were Bob Dole and Indiana's Richard Lugar. If Lugar had been elected majority leader, he would have been ineligible to chair a committee. In that case, many expected Helms to exercise his committee seniority to head Foreign Relations in order to block Maryland's liberal Charles McC. Mathias, Jr., who ranked just behind Lugar. The conservatives already had engineered a comparable maneuver in 1980 to prevent Mathias from taking over Judiciary. Some senators reportedly were reluctant to make Lugar party leader because they did not want to risk having either Helms or Mathias chairing Foreign Relations. When Dole was elected leader, Helms still had the option of picking Foreign Relations. That ran head-on into his promise to Tarheel voters, and as a result, Lugar got the post.

Almost flirtatiously, Helms told his admirers at the Conservative Caucus, "That commitment cost me, for the time being at least—and listen to me carefully: for the time being, at least—the chairmanship of Foreign Relations. But remember, I am still the ranking member . . ."

Helms dangled that prospect, or threat, before both friends and enemies as the Ninety-ninth Congress began. Although he was not committee chairman, he created more ruckus and got more publicity than Chairman Lugar did. He was in the middle of controversy as head of the Latin American subcommittee. Often he would take stage center by calling a witness back for further questioning in a separate session, after his colleagues were through. He found ways to use his Agriculture chairmanship to veer off into foreign affairs. Repeatedly, he exercised—many said he abused—his personal senatorial prerogative to put a "hold" on one or a platoon of administration diplomatic appointees until he got his way on an issue or some other appointment. Ignoring other senators' annoyance and effectively thumbing his nose at Ronald Reagan, he continued to go his own way, with his own personal foreign policy.

Late one afternoon in the summer of 1985, Helms picked up his pencil and threw it down on the long, high desk behind which he sat as he questioned an ambassador. As they talked back and forth, he threw it down again and again. Each time, the sound cracked through the microphone and around the committee hearing room as if he were slapping a ruler on the desk.

Calmly, stubbornly, the ambassador still refused to answer. "That's between me and the secretary of state," he said.

The senator's face reddened. His narrow mouth turned down deeper at the corners. He made a steeple of his fingertips and peered over them. He leaned his head back and pulled impatiently at his wattles as he stared at the ceiling. Then he glared at the ambassador.

"I belong to that hardy band of citizens who believe things should not be classified unless they involve the security of the United States," he said in a warning tone.

Just when it seemed civility would be abandoned, the ambassador relaxed the tension by saying he meant nothing personal, but that his diplomatic communications with the secretary of state were supposed to be non-public. He wouldn't mind at all telling the senator if an exception could be arranged. The hearing trailed off after that.

That was not the first time Helms had confronted Thomas R. Pickering, a career diplomat then on his way to his fourth ambassadorial post. Earlier, he had held up Pickering's confirmation as envoy to El Salvador. He had used his leverage as subcommittee chairman to try to drag in George Shultz, the secretary of state himself, to be interrogated on Latin American policy. In effect, he had held the Pickering nomination hostage for a Shultz appearance. Meanwhile, the United States had done without an ambassador in one of the most feverish crisis spots on the map.

Once Pickering got to El Salvador, Roberto D'Aubuisson's right-wing party there asserted that the ambassador was interfering in elections in favor of the centrist candidate, José Napoleon Duarte. Some of D'Aubuisson's associates, in fact, were implicated in an apparent plot to get Pickering out of the way by assassinating him. Helms demanded Pickering's recall. Eventually, with the Reagan administration's backing, Duarte did win the election, and that further angered Helms.

Now that Pickering had left El Salvador, Helms took another opportunity to slice at him as the veteran troubleshooter headed to be ambassador in another crisis spot—Israel—at another critical moment. In two consecutive hearings, most of the senator's opening questions were indeed about Israel. He even went through the motions of being in good humor. He told a favorite story about how "in my home town of Monroe, we had an old gentleman ninety-some-odd years old, who had fought in the Civil War, and he was always working on a book. He said it would be 'an objective assessment of the War Between the States from the southern viewpoint.' " That's the kind of objective responses he himself was expecting, Helms said. Some of those listening chuckled dutifully. Then, relentlessly, Helms turned the conversation back to Central America.

He led the ambassador into an exchange about the "death squads" that plague El Salvador. Repeatedly, Helms, the chairman of the subcommittee on Latin America, mispronounced even the simplest Spanish names, of men he had been hearing about for years. When he kept misplacing the accent on Avila, Pickering corrected him patiently for a while, and then gave up. "That's good enough," he said. "We know what you mean."

Only someone familiar with the Helms-Pickering confrontations of the past, familiar with the Helms role in creating D'Aubuisson as a power in Salvadoran politics, could appreciate that high tension underlay their dialogue. Helms asked whether Pickering had recommended that the right-wing candidate, often said to be linked to the Salvadoran "death squads," be denied a visa to the United States. That was when Pickering refused to answer, and Helms began his impatient whacking of his pencil on the desk, finally halted by Pickering's assurance that he meant nothing personal.

When Helms adjourned the hearing, it seemed an anticlimactic end to one more step in the ambassadorial confirmation process. But it was not ended at all. It was nothing personal, as Helms assured Pickering in return. Of course it was deeply personal, but it was not exceptional. At the same time, the senator had put a hold not just on Pickering but on twenty-seven other State Department nominations. He was objecting to what he considered a purge of hard-line officials from the foreign service. In holding up Pickering, Helms was preventing U.S. ambassadorial representation in Israel at the height of the crisis over the TWA hostages at the Beirut airport. Prisoners held by Israel were a critical factor in the negotiations. None of that dissuaded Helms.

Nor did he allow larger matters to override his personal pique that fall, when he prevented U.S. ambassadorial representation in China during Vice President George Bush's formal visit to Peking. Helms held up that ambassador, Winston Lord, ostensibly because he was unhappy with administration policy toward China's family planning program. Weeks after Lord had been endorsed by a 16 to 1 vote of the Foreign Relations Committee, Helms and four Senate friends wrote Reagan that they objected to China's "inhuman" one-child-per-family policy. As long as U.S. funds continued to go indirectly to the Chinese program, and as long as Lord supported that policy, it would be "inappropriate" for him to proceed to Peking, the letter said. Like the other contingent of Helms hostages, Lord was finally cleared—but only after Helms told the Senate that the president had personally assured him on the birth-control policy. Just before the Senate voted, Helms professed to be upset about the press coverage that belatedly brought the Lord impasse to wide attention. Defiantly, he said, "I have news for Mr. Lord and for the major news media: I am beyond your reach."

Helms thrived on the hubbub created by his one-man crusades. The image of him standing alone against the waves of communism and immorality endeared him to his fans, provided new grist for his fund-raising literature. So the Lord episode was barely past when he strode into another controversy—this time with many liberals, moderates, and conservatives all supporting him for defying the Reagan administration.

Just before Reagan went to meet Mikhail Gorbachev at Geneva in November, 1985, a Soviet seaman named Miroslav Medvid leaped off a ship in the Mississippi River and swam ashore, apparently seeking political asylum. After questioning by U.S. authorities he was sent back to his ship, but jumped overboard again as the boat neared the Soviet freighter. Finally the Border Patrol dragged him back yet again, provoking protests from all political directions. Helms was infuriated. As chairman of the Agriculture Committee, he issued a subpoena for the seaman, on the premise that the case could affect U.S.-Soviet grain trade. "It's clear to me that [Medvid's] life is in danger the second that ship hits the high seas," he said. He was not supported unanimously by his committee: one Republican said, "As far as I'm concerned, there is only one president at a time, and I'm picking Ronald Reagan over Jesse Helms." Taken aback by Helms's action, the White House delayed a decision on letting the ship sail. But finally a Reagan spokesman said, "The case is closed," and it was. The Soviet captain ignored the subpoena and departed with Medvid, leaving Helms, the right wing, and many others frustrated and angry.

Again, Helms had forced a choice—between his concepts of right and wrong, communism and freedom, even between himself and his president. He leaves no one indifferent. Americans were still talking about the showdown over Medvid the night Reagan flew home from the Geneva summit, the same night when Helms spoke to devoted fans at a Capitol Hill hotel.

"President Pat Robertson! Doesn't that have a nice ring?"

As Helms said it, he turned toward the ruddy, smiling television evangelist who sat farther down the head table. A ripple of laughter and applause ran through the audience.

They had gathered, ostensibly, to "roast" Jesse Helms. The idea seemed a natural, because he is so eminently roastable. But nobody was willing to turn up the heat high enough to roast or even singe the senator. All the jokes were lukewarm, except the ones pointed at absent villains. In sum they were glowing tributes rather than insults, and at the end Helms stood up and paid tribute in turn to all those who had praised him. The expression on his face throughout made clear that that was the kind of roast he liked.

The date of the Helms roast, to raise funds for a conservative youth political action committee, had long been fixed when the president decided to fly directly from Andrews Air Force Base by helicopter that night to give Congress a prime-time report on the summit meeting. The crowd at the Helms roast, four blocks from the Capitol, barely filled twenty widely spaced tables of ten $125 seats each. The president's speech, and Congress's late hours before the Thanksgiving holiday, made good excuses for most Republican legislators to stay away. The few who came ducked out early. Nor was there anyone notable from the White House.

Senator Bob Dole, majority leader, came to say his piece and then rush back to the Capitol. Education Secretary William Bennett was there till he too left to welcome Reagan. But beyond them there was only a hard core of the most faithful. At tables paid for by R.J. Reynolds, the Coors beer family, and other wealthy fans of Helms, there sat dozens of intense young people, junior officers of the New Right army. The organizers of the roast had tried to get some prominent liberal to take part as a novelty, but one after another had turned them down. No matter. It was better, purer, that way.

Pat Robertson, toying with the idea of running for president, came early and stayed late, knowing that if he took his political venture further, Helms's good will would be invaluable. Robertson's toe-dabbling might be merely that, merely a way to attract attention to raise more money through his 700 Club and Christian Broadcasting

Network. It could be a serious effort to use that most popular evange-
listic TV show to force the Christian right openly, formally onto the
Republican Party's 1988 ticket—although Robertson, son of a long-
time Virginia politician, should have been more realistic than that.
Or it could be a way overtly to expand his and the evangelists'
influence in the party, to put himself in position to exercise a veto
over the candidate or the platform next time.

Robertson is a remarkable combination of sophistication and su-
perstition, a broadcaster who speaks with seeming authority about
world affairs one minute and the next is closing his eyes and describing his God-given vision of some woman in Kansas miraculously
rising from her death bed, some elderly communicant in Georgia
suddenly solving his debt crisis. In politics, Robertson was doing as
Helms had done for more than a dozen years, pushing the same
issues, feeling for opportunities. By 1988, that could make them rivals
as easily as partners. It occurred to some that Helms, in his take-no-
prisoners style, may have opened the path toward high office for
someone like Robertson to carry on beyond him—charming his way
to heights the slugging Helms could never reach.

Thus both men seemed wary in their graciousness toward each
other. Robertson "roasted" Helms by describing him as "dedicated
Christian, loyal American, devoted father and husband, fearless
fighter, man of honor and integrity, true public servant in the very
best sense of the word." Helms, at the end, spoke of "President Pat
Robertson . . . a fellow who really knows what America is all about,"
who "has a unique ability to communicate, whether it be about
Central America or the economy or morals or spiritual concerns. I'm
amazed at the breadth of this man's knowledge and understanding.
I like Pat Robertson."

It was not precisely an endorsement of Robertson's feeler for the
presidential nomination. There are many competing cults of personality swinging emotion and potentially votes out there in TV land,
not only Robertson but Roberts, Robison, Falwell, Swaggart, Bakker, dozens more. Helms was staying on good terms with all of them
by being praiseful but noncommittal about Robertson. He was not
nearly ready to bow gracefully off stage and pass on to a younger man
his role as the political embodiment of the Christian right.

One by one, the roasters took their turns warming Helms. It became
a modified "This is Your Life" show, not reaching back in time but

touching all the facets of his present and future—his ties with evangelical politics, his love-hate relationship with the Reagan administration and the Republican majority in the Senate, his central role in the New Right, his determination to dominate the political process in his home state, his unremitting war against the media.

Bob Dole, before he rushed back to the Senate, kept his tart tongue under close control. He said none of the many things he as party leader could have said about Helms's obstructionism, about the farm bill Helms was fighting against that very day. Dole too was ambitious. If his ambitions were to go any further in the Republican Party of the eighties, he would have to be gentle. He called Helms "the Rambo of the Geritol generation," and said, "I promised to campaign for him in '84 if he would promise to stay away from Kansas in '86."

That was as rough as the roast got.

Paul Weyrich, the busy New Right organizer, said he was just back from a trip into the future, wherein Helms had been elected president in 1993. President Helms had picked as vice president Phyllis Schlafly, the anti-women's rights entrepreneur; as secretary of state, Seaman Medvid, the would-be Soviet defector whom Helms had just tried to rescue; as disarmament director, Daniel Graham, chief lobbyist for the Reagan "Star Wars" strategic defense scheme; as interior secretary, Jim Watt, who eventually became too controversial for Reagan—and for the Helms Supreme Court, New York's subway vigilante, Bernhard Goetz. President Helms had held his first press conference at Right-to-Life headquarters, and annexed Taiwan as the fifty-first state. Tobacco stock prices had soared . . . But then Weyrich's dream was over, and the evening returned from heaven to earth.

Secretary of Education William Bennett, whose earlier promotion Helms had opposed till Bennett demonstrated his own spirited conservatism, was the sole ranking administration figure. Helms's problem with Bennett had been that he held two jobs with a suspicious word in their titles (as head of the National Humanities Center in North Carolina and the National Endowment for the Humanities in Washington: the objectionable word was not "national," but "humanities," which sounds like "humanism," which linked with secularism could equal "secular humanism," the hobgoblin of the Christian right). Not only that, but Bennett now headed a department that the GOP platform, inspired by Helms, had pledged to eliminate. But he had proven himself: he was strong for school prayer, private school tuition tax credits, and teaching the basics—and against busing. Helms said that "if Bill Bennett continues to make sense as he has been doing as secretary of education, we may never be able to abolish that department."

David Funderburk was the least familiar figure among the roasters. He had been a history professor in North Carolina when he produced an anti-communist tract for Helms's use in the 1978 campaign. When the Republicans won the White House, Helms got him an ambassadorship, to Romania. Now Funderburk had quit, with a blast at how George Shultz's (not Reagan's, but Shultz's) State Department was soft on human rights violations in Eastern Europe. Back home, he was considering a try for Congress when Helms's ailing colleague John East decided not to run again. Helms and Ellis ordered a poll and concluded they needed a newcomer, someone with no vulnerable political record, as a senatorial candidate. They tapped Funderburk, who like East in 1980 was almost a blank slate compared to his competition.

Veteran GOP Congressman James T. Broyhill, a traditional, business-oriented conservative, announced against him. That set up the most serious primary fight any major Congressional Club candidate had ever faced. Rich and powerful as it was, the Helms machine had won its reputation in general elections, drawing decisive numbers of crossover "Jessecrats" with its anti-liberal, racially tinged campaign tactics. Whether GOP primary voters would respond the same way to attacks on a man who had served their party faithfully since long before either Helms or Tom Ellis became Republicans was a different question.

When the forty-one-year-old Funderburk stood before the mostly young, bright-eyed zealots at the Helms roast, he seemed one of them. He was rather pale and bespectacled, of medium height, with his dark hair plastered over his right temple. He had studied his subject: he quoted Helms's old television stand-in, the Carolina character "Chub" Seawell, who had dubbed the future senator "Cousin Jesse Jeremiah Horatio-at-the-Bridge Helms." He maintained that in the last election, the Shultz State Department had tried to defeat Helms by objecting to the unorthodox endorsement of the senator by two dozen active ambassadors.

Neither Helms nor his fans were in a kindly mood toward the State Department that week. First there had been the Seaman Medvid affair, then the world's living rooms had been engulfed by pictures of Reagan—obviously under the influence of professional diplomats who were soft on communism—chatting and smiling with Gorbachev in Switzerland. Clearly, the Medvid fiasco and the Geneva pleasantries would not have happened if Helms and his man David Funderburk and their fans at the Helms roast were running things. Funderburk, the senator said, "is the kind of diplomat we need more of—but if George Shultz had his way, there would soon be none of."

But the most pointed line in their exchange was Funderburk's promise, "When I get to the Senate, Jesse will be the *liberal* senator from North Carolina."

But that was not to be. Although Funderburk and the Congressional Club tore at Broyhill's record and mounted another all-out effort to energize fundamentalist voters, Helms remained formally neutral in the 1986 primary. Party-line Republicans stuck with Broyhill, and nominated him by a 2 to 1 margin. That pitted the congressman (appointed senator after East committed suicide) against the Democrats' ex-Governor Terry Sanford in the fall. It also demonstrated, as had the 1982 congressional elections, that Helms's strength was most decisive when it was wholly committed; his familiar voice and combative stands could do what his club and its money could not always do.

At that November Helms roast, before the senator stood to acknowledge his admirers' tributes, the master of ceremonies read one more, a flowery cable from Reagan. "We can depend on you when it counts," it said, "—when we need you, when it's a matter of principle, when others may be reluctant to take the lead." With a hint of irony, it added, "I am grateful for all you have done to help my campaign and my administration . . ."

Even in the mood set by that polite, carefully phrased praise, Helms himself could not keep things entirely light and pleasant. His audience would have been disappointed if he had; it would have been out of character. He slipped in digs at Dan Rather, Pat Moynihan, and Ted Kennedy. But it was not his humor that wowed his listeners. They liked to see him scowl. He complained about the farm bill, which again was moving beyond his control as Agriculture chairman. He said unhappily that "the very same senators who have gone home time and again, delivering their rhetoric about how we must have a balanced budget," were "voting every time to increase spending and thereby make a terrible farm bill worse." He could not mention Dole, "a delightful man," without adding, "He's a pretty good guy, but if you agree he ought to forget about that genocide treaty, would you just say so?" They did, with a brisk surge of applause. (Months earlier, the Foreign Relations Committee had approved the long-pending treaty that would submit allegations of genocide to the World Court. Conservatives opposed it because they suspected it would ignore U.S. sovereignty and become a propaganda vehicle for anti-American Third World countries.) Dole "may as well forget it," Helms warned, "because if he doesn't, he's got a filibuster on his hands." They clapped again. Even in fun, he had not let them down.

There was something almost poignant about the way Helms waved goodbye to the sparse crowd of mostly unfamiliar faces, his own faithful, and then rushed out the door and up the escalator toward the Capitol to welcome his president back from Geneva. He was opposed in principle to civil relations with the Russians, and yet it was his duty and pleasure to be there, to be seen applauding Reagan for his extended communion with Gorbachev. However distasteful the substance of it, he cherished his place among the powerful, amid all the trappings of his office and seniority. Yet they were not the sources or even symbols of his own power.

Helms's strength was not there at the Capitol among his colleagues, among the other chairmen, the cabinet, and the diplomatic corps assembled in the House chamber to hear the president. It was not in his long, erratic relationship with Ronald Reagan. Instead, it was among America's outsiders, those socially and culturally aggrieved who believed that no one else stood up for them.

Although the most conservative president in their lifetimes had held office for five years, many of them felt betrayed by the way Reagan had dealt with the realities of the world. But while Reagan may have let them down, Helms had not. If he represented any part of the Bill of Rights above all others, it was that phrase of the First Amendment that guarantees the right "to petition the government for a redress of grievances." If he represented any figure in the folklore of America, it was the lone sheriff bringing law and order to a cowtown—or the tough police chief keeping blacks in their place in a county seat in the South. He wore the sobriquet of "Senator No," meant to be an insult, as if it were a badge of honor.

Helms has done what he urged upon the then-lonely right more than a decade ago, when he said it should reach out to "not only our trusty band of ideological conservatives, but non-political people who are grappling in their own communities with issues such as pornography, the right to life, school textbooks, community control of schools." "The most fertile ground for political action," he said then, "lies with the millions who are completely disgusted with both major parties." It lay out beyond the Capital Beltway, among the newly organized fundamentalists, who for generations stayed out of politics and watched in frustration as their country slid downhill into modern times. It lay with the millions who responded to simple red-white-and-blue, with-us-or-against-us patriotism, who could not abide the compromises that ease life between contending superpowers.

At the start, unbelievers had classed Helms as a kook, scoffed at him and his dream. But he understood, as they did not, the reach of that farspread resentment. They could not imagine the scale on which those millions of the uninvolved could be mobilized. For Helms and his allies had tapped more than mere undisciplined numbers. They had energized a hidden reserve of brains and fervor, inspired a cadre of educated, determined young people like those at the Helms roast—the ones who stayed behind when he left and watched Reagan on television, and hissed when the cameras panned past George Shultz, and when the president talked about further meetings with the men of the Kremlin. Helms had been the guiding spirit to formation of a long list of New Right organizations. Through them, such talented, long-frustrated young people had raised the money to find and register the resentful millions.

Helms's own complex of political action committees, institutes, and foundations was copied by other major reachers for the White House, liberal and conservative alike. He and canny men like Tom Ellis, Richard Viguerie, Paul Weyrich, and Jerry Falwell had become masters of media that outdated the TV networks and newspapers they maligned so methodically. While attacking the credibility of those by-now traditional forms, Helms streamlined another old medium, direct mail. It flooded the nation with his own revealed truths and at the same time raised immense sums of money for further propagandizing. These weapons have made Helms a force in

American politics that cuts across regions and party lines. But more than his machinery or his money, it is his personal refusal to compromise, his reputation as the one unshakable keeper of the true faith, that is Jesse Helms's strength. The way he has combined the primeval determination to be right and state-of-the-art fund-raising technology suggests an answer to whether Helms is true believer or cynic: Why not both?

He and his movement ascended with Ronald Reagan, then began to turn away from him as Reagan in office wandered away from Reagan the candidate. That split widened as the president neared the end of his term and the path to the right led on beyond his administration. Helms, those who prospered with him, and those who struggled against them all understand that 1988 will be a year of decision, when the nation will decide whether the rise of the right was the genuine political realignment Jack Kemp had cheered, or a passing phenomenon tied too close to the genial charisma of an aging movie star. It is increasingly clear that in competing to succeed Reagan, some of his erstwhile champions will be running against Reagan's works—against his vice president and heir presumptive, against his summit trips, his economic compromises, his failure to sacrifice all else for the sake of school prayer and an anti-abortion amendment. Helms will lead this offensive because he already is so far out front of the rest, beginning the day Reagan was sworn in. Already he has pointed the way his party moved, and determined by his veto power what it said in its quadrennial statement of principles. Now, with Reagan moving on, Helms will insist that after all the Second American Revolution must be a victory of principle and not mere personality.

Whether he himself stands up as candidate or plays Horatio to block the rise of someone inadequately faithful, Jesse Helms will fight over the way his party and his country move beyond the 1980s, and that will affect all our fates, into the next century.

Acknowledgments

This project has been made easier by the fact that everyone who knows anything at all about Jesse Helms feels strongly about him, and many who have known him through the years are eager to talk about him. Especially in North Carolina, it seems that thousands of people have been waiting eagerly for someone to come along and ask them about their senior senator. However, many of those whose feelings are strongest are not eager to have their names associated with what they think and say. That is particularly true in Washington, where his colleagues realize they will have to work with him for years to come, and Senate staff members know that as his seniority and influence grow, Helms's good or bad will could have decisive effect on their careers. Thus the persons whose help I acknowledge directly are no more than half those who have aided me since I began my research.

I am indebted to the newspapers of Helms's home state, particularly the *Raleigh News & Observer.* Growing up nearby, with many friends who are present and former journalists there, I have known all my life that North Carolina is probably the best newspaper state in America. Today's reporters and editors there continue that enterprising tradition. Many of them have shared their work and insights, for which I am especially grateful.

Professors and preachers in Carolina also have been generous with their time and experience. In fact, I see now that in putting together this first book about the Helms phenomenon, I have been the instrument for a community of journalists, academics, and clergymen who would be eager to do the job themselves if their situations were different.

My particular thanks go to Ferrel Guillory, associate editor of the *News & Observer,* for making available his personal files, giving me initial entree to his paper's records, and sharing his seasoned political judgment. That paper's editorial director, Claude Sitton; its managing editor, Bob Brooks; and Colline Roberts, Laney McDonald, and Betsy Marsh of its news library also were especially helpful.

H. G. Jones, professor of history and curator of the North Carolina Collection at the University of North Carolina in Chapel Hill, not only opened the way into that outstanding collection but made available his own deep background in Carolina history.

Among the many others who helped, some by putting me in touch with valuable sources, others with long interviews, a few by assembling important substantive research, were:

Hoover Adams, Claude Allen, Robert Anthony, Pou Bailey, James David Barber, Martha Bergmark, Thad Beyle, Merle Black, Alex Brock, John Carbaugh, Roland H. Carson, Jim Chaney, Scott Cohen, Richard R. Cole, Daniel T. Crisp, John Cyrus, Grady Davis, Judith Davison, Fred Eiland, Thomas F. Ellis, Daniel J. Evans, W. W. Finlator, Harry Fleming, Fred Fletcher, William C. Friday, Sam Fulwood III, Nick Galifianakis, Jesse Glasgow, Harry Gatton, Mary Gatton, Frank Griffin, Fred Hartmann, Margaret Hayes, Robert Greenstein, Barry Hager, Peter Hart, Paul Hoover, Ann Hubbard, Jay Jenkins, William Joslin, Chancy Kapp, Cyrus Baldwin King, John M. Lewis, Charles McC. Mathias, Jr., Wes McCune, A. L. May, Lamarr Mooneyham, Robert B. Morgan, the North Carolina Bankers Association, Don Oberdorfer, Herbert O'Keef, Gary Pearce, Delton Ponder, R. G. Puckett, Sam Ragan, Bari Schwartz, Murray Seeger, Gladys Segal, Marsha Simon, William D. Snider, Sharon Snyder, Robert Timberg, Malcolm Tolbert, Ruel W. Tyson, Jr., Paul Vandergrift, Wesley Wallace, and John Winters, Sr.

Sources

Chapters One and Two are based mostly on my own observations, and conversations with politicians who have known Helms. Reaction to Helms's use of the Grenfell family photo was described by Sherry Jacobson in the *Rochester Times-Union,* October 13, 1983. For comparing Helms with other politicians, I found useful Richard Rovere's *Senator Joe McCarthy* and Marshall Frady's *Wallace.*

Chapters Three, Four, Five, and Six, like many later chapters, draw heavily on Helms's own huge written record—specifically, the columns and editorials he did from 1953 through 1960 for the *Tarheel Banker,* and the Viewpoint editorials he broadcast for WRAL-TV from 1960 to 1972. The *Tarheel Banker* material is on file at the headquarters of the North Carolina Bankers Association in Raleigh, and the 2,761 Viewpoint editorials are in the North Carolina Collection at Chapel Hill. Most unattributed quotations in the early chapters are from these writings, or from the published articles listed with the Bibliography.

The sketch of Monroe in the twenties is based partly on the Monroe and Union County magazine section of the *Monroe Journal,* October 23, 1925. The description of the anti-evolution controversy of that period relies on "Professors, Fundamentalists and the Legislature," by Willard B. Gatewood, Jr., in *The North Carolina Experience.* George B. Tindall's "North Carolina, from Lubberland to Megastate" and H. G. Jones's *North Carolina Illustrated* also were useful for historical background.

Chapter Four was aided substantially by Helms's recollections about his early career in a "North Carolina People" television interview conducted by William C. Friday, the president of the University of North Carolina, on WUNC, the Chapel Hill public television station, April 9, 1984, and a "State Line" interview by Lew Gitlin for WUNC, September 21, 1984. There are numerous accounts of the 1950 Smith-Graham primary in the North Carolina Collection. One of the most recent summaries was by Jim Chaney, who covered the 1950 race, in the *News & Observer*'s comprehensive state anniversary edition, *400 Years,* published in July, 1984. Another detailed reconstruction of that race was by Chris Simmons in *The Phoenix,* August 20, 1984.

It is appropriate here to credit the remarkable succession of newspaper reporters who through the years have helped make North Carolina one of the most politically conscious states and Jesse Helms one of the most thoroughly tracked politicians in the country. For purposes of this book, they begin with men like Jim Chaney, Herb O'Keef, Jay Jenkins, C.A. McKnight, Bill Snider, and my late friend, Simmons Fentress. They include Ferrel Guillory, A.L. May, Bill Arthur, Jesse Poindexter, Daniel C. Hoover, Rob Christensen, Charles Babington, Richard Whittle, and no doubt others I have overlooked.

Chapter Five is based mainly on Helms's own writing at the North Carolina Bankers Association. Harry Gatton, who succeeded Helms as a senatorial staffer and later at the Bankers Association, was most helpful for the period of the forties and fifties.

The backbone of Chapter Six is Helms's WRAL-TV editorials. Calvin Trillin's *New Yorker* piece on the racial trouble in Monroe is reprinted in his *U.S. Journal*. Milton O. Gross located material in the files of the Federal Communications Commission (Report no. 5183, July 30, 1964, and Memorandum Opinion and Order adopted July 5, 1967). Thomas C. Parramore's "Sit-Ins and Civil Rights," in *The North Carolina Experience*, provided historical background to Helms's commentaries. Helms's suggestion that Nixon's Kansas State speech helped persuade him to switch parties came in an interview with Jack Bass on March 8, 1974, on file with the Southern Oral History Project, in the Southern Historical Collection at Chapel Hill.

For Chapter Seven, my conversation with Tom Ellis was particularly helpful. Here and throughout, especially for Helms's later political career, Bill Snider's book, *Helms and Hunt*, proved invaluable.

From the moment of Helms's arrival in the Senate, his public doings have been tracked in detail not only by the press, but by his political rivals. The North Carolina Democratic Party's research director, Ann Hubbard, presided over a major collection of Helms material at party headquarters in Raleigh. The research office of the AFL-CIO's Committee on Political Education in Washington maintains an extensive Helms file. Wes McCune of Group Research, Inc., in Washington, has unique records on the senator's many associations on the extreme right, and material published by Helms and his staff in right-wing periodicals. *Congressional Quarterly*'s weekly service has methodically recorded Helms's votes, bills, and amendments. His floor speeches and maneuvers are set down verbatim in the *Congressional Record*. And once he was elected, Helms became a magnet for attention from the national press, particularly the *Washington Post* and the *New York Times*. Articles of unusual interest are listed in the Bibliography. All of these sources, and particularly the *News & Observer*'s files, backstopped my reporting from Chapter Eight through Seventeen.

My colleague Robert Timberg not only did excellent investigative work on the Helms political-financial machine, but shared with me his research on the subject. Fred Eiland and his associates at the Federal Election Commission were helpful as always in tracking election spending.

Bibliography

Barone, Michael, and Grant Ujifusa. *The Almanac of American Politics 1986.* National Journal, 1985.

Barrett, Laurence I. *Gambling With History: Reagan in the White House.* Doubleday, 1983.

Bass, Jack, and Walter DeVries. *The Transformation of Southern Politics.* Basic Books, 1976.

Butler, Lindley, and Alan D. Watson, eds. *The North Carolina Experience: An Interpretive and Documentary History.* University of North Carolina Press, 1984.

Cannon, Lou. *Reagan.* Putnam, 1982.

Cash, W.J. *The Mind of the South.* Alfred A. Knopf, 1941.

Clabaugh, Gary K. *Thunder on the Right: The Protestant Fundamentalists.* Nelson-Hall, 1974.

Cook, Fred J. *The Nightmare Decade: The Life and Times of Senator Joe McCarthy.* Random House, 1971.

Crawford, Alan. *Thunder on the Right: The 'New Right' and the Politics of Resentment.* Pantheon, 1980.

Drew, Elizabeth. *Politics and Money.* Macmillan, 1983.

Daniels, Jonathan. *Tar Heels: A Portrait of North Carolina.* Dodd, Mead, 1941.

———. *A Southerner Discovers the South.* Macmillan, 1938.

Falwell, Jerry, ed. *The Fundamentalist Phenomenon,* Doubleday, 1981.

Forster, Arnold, and Benjamin R. Epstein. *Danger on the Right: The Attitudes, Personnel and Influence of the Radical Right and Extreme Conservatives.* Random House, 1964.

Frady, Marshall. *Southerners: A Journalist's Odyssey.* New American Library, 1980.

———. *Wallace.* World, 1968.

Greenhaw, Wayne. *Elephants in the Cottonfields.* Macmillan, 1982.

Gunther, John. *Inside USA.* Harper & Row, 1946.

Helms, Jesse. *When Free Men Shall Stand.* Zondervan, 1976.

Hudson, Winthrop S. *Religion in America.* Scribner's, 1973.

Johnson, Gerald W. *The Lunatic Fringe.* Lippincott, 1957.

Jones, H. G. *North Carolina Illustrated 1524–1984.* University of North Carolina Press, 1984.

Katz, Harvey. *Give! Who Gets Your Charity Dollar?* Anchor Press/Doubleday, 1974.

Kempton, Murray. *America Comes of Middle Age.* Little, Brown, 1963.

Kennedy, Stetson. *Southern Exposure.* Doubleday, 1946.

Key, V. O., Jr. *Southern Politics in State and Nation.* Alfred A. Knopf, 1949.

Kilian, Michael and Arnold Sawislak. *Who Runs Washington?* St. Martin's, 1982.

Lipset, Seymour Martin and Earl Raab. *The Politics of Unreason: Right-wing Extremism in America, 1790–1970.* Harper & Row, 1970.

Lubell, Samuel. *The Future of American Politics.* 3d ed., rev. New York: Harper & Row, Colophon, 1965.

Manchester, William. *The Glory and the Dream: A Narrative History of America 1932–1972.* Little, Brown, 1974.

McEvoy, James III. *Radicals or Conservatives? The Contemporary American Right.* Rand McNally, 1971.

McGill, Ralph. *The South and the Southerner.* Little, Brown, 1964.

Muse, Benjamin. *Ten Years of Prelude: The Story of Integration Since the Supreme Court's 1954 Decision.* Viking, 1964.

———. *Virginia's Massive Resistance.* Indiana University, 1961.

Nordhoff, Grace, ed. *"A Lot of Human Beings Have Been Born Bums: 20 Years of the Sayings of Senator No."* N.C. Independent, 1984.

Phillips, Kevin P. *Post-Conservative America: People, Politics and Ideology in a Time of Crisis.* Random House, 1982.

Raines, Howell. *My Soul is Rested: Movement Days in the Deep South Remembered.* Putnam, 1977.

Rather, Dan. *The Camera Never Blinks.* Morrow, 1977.

Reichley, A. James. *Religion in American Public Life.* Brookings, 1985.

Reinhard, David W. *The Republican Right Since 1945.* University Press of Kentucky, 1983.

Robinson, Blackwell P., ed. *The North Carolina Guide.* University of North Carolina Press, 1955.

Rovere, Richard H. *Senator Joe McCarthy.* Harper & Row, 1959.

Rusher, William A. *The Rise of the Right.* Morrow, 1984.

Rustin, Bayard. *Down the Line.* Quadrangle, 1971.

Sale, Kirkpatrick. *Power Shift: The Rise of the Southern Rim and Its Challenge to the Eastern Establishment.* Random House, 1975.

Sherrill, Robert. *Gothic Politics in the Deep South.* Ballantine, 1969.

Sims, Patsy. *The Klan.* Stein and Day, 1978.

Snider, William D. *Helms and Hunt: The North Carolina Senate Race, 1984.* University of North Carolina Press, 1984.

Terkel, Studs. *American Dreams: Lost & Found.* Pantheon, 1980.

Tindall, George Brown, ed. *A Populist Reader.* Harper & Row, Torchbooks, 1966.

Trillin, Calvin. *U.S. Journal* Dutton, 1971.

Viguerie, Richard. *The New Right: We're Ready to Lead.* Viguerie Company, 1981.

Wagner, Susan. *Cigarette Country.* Praeger, 1971.

Watters, Pat. *The South and the Nation.* Random House, Vintage, 1969.

White, Theodore H. *The Making of the President 1972.* Athenaeum, 1973.

Williams, T. Harry. *Huey Long.* Knopf, 1969.

Williams, Robert F. *Negroes with Guns.* Third World Press, 1962.

Young, Perry Deane. *God's Bullies: Native Reflections on Preachers and Politics.* Holt, Rinehart, and Winston, 1982.

Articles

Andersen, Kurt, with Joseph N. Boyce, Joseph J. Kane, and John F. Stacks. "To the Right, March!" *Time,* 14 September 1981.

Anderson, Jack, and Les Whitten. "Sale Cancelled; Helms Assessed." *Washington Post,* 13 June 1977.

Arieff, Irwin, Nadine Cohodas, and Richard Whittle. "Special Report: The Helms Network." *Congressional Quarterly,* 6 March 1982.

Arthur, Bill. "Few Congressional Club Dollars Reach Candidates." *Charlotte Observer,* 10 April 1983.

―――. "Helms: Outspoken Symbol of the Right." *Charlotte Observer,* 12 February 1984.

Averill, John. "Helms Leads Conservative Bloc." *Los Angeles Times,* 8 June 1975.

Bender, Gerald J. "Secretary of State Helms." *New York Times,* 10 June 1981.

Bonafede, Dom. "Though He's Riding a Conservative Tide, Jesse Helms Remains the Lone Maverick." *National Journal,* 18 July 1981.

Brinkley, Joel. "Helms and Rightists: Long History of Friendship." *New York Times,* 1 August 1984.

Chaney, Jim. "Graham and Smith: A Sizzling Campaign for U.S. Senate Seat." *Raleigh News & Observer,* 400th Anniversary Edition, July 1985.

Christensen, Rob. "Helms Spawns Passions Among Supporters, Detractors" and "Helms' Career in Senate Series of Ideological Stands." *Raleigh News & Observer,* 23 September and 21 October 1984.

―――. "Helms Courting Latin Right 'To Keep Communism Out.'" *Raleigh News & Observer,* 25 April 1982.

Cohodas, Nadine. "The Junior Senator, John East." *Tar Heel* magazine, August 1981.

Conway, John. "What Makes N.C. Senator Jesse Helms Tick?" *Daily Tar Heel,* 15 February 1985.

Drew, Elizabeth. "A Reporter at Large: Jesse Helms." *The New Yorker,* 20 July 1981.

Dunn, J.A.C. Helms profile. *Chapel Hill Newspaper,* 25 September 1972.

Edsall, Thomas B. "Onward, GOP Christians, Marching to '88." *Washington Post,* 30 June 1985.

―――, and David A. Vise. "CBS Fight a Litmus Test for Conservatives." *Washington Post,* 31 March 1985.

Ellerin, Milton, and Alisa H. Kesten. "The New Right: An Emerging Force on the Political Scene." Report for The American Jewish Committee, 18 November 1980.

Evans, Stanton. "Sen. Jesse Helms: A New Kind of Politician." *Human Events,* 5 August 1978.

Furgurson, Ernest B. "Newcomers to South Likely To Be Republicans Who Vote." *Baltimore Sun,* 28 March 1981.

Goshko, John M. "Transition's Carbaugh Alarms State Dept." *Washington Post,* 23 November 1980.

Guillory, Ferrel. "National Attention Focuses on Helms-Ingram Senate Race." *Raleigh News & Observer,* 5 November 1978.

―――, "Hunt Season: Can Jim Bag Jesse?" *The New Republic,* 4 July 1983.

Gunter, Rick. "1950 Senate Race Revisited." *Asheville Citizen,* 11 September 1984.

Helms, Jesse. "A New Policy for Latin America." *Journal of Social and Political Affairs,* January 1976.

Hoffman, Peggy, and others. "A Peculiar People." Drama celebrating history of United Church, Raleigh, N.C.

Hoover, Daniel C. "Mastermind of the Right." *Raleigh News & Observer,* 25 November 1979.

———. "Helms Denies Role in 'Dirty' 1950 Race," *Raleigh News & Observer,* 9 August 1981.

Hunt, Albert R., and James M. Perry. "Man on the Right." *Wall Street Journal,* 16 July 1981.

Jacobs, Barry. "A Tar Heel Interview with Thomas Ellis." *Tar Heel* magazine, March 1980.

Jacobson, Sherry. "Grenfell Photo Used by Helms." *Rochester Times-Union,* 13 October 1983.

Kilpatrick, James J. "Bitter Cooley Seeks Revenge." *Washington Star,* 28 February 1967.

Kincaid, Cliff, and Richard F. LaMountain. "Interview: Senator Jesse Helms on America's Retreat from Communism." *New Guard,* Fall 1979.

Langston, Kenneth T. "Baptists and the New Right: A Theoretical and Political Examination of a Complex Relationship." Honors essay, political science department, University of North Carolina, 1984.

Lemann, Nicholas. "Trying to Turn a Collective Sentiment into a Government." *Washington Post,* 2 February 1981.

Lichter, S. Robert, and Stanley Rothman. "Media and Business Elites." *Public Opinion,* Oct./Nov. 1981.

Marty, Martin E. "Fundamentalist Politics: A Historian's View." *Liberty,* November/December 1982.

Massing, Michael. "CBS Under Siege." *The New Republic,* 6 May 1985.

May, A.L. "Black Voter Registration Could Be N.C. Key in '84." *Raleigh News & Observer,* 12 June 1983.

———. "Helms Action Shows Shift Toward Israel." *Raleigh News & Observer,* 20 October 1985.

Maynes, Charles William. "The Helms Syndrome: Feeding the American Public With Fear." *Denver Post,* 12 July 1981.

Maynor, Joe. "His Name was Papa and to Jesse Helms He Was Always Right." *Conservative Digest,* May 1981. Reprinted from *Charlotte* magazine, September /October 1980.

Pachino, Marcie, Ruth Ziegler, and Campaign Finance Project, Institute for Southern Studies. "Jesse Helms: The Meaning of His Money," "Who's Playing Right Field," and "Researching the Contributors." *Southern Exposure,* February 1985.

Perry, Alfred Clinton. "Jesse Helms: The Man and his Club." Honors essay, Political Science Department, University of North Carolina, 1982.

Pinsky, Mark. "Senator Helms in Command." *Boston Globe,* 17 May 1980.

Poindexter, Jesse. "Helms Stands Rigidly Uncompromising." *Winston-Salem Journal,* 28 October 1984.

Pyes, Craig. "Salvadoran Rightists: The Deadly Patriots." Reprint of a 1983 series, *Albuquerque Journal*

Range, Peter Ross. "Thunder from the Right." *New York Times Magazine,* 8 February 1981.

Robinson, Michael J. "Jesse Helms, Take Stock . . . ." *Washington Journalism Review.* April 1985.

Saracino, Bill. "Jesse Helms: Embattled Pro-Gunner vs. Big Name, Leftist Smear Artists." *Gun Owner* magazine, 3d quarter 1984.

Scism, Jack. "Nick Thrives on Campaigning." *Greensboro Daily News,* 5 October 1972.

Shaw, Robert D., Jr. "New Right Gave Candidates Little" and "Fund Raisers Take Big Bite of Funds Raised." *Miami Herald,* 29 and 30 March 1981.

Simmons, Chris. "Two Souths in Tension: Liberalism Meets the Antebellum Code." *The Phoenix,* 20 August 1984.

Spence, Susan, and Howard Troxler. "The Right and the Power." *Tar Heel* magazine, March 1982.

Swofford, Stan, and others. "Tobacco: A Golden Currency for N.C." Reprint of a series. *Greensboro News & Record,* 23–30 September 1984.

Taylor, Paul. "Helms Modernizes GOP Political Machine for the Electronic Age." *Washington Post,* 15 October 1982.

Thompson, Roy. "Smith vs. Graham Free-for-All a Tar Heel Legend." *Winston-Salem Journal,* 30 October 1983.

Timberg, Robert. "New Right Campaign Operation Bypasses Election Laws." *Baltimore Sun,* 17 October 1982.

———. "The New Right: A Political Crusade." *Baltimore Evening Sun,* 19–24 Jan. 1981.

Tindall, George Brown. "North Carolina, from Lubberland to New Megastate." *Raleigh News & Observer,* 400th Anniversary Edition, July 1985.

Tonelson, Alan. "Battling Modern Diplomacy." *Foreign Service Journal,* October 1981.

Valentine, Paul W. "The Fascist Specter Behind the World Anti-Red League." *Washington Post,* 28 May 1984.

Whiteley, Michael. "Helms Honed Beliefs on TV, City Council." *Raleigh Times,* 1 November 1984.

Whittle, Richard. "Aide Details Funding for Helms-Backed Foundations." First in a series of ground-breaking reports. *Raleigh News & Observer,* 22 September 1979.

Winston, Diane. "Christians Get Campaign Tips at Conference." *Raleigh News & Observer,* 20 October 1985.

Index

Abernathy, Ralph, 214–15, 242
abortion, 16, 110–11, 159–60, 243
Adams, Hoover, 49, 264, 266–67
  on Smith-Graham campaign, 51–55
Adelman, Kenneth, 204
Africa, 14, 202–3
  see also South Africa
Agnew, Spiro T., 88, 99, 252, 253, 261
alcohol, see drinking
Allen, Claude, 176, 180, 226, 232
Allen, James, 104–6
Amalgamated Clothing and Textile Workers
  Union, 149
ambassadorial appointments, 272–75
amendments to bills, 24, 104–6, 110–11, 121–22,
  160–61
American Coalition for Traditional Values
  (ACTV), 171, 249
American Enterprise Institute, 266
American Family Institute, 134, 198, 199
American history, fundamentalist interpretation
  of, 239, 245
American Opinion (magazine), 191
American Patriot Party, 173
Anderson, Carl, 198
Anderson, Jack, 15, 121
Anderson, Tom, 115–16
Andrews, Ike, 150–51
Argentina, 188–89, 196, 197
Arthur, Bill, 230
Aspen Institute for Humanistic Studies, 244
Atlanta Constitution (newspaper), 213

Bailey, Pou, 49, 250
  poker club of, 61
  on Smith-Graham campaign, 53–55
Baker, Bobby, 90
Baker, Howard, 159–60, 270
Baker, Lenox, 75, 85
Bakker, Jim, 235–36
Ball, Ed, 50
Baltimore Sun, 147
Baptist Church:
  beliefs of, 241
  politicization of, 248–51
  school prayer issue and, 241–42
  youth camp, 75–76
  see also Southern Baptist Convention
Baptist Joint Committee on Public Affairs, 250
Baptist State Convention, 34, 251
Beasley, Rowland, 37
Belk, Henderson, 250
Bender, Gerald J., 202–3
Bennett, William, 278–79

Bible, the:
  fundamentalists and, 245
  literal belief in, 237
  red, white and blue, 234–35
"Biblical Position Rating," 246
Biblical Recorder, 241
Biden, Joseph, 221–24
Bill of Rights, 189–90
birth control, China's policy on, 274–75
blacks, 14, 16
  personal relationships with, 33, 229–30
  registration of, 169
  rights of, 211
  vote of, 26, 224–25
  see also busing; civil rights movement;
    desegregation; racism; segregation; Voting
    Rights Act
"bloc vote," 87, 224–25
Board for International Broadcasting hearings,
  220–24
Bolivia, 204
Bond, Julian, 176
Booe, Bill, 97
Bowls, Hargrove, 102
Bradley, Bill, 177
Brazil, 188–89
Brinkley, Joel, 197
broadcasting career, Helms's, 44–45, 50, 255–59
  radio, 45–55
  TV, 69–91
  see also WRAL editorials
Brock, Alex, 168
Broughton, Melville, 47, 224–25
Broyhill, James T., 95, 279, 280
Buckley, William F., Jr., 263
Buckley, James, 101, 103–4, 115
Bumpers, Dale, 161
Bunche, Ralph, 238
Bush, George, 139
busing, 16, 64, 106
  Reagan's comments on, 185
"By Jesse Helms" (column), 60, 61
Byrd, Harry F., 216
Byrd, Harry F., Jr., 108

campaigning:
  "retail," 98
  see also specific campaigns under e.g.,
    senatorial election
Campbell College (later Campbell University), 75
Cannon, Lou, 118
capitalism, see free enterprise; property, right to
  own
Carbaugh, John, 193–95, 198, 200–201

Carson, R. H., on Smith-Graham campaign, 54–55
Carter, Jimmy, 203
  1978 senatorial campaign and, 128
  North Carolina and, 130, 143
  Rhodesia and, 194–95
CBS, campaign for control of, 14, 16, 252, 255, 262–69
  countersuit by CBS and, 264–65
  results of, 268–69
  Turner and, 267
Centre for a Free Society, 134, 198
  investigation of, 199
change, fighting, 69–70
Chapel Hill Newspaper, 98
charities, 74–76
Charlotte Observer, 109, 230
Chatham, Hugh, 85
Chile, 188–89, 197, 204
China, 274–75
Christensen, Rob, 156, 161
"Christian America," 28, 246–47
Christian Broadcasting Network, 276–77
Christianity:
  definition of, 238
  nationalism and, 236–37
Christian Voice, 246
churches:
  integration of, 227
  see also specific churches
church and state, separation of, 33–34, 171, 233–34
  civil rights movement and, 238, 242–43
  Graham on, 244–45
  Helms's position on, 238–39, 242–43
Citizen (magazine), 84, 216–17, 218
Citizens for the Preservation of Constitutional Government, 85, 221–22
Civil Rights Act (1964), 86, 212
civil rights movement, 26, 76
  communism and, 77–78, 210–14
  discrediting of, 212–13
  non-violence of, 214–15
  religion and, 238, 242–43
  Schuyler and, 211
  see also busing; desegregation; King, Martin Luther, Jr.; Voting Rights Act
Clancy, Paul, 109
Coalition for Freedom, 150, 265
Cobey, William W., Jr., 150, 226
Coble, Jacob, 46
Cole, Willard, 258
Columbia Broadcasting System, see CBS
Committee on Conservative Alternatives, 115
Commodity Credit Corporation (CCC), 155
communism, 16–17, 26
  civil rights movement and, 64, 77–78, 210–14
  the media and, 253–54
  at University of North Carolina, 78–79
compromise, 236
computers, New Right's use of, 124–25
Confederacy, romance of, 35, 40
Congressional Club, 115, 248
  accomplishments and goals of, 160
  anti-labor activities of, 148–49
  campaign tactics of, 150
  distribution of money raised by, 147
  fundamentalists and, 245–46
  1980 presidential campaign and, 144
  1982 congressional campaign and, 150–51
  reorganization of, 133
  see also North Carolina Congressional Club
congressional election (1982), 150–51
congressional election (1986), 279–80

Congressional Quarterly, 199, 200
Congressional Record, 215
Conservative Caucus, 28, 271
Conservative Political Action Conference, 111, 253
conservatism (conservative movement):
  of New Right, 124
  1976 presidential primary and, 118
  1980 presidential campaign and, 139–40
  opponents of, 24, 104–6, 110–11, 121–22, 160–61, 243–44
  politicization of, 111–12
  radicalism of, 29
  Reagan and, 281–83
  Republican Party and, 111
  unification of, 109–10
  see also right, the; and specific groups and movements
Constitutional system, Helms's attitude toward, 23–24
Cooley, Harold D., WRAL editorials and, 81–82
Council on National Policy, 222
Covington & Burling, 133
Crisp, Dan, 50, 51, 54–55
Criswell, A. C., 183
Crocker, Chester, 202
Cronkite, Walter, 261
Currin, Sam, 249–51
Curtis, Carl, 109
"cussing," 57

Daniels, Jonathan, 43, 47–48, 256
Daniels, Josephus, 43, 256, 257
Danielson, John, 62–63
D'Aubuisson, Roberto, 182, 195, 204, 273, 274
death squads in El Salvador, 181–82, 274
Debnam, W. E., 46
Delahoyde, William, 250
Democratic National Convention (1968), TV coverage of, 261
Democratic party:
  demoralization of, 270
  fund-raising literature of, 158–59, 166
  Ku Klux Klan on, 174
  1952 convention, 58–59
  in 1960s, 89
democratic process, 28, 189–90
democratic values, "basic American" values vs., 189–90
Denton, Jeremiah, 143–44
desegregation, 61–62, 210
  communism and, 64
  Kilpatrick and, 216
  private schools and, 94
détente, 100, 108, 114
"devil figures" of New Right, 145, 262
direct-mail campaigns, 13, 125
  compiling mailing lists for, 135
  content and style of letters, 144–45
  "devil figures" in, 145, 262
  distribution of funds raised by, 145–48
  Hunt's, 179
  investigations into, 144, 146–48
  organizations involved in, 135
  paranoia aroused by, 145
  potential of, 132
  psychology of donors, 145
  response to, 145
  targets of, 144
  techniques used in, 146–47
  voting record of opponents and, 104–6, 110–11, 160–61, 243–44
Dolan, Terry, 125, 143
Dole, Bob, 158, 270–72, 278
Draper, Wycliffe, 220

Drew, Elizabeth, 146–47
drinking, 22, 32, 43, 57
Dunlop, George, 183
Duarte, José Napoleon, 195, 204, 273
Dunn, J.A.C., 98
Dunn Daily Record, 22, 266–67

Eagleburger, Lawrence S., 202
Eagleton, Thomas, 23, 156–58
Earl, Charles, 227
East, James T., 162, 165
East, John P., 23, 119, 150, 156–58, 202, 205
  ideology of, 140–41
  1980 senatorial campaign and, 140–43
Eastern Europe, 205
economic policies, Wallace's vs. Helms's, 25–26
Eisenhower, Dwight D.:
  attack on the press by, 253
  McCarthy and, 203–4
elections, *see* congressional election; gubernatorial election; senatorial election
Ellis, Thomas F., 49, 132, 134–37, 180, 190, 219–24
  background of, 93
  Citizens for the Preservation of Constitutional Government and, 221–22
  conservative campaigns and, 94
  desegregation and, 221
  Fairness in Media and, 263
  1968 senatorial campaign and, 93
  1972 senatorial campaign and, 93
  1976 presidential primary and, 116, 118
  1978 senatorial campaign and, 140–41, 146–51
  Pioneer Fund and, 220, 264
  racial genetics and, 220–21
  on Smith-Graham campaign, 52–55
  South Africa trip of, 222
El Salvador, 181–82, 195, 204, 273–74
Enders, Thomas, 202
Equal Rights Amendment (ERA), 138
Ervin, Sam J., Jr., 33, 107, 232
Eutsler, Fred, 238
evangelical movement 1980 presidential campaign and, 138–39
  politicization of, 237
  TV evangelists, 124–25
  see also fundamentalism
evolution, theory of, 193
  North Carolina bill against teaching of, 33–34

Fairness in Media (FIM), 255
  CBS and, 16, 262–69
  Ellis and, 263
Falklands war, 196
Falwell, Jerry, 14, 28, 124, 167–68, 183, 247–49
family, the, 15–16
farm bill, 280–81
far right, leadership of, 103–4
Federal Communications Commission (FCC)
  encouragement of broadcast editorializing by, 73, 258
  fairness doctrine of, 80
  on complaints versus Helms, 80–82
Federal Elections Commission, 133, 148, 184
Fediay, Victor, 113, 198
Ferraro, Geraldine, 185
Finlator, W. W., 245
Finley, A. E., 84–85
First Baptist Church (Raleigh, N.C.), 227
Fletcher, A. J., 45, 48, 65–68, 70–72, 257
  Helms's decision to run for Senate and, 95–96
  personal characteristics of, 65–66, 71
Fletcher, Fred, 70–71
food stamp program, proposed cuts in, 110, 152–53

Ford, Gerald:
  moderation of, 111
  1976 election, 112–20
  Rockefeller and, 108–9
foreign policy:
  ambassadorial appointments and, 272–75
  domestic politics and, 203
  Helms's interference in, 188, 194–96
  Latin America and, 188–89
  1976 presidential campaign and, 119–20
  rational, 192–93
  Reagan's nominees for, 201–5
  Soviet Union and, 203
  see also specific topics
Foreign Policy (magazine), 206
foreign travel, financing of, 196
Founding Fathers, religion and, 239, 245
Frazier, Anne, 250
Freedom Riders, 76–77
free enterprise, 67–68
Friends of Life and Liberty, 246
Fuller, Clint, 191
Fulton, Catherine, 258
fundamentalism (fundamentalist movement):
  Baptist church and, 241, 248–51
  beliefs of, 237
  believers vs. nonbelievers in, 238, 239
  the Bible and, 245
  Congressional Club and, 245–46
  humanism and, 245
  interpretation of American history by, 239, 245
  politicization of, 237, 285
  rational thinking and, 238
  Shi'ite Moslems compared to, 245
  voter registration by, 169–71
  see also evangelical movement
Funderburk, David B., 186, 205, 279–80
fund-raising letters, 18–20
  CBS stock and, 262–63
  Falwell letter, 247
  KAL Flight 007 letter, 18–20
  see also direct-mail campaigns

Galifianakis, Nick, 100–3
gambling, 43
gasoline-tax filibuster, 163, 166, 178
Garn, Jake, 18
Gatton, Harry, 44
Gemma, Peter, 161
genocide treaty, 281
Goldwater, Barry, 24, 86–87, 103, 115, 122
Gomez, Luis Arce, 204
Gorbachev, Mikhail, 280
Goshko, John, 200
Graham, Billy, 57–59, 244–45
Graham, Frank Porter:
  alleged communist associations of, 49
  conservative resentment of, 47
  Jonathan Daniels on, 47–48
  Senate and, 48
  see also Smith-Graham campaign
Grant, Marse, 241–42, 258
Great Britain, Rhodesia negotiations and, 195
Greensboro, N.C., 173
Greensboro News and Record, 182
Grenfell family, campaign letter about, 18–19
Grove City College decision, 225
gubernatorial election (1960), 66–67
gubernatorial election (1980), "Biblical Position Rating" and, 246
gubernatorial primary (1964), black vote and, 224
Guillory, Ferrel, 158
guilt by association, 217–18

Haig, Alexander M., Jr., 201
Hardison Corporation, 133
hard work, philosophy of, 37-38
Harriman, Pamela, 179
Harris, Bob, 179-80
Hart, Peter, 178, 185
Harvey, Paul, 96, 260
Hatch, Orrin, 159-60
Hayes Barton Baptist Church, 227, 233-35
Heath, Lura, 35
Heath, Major, 35-36
Helms, Charles, 74-75
Helms, Dorothy, 44, 67, 155
Helms, Jesse:
    childhood of, 30, 32-35, 40
    mother of, 33
    physical appearance of, 13, 98-99
    popularity of, 205-6, 281-83
    speaking style of, 15
    see also specific topics
Helms, Jesse, Sr. (father), 30-32
    blacks' view of, 39
    Ray House on, 40
    the poor and, 39
Helms, Nancy, 89, 90
Helms and Hunt: The North Carolina Senate
    Race, 1984 (Snider), 90, 127
Helms family, history of, 30-31
history, fundamentalist view of, 239, 245
Hodges, Luther, Jr., 94, 126-28
Hoey, Clyde R., 58
Holshouser, Jim, 117, 119
homosexuals, 181, 185-86
Hoover, Daniel C., 148
Hoover, Herbert, 34
Hoover, J. Edgar, 215
Hoover, Paul, 63-64
Hormats, Robert, 202
House, Ray, 36-38, 40
House Un-American Activities Committee, 84
Hufstedler, Shirley, 244
Human Actions (von Mises), 46
Human Events (newspaper), 203
humanism, "secular," 193, 224, 244, 245
human rights, 204, 205
Humphrey, Hubert, 87
Hunt, Jim, 38
    attacks on Helms by, 179
    "Biblical Position Rating" score, 246
    Mondale and, 180, 184-85
    1980 gubernatorial election and, 143
    1984 senatorial election, 165-87
    shifting position of, 180

Ingram, John, 236
    1978 senatorial campaign and, 127-30
Institute of American Relations, 134, 197-200
Institute of Religion, 64-65, 238
Institute on Money and Inflation, 134, 198
Israel, 197, 274
integration, see desegregation

Jackson, Henry M., 114
Jackson, Jesse, 1984 senatorial campaign and,
    167-71, 176, 177, 187
Jackson, Miss., 216
Jackson Southern Crusade, 170
Jefferson Marketing, Inc. (JMI), 133, 248
    anti-labor activities of, 148-49
    investigation into, 184
    services provided by, 147-48
Jensen, Arthur, 220
Jews, 172, 247
John Birch Society, 84, 191

Johnson, James, 97
Johnson, Lyndon B., 87, 88, 90
Jones, J. Robert, 219
Jordan, B. Everett, 90-92, 95, 98
journalism, Helms's career in, 252, 255-59
    at Monroe Journal, 36-37
    radio, 45-55
    at Raleigh News & Observer, 42-43
    at Raleigh Times, 42, 44
    as sports writer, 36-37, 42, 43
    at Tarheel Banker, 60-62, 256, 257
    TV, 69-91
Journal of Social and Political Affairs, 188

Keefer, Patricia, 166
Kennedy, Edward, 13, 14, 24, 105
Kennedy, John F., 86, 214
Kennedy, Robert, 87, 212, 214
Key, V.O., Jr., 47
Kilpatrick, James Jackson, 74, 81-82, 166, 191,
    215-17, 260
King, Martin Luther, Jr., 78, 213-15, 242
    communism and, 213-14
    guilt by association and, 217-18
    John Kennedy and, 214
    letter about, 64-65
    see also Martin Luther King Day
Kiracofe, Clifford, Jr., 202
Kissinger, Henry, 107, 192
    criticism of, 112-13
    1980 presidential campaign and, 139
    Solzhenitsyn visit and, 113-14
Knott, Joseph T., III, 250
Koop, Everett, 156
Korean Air Lines (KAL) Flight 007, 17-20
Ku Klux Klan, 76, 84, 172-76, 182
    constitutional rights of, 218-19
    Reagan and, 175
    support of Helms by, 219
    voter registration drive of, 172-74

labor movement, 94, 110, 114, 128, 148-49
Laetrile, 121
LaHaye, Tim, 171
Lake, I. Beverly, 66-67, 94
Lake, I. Beverly, Jr., 140, 246
Landry, Tom, 17
Langston, Kenneth T., 237
Latin America, 26, 188-89, 195-96, 204
    See also specific countries and subjects
Laxalt, Paul, 116
Lee, Annie, 36
left, radical, University of North Carolina and, 78-79
legislative agenda:
    conservative issues, recording of votes on, 24,
        104-6, 110-11, 160-61, 243-44
    control of state department and, 191
    foreign policy and, 271-75
    North Carolina's interests and, 158, 271
Lennon, Alton, 60, 212
Lewis, Fulton, Jr., 27, 46, 79
Lewis, John M., 227
letter-writing campaigns:
    anti-Helms, 158-59, 161
    See also direct mail campaigns; fund-raising
        letters
liberalism:
    the media and, 253-69
    in postwar North Carolina, 46-47
    Watergate scandal and, 108
Lichter, Robert, 254
Livingstone College, 186, 231
Long, Huey, 129
Lord, Winston, 274-75

Lucier, James P., 191–95, 198, 200
Lugar, Richard, 271–72
"Lunatic Thesis of Human Equality, The"
(Kilpatrick), 216

McCarthy, Eugene, 87
McCarthy, Joseph R. (McCarthyism), 25–28, 101,
156, 203–4, 256
McCormack, Richard T., 205
McGill, Ralph, 213
McGovern, George, 99–100
Mangum, Erbie and Linda, 75
Manion, Christopher, 183, 195–96
Manion, Dean Clarence, 85, 110, 211
Martin, Jim, 187
Martin Luther King Day, 176–78, 226
Marty, Martin E., 245
Marvell, Andrew, 83
Marxism, *see* communism
Mathias, Charles McC., Jr., 272
Maupin, Armistead J., 85
Maupin, Taylor and Ellis, 93–94
Maynes, Charles William, 206
Meany, George, 114
media, the, 252–69
  Agnew and, 261
  belief in, Helms's, 65
  bias of, 70
  blaming of, 157–58, 271
  communism and, 253–54
  conservatism of, 259–60
  as "devil figure," 262
  "elite," 254, 259, 260
  exploitation of, 253
  freedom and, 254, 257, 259
  ideals of, 258
  Jews and, 172
  moral issues and, 254
  New Right's attitude toward, 13, 16
  Watergate and, 107–8
  see also broadcasting career; journalism; press,
  the; television
Medvid, Miroslav, 275–76
Memory, Jasper "Bull," 42
Metzenbaum, Howard, 156
Miller, Glenn, 172–76
Miller, Richard W., 144
Milliken, Roger, 102
Minow, Newton, 73, 258
Mises, Ludwig von, 46
Mondale, Walter, 180, 184–85
Monroe, N.C., 30–40, 76–78, 207–9
Monroe Journal, 36–37
Mooneyham, Lamarr, 167–71, 236
Moore, Dan K., 80
Moorer, Thomas H., 199
moral issues (morality):
  China's birth control policy, 274–75
  human rights, 204, 205
  "new," 88
  pornography, 15–16
  the press and, 254
  rating of politicians' views on, 246
  see also abortion; busing; church and state,
  separation of; communism; religion; values
Moral Majority, 168–71, 236, 245
Morgan, Robert, 140–43, 246
Motley, Constance Baker, 213
Moynihan, Daniel Patrick, 161
Murray, Madalyn (O'Hair), 240
Muzorewa, Abel, 194

National Association for the Advancement of
Colored People (NAACP), 76, 212

National Association for the Advancement of
White People (NAAWP), 175
National Conservative Political Action
Committee (NCPAC), 28
National Council of Churches, 88, 243
nationalism, Christianity and, 236–37
National Religious Broadcasters, 13–18
Nationalist Republican Alliance (ARENA), 182,
195
National Review, 263
National Right to Life Committee, 166
National Voter Registration Manual, 171
National Youth Administration, (NYA), 42
"Nation Needs to Know of Red Involvement in
Race Agitation" (Helms), 84
Navy, U.S., 44
"New Policy for Latin America, A" (Helms),
188–89
New Right:
  abortion and, 243
  conservatism of, 124
  development of, 111–12
  "devil figures" of, 145
  members of, 123–24
  1978 senatorial campaign and, 131
  1980 senatorial campaign and, 143
  North Carolina's interests and, 158
  Old Right vs., 122
  political potential of, 285
  populism of, 206
  as radical movement, 29
  traditional Republicans and, 123
New Right, The: We're Ready to Lead (Viguerie),
123
New Yorker, The, 146–47
New York Times, 260
Nixon, Richard M. (Nixon administration), 86–88
  congressional campaign of, 56
  foreign policy of, 100, 108
  Kansas State University speech, 89
  1972 senatorial campaign and, 99–100
  Willis Smith and, 56
  Supreme Court nominees of, 92
  Watergate and, 106–8
Nofziger, Lyn, 117
nominations, blocking of, 63, 201–5, 272–75
North Carolina:
  anti-Darwinism in, in 1920s, 33–34
  interests of, 153–58, 271
  liberalism in, 46–47, 258
  New Right and, 158
  1982 tax bill and, 162
  politics of, in 1920s, 33–34
  tobacco industry in, 154–55
  voter registration drive in, 168–69
North Carolina, University of:
  academic freedom at, 82–83
  communism at, 78–79
  conservative resentment of, 47, 78–79
  liberalism of, 47–48
  literary magazine controversy at, 82–83
  radical left and, 78–79
  reaction to Helms's editorials at, 78
  speaker ban at, 78–79
North Carolina Advisory Commission on
Education, 221
North Carolina Bankers Association, 60
North Carolina Cerebral Palsy Hospital, 75
North Carolina Congressional Club, 125
  funds raised for 1978 campaign by, 127
  see also Congressional Club
North Carolina Fund for Individual Rights
(NCFIR), 149
North Carolina State University, 81–82

obstruction tactics:
  amendments to bills, 24, 104–6, 110–11, 121–22, 160–61, 243–44
  filibusters, 163, 166, 178
  nominations, blocking of, 63, 201–5, 272–75
O'Dell, Jack, 213

PACs (political action committees), 145–46
Panama Canal treaties, 194, 196
Paraguay, 188–89
paranoia, direct-mail campaigns and, 145
Park, John A., 44
Parker, Roy, Jr., 267
Parramore, Thomas C., 79
paternalism, 227–29
Paull, Michael, 83
Pearson, Roger, 188
Pepper, Claude, 50
Percy, Charles H., 201, 271
personal attacks, 49–55, 100–102, 109, 157
Peterson, Bill, 162
Phillips, Howard, 124, 271
Pickering, Thomas R., 272–74
Pioneer Fund, 220
  Ellis and, 264
  Washington Post investigation of, 264–65
political action committees, *see* PACs
political ideology, formation of, 46
political issues
  as religious issues, 244
  see also specific issues
political organizations, Helms's, 133–34
  see also specific organizations
political style, Helms's:
  aggressiveness, 105, 156
  consistency, 69–70, 237–40
  guilt by association, 217–18
  "hardball" tactics, 161
  media, blaming of problems on, 157–58, 271
  network of allies and, 26
  personal attacks, 49–55, 100–102, 109
  public vs. private aid, 153
  Senate rules, abuse of, 23–24, 104, 271–72
  speaking style, 15, 71
  uncompromising, 236
  "wholesale" campaigning, 98
  see also direct mail campaigns; obstructionist tactics
politico-religious alliance, 28
Ponder, Delton, 152–53
poor, the:
  aid for, 106, 225
  Helms Sr. and, 39
  see also food stamp program
Poor People's March (1968), 215
popularity, 162, 166, 205–6, 281–83
populism, New Right and, 206
pornography, 15–16
prayer in public schools, 16, 22, 110, 216–17, 270–71
  Baptist Church and, 241–42
  Reagan and, 242
  Supreme Court decision on, 239–40
preaching, 236–37
pre-political vs. rational politics, 191–92
presidential candidacy:
  Helms and, 22, 115–16
  Robertson and, 276–77
presidential election (1968), 87–88
presidential election (1980), 135–40
  Bush and, 139
  "Christian nation" issue and, 246–47
  Congressional Club and, 144

conservatives and, 139–40
evangelical movement and, 138–39
Kissinger and, 139
Republican platform, 138
vice presidency and, 136–40
presidential primary (1976):
  Ford's victories in, 117
  Reagan's North Carolina victory in, 118
press, the:
  blaming of problems on, 271
  conservative viewpoint in, 257
  freedom of, 28, 189
  TV vs. writing, 261
  see also journalism; media, the
Preyer, Richardson, 224
Price, Gene, 258
privacy, right of, 63, 243
private schools, 236
  funding of, 94, 239
Privette, Rev. Coy, 248, 250, 251
property, right to own, 189–90
PTL Network, 130, 235–36
public good, spending on, 63
public image, 13, 41
public opinion polls, 166, 178
public policy, private gestures vs., 153
Puckett, R. G., 248

quality of life, spending on, 63

race, question of:
  genetics and, 220–21
  Helms's views on, 226–32
  in Ellis's senate hearings, 219–24
  in Helms's political constituency, 26
  Smith-Graham campaign and, 49–55
  Tarheel Banker editorials and, 61–62, 210
racism, 207–9, 217–18
  see also Ku Klux Klan; segregation
radical left, 78–79
radio, 44
  See also WRAL editorials
Raleigh City Council, 63
Raleigh News & Observer, 22, 42–44, 52, 54, 62, 65, 73, 82, 83, 128, 148, 157, 166, 200, 257
  politics of, 43, 256
  racial policy of, 209
  Tarheel Banker editorials and, 62
Raleigh Times, 44, 45, 73–74
Rashish, Myer, 204
Rather, Dan, 14, 16, 263, 265–69
rational vs. pre-political politics, 191–92
Reader's Digest, 259
Reagan, Ronald (Reagan administration), 15, 115, 117–18
  affinity of Helms and, 117
  conservatives' disappointment with, 281–83
  foreign policy nominees of, 201–5
  Ku Klux Klan and, 175
  letter supporting 1978 campaign, 126
  1984 senatorial campaign and, 187
  political survival of, 28
  school prayer issue and, 242
  Soviet seaman incident and, 275–76
Reds in America (Whitney), 211
Rehnquist, William, 199
religion, 233–51
  civil rights movement and, 238
  Founding Fathers and, 239, 245
  see also specific subjects
religious experiences, 235–36
Republican National Convention (1976), 119–20
Republican National Convention (1980), 137–40

Republican National Convention (1984), 183
Republican party:
  conservatives and, 109–11, 114–15
  Ku Klux Klan on, 174
  New Right and, 123, 271
  in North Carolina, 34
  switch to, in South, 24, 87, 89–90
  after Watergate scandal, 109–10
Republican Steering Committee, 109
Reynolds, Robert Rice, 48
Rhodesia, 14, 194–95
Richmond, Fred, 156–58
Richmond News Leader, 74, 191, 215
right, the:
  backlash against, 248–51
  old, 122
  religious, 29
  see also conservatism; New Right; *and specific groups*
Robertson, Pat, 28, 124–25, 136, 270, 276–77
Robinson, Michael J., 266
Rockefeller, Nelson, 108
Roe v. *Wade,* 16
Romania, 205
Roosevelt, Eleanor, 42, 46
Rose, Charles, 184
Rostow, Eugene, 204
Rotary Club, 86
Rothman, Stanley, 254
Russell, Richard B., 25, 58–60, 209, 256
Rustin, Bayard, 213

Safire, William, 260
SALT II treaty, 199, 202
Sanford, Terry, 66–67, 69, 78, 97
Scales, Junius, 78
schools, *see* desegregation; prayer in public
  schools; private schools
Schuyler, George, 211
Schweiker, Richard, 119
Scopes trial, 34
Scott, Kerr, 46, 47
Scott, William, 109
Sears, John, 119, 135–36
Seawell, H. F. "Chub," Jr., 96–97, 175, 279
Seawell, Malcolm, 218
secular humanism, 193, 224, 244, 245
Segermark, Howard, 198
segregation, 38–39
  See also desegregation; racism
Selma, Alabama, march (1965), 214
Senate, U.S.:
  Agriculture Committee, 154–58, 271–72
  atmosphere of, 156
  cooperation with Helms in, 270
  discipline in, 24
  first-year achievements in, 105
  Foreign Relations Committee, 195–96, 271–72
  Helms's use of, for his own ends, 23–24
  rules of, 104, 272
  tactics used by Helms in, 110–11, 160–62
  unpopularity of Helms in, 162, 166
senatorial election (1950), 41
senatorial election (1972)
  advertising campaign in, 100–3
  competition in, 97
  decision to run in, 92–93, 95
  financing of, 95
  Fletcher's reaction to, 95–96
  Jordan and, 92, 95, 98
  Nixon and, 99–100
  primary, 97–98
  public reaction to, 97

religious experience and, 235–36
Seawell and, 96–97
Wallace and, 98
senatorial election (1978), 125–30
  direct mail campaign and, 127
  Carter and, 128
  Ingram and, 127–30
  Luther Hodges, Jr. and, 127–28
  money issue in, 128
  New Right and, 131
  organization of, 129
  Reagan's letter of support for Helms in, 126
  spending in, 130
  tobacco industry and, 128
senatorial election (1980), 140–43
senatorial election (1984):
  ambassadorial endorsements in, 186
  anti-Hunt ads in, 169
  debates during, 184
  El Salvador ad and, 181–82
  Falwell and, 247–48
  gasoline tax filibuster and, 178
  gimmicks used in, 182
  homosexual letter incident in, 185–86
  Jackson and, 176, 177, 187
  Martin Luther King Day and, 178
  race issue in, 230–31
  Reagan administration and, 187
  voter registration drives and, 168–69
Sensing, Thurman, 74
700 Club, 276, 720
Shales, Tom, 264
Shi'ite Moslems, 245
Shockley, William, 220–21
Shultz, George, 279–80
Silent Scream, The (film), 16
Simon, Paul, 23
Simpson, Alan, 163–64
sixties, the, 69
"Sixty Minutes," 180
Smathers, George, 50
Smith, Alfred E., 34
Smith, Ian, 194–95
Smith, Willis, 48–55, 209
  1950 primary and, 41
  Nixon and, 56
  as senator, 56–58
  see also Smith-Graham campaign
Smith-Graham campaign, 255–56
  Ball and, 50
  Crisp and, 50, 51, 54–55
  historical view of, 50
  race issue in, 49–55
  role of Helms in, 52–55
Snider, William D., 90
socialism, *see* communism
social programs, opposition to, 225
Solzhenitsyn, Alexander, 113–14
South, the:
  liberal intellectualism and, 47
  Republican party in, 24, 87–89
  romance of the Confederacy in, 35, 40
  Russell and, 58–59
  Voting Rights Act and, 116
South Africa, 14, 191, 202
  Ellis's trip to, 222
Southern Baptist Convention (SBC), 28, 241
Southern Employees Education Fund (SEEF), 149
Southern Politics in State and Nation (Key), 47
Southern States Industrial Council, 74
Soviet seaman incident, 275–76
Soviet Union, 204
  summit meeting with, 280

Soviet Union*(continued)*
  U.S. foreign policy and, 203
speaker ban at University of North Carolina, 78–79
speechwriting, Willis Smith's, 57
sports journalism, Helms's career in, 36–37, 42, 43
Stanley, Charles, 250
State, U.S. Department of, 26, 191, 200, 279–80
State championship story, 36
Stennis, John C., 226
Stevens, J. P., 148, 149
Stevenson, Adlai, 59
summit meeting (1985), 280
Supreme Court, U.S.:
  abortion and, 16
  Nixon's nominees to, 92
  school prayer and, 22

Taft, Robert A., 25
Talmadge, Gene, 25
Tarheel Banker, 60–62, 210, 256, 257
Tar Heels (Daniels), 47
Taxpayers' Educational Coalition, 150
teachers, influential, 35–36
technology, 45, 124–25
  see also direct mail campaigns; television
television:
  1968 Democratic National Convention coverage by, 261
  New Right's use of, 124–25
  news coverage by, 261–62
  see also CBS, campaign for control of; media, the; WRAL editorials
  television evangelists, 124–25, 260, 277
  see also individual evangelists
Teresa, Mother, 199
Thomas, Cal, 263–64
Thunderbolt, The (newspaper), 172, 175
Thurmond, Strom, 25, 87, 89, 159
  1948 presidential election and, 46
  moderation of, 103
  Voting Rights Act and, 25, 225
Timberg, Robert, 147–48
tobacco industry:
  federal support of, 154–58
  1978 senatorial campaign and, 128
  1982 tax bill and, 162
  North Carolina and, 154–55
Tobacco Stabilization Corporation (TSC), 155
"To His Coy Mistress" (Marvell), 83
Tolbert, Malcolm, 233–35
Tonelson, Alan, 192–93
Touchton, Robert, 248
Tsongas, Paul, 161, 205, 220–21, 223
tuba story, 36
Turner, Ted, 267
TV Guide magazine, study of network news by, 263, 265, 266

Union County, N.C., 76
unions, *see* labor movement
urban renewal programs, 63
Uruguay, 188–89

values:
  democratic vs. basic American, 189–90
  fundamental American, 27

Vesco, Robert, 199
vice-presidency, rationale for seeking, 136–37
Viguerie, Richard, 118, 123, 136
voter registration:
  Jackson's vs. Moral Majority's strategy for, 168–71
  1984 senatorial campaign and, 245
Voting Rights Act, 103, 116, 160
  politics of race and, 25–26, 225–26
voting record, 110, 161, 177
  of opposition, 24, 104–6, 110–11, 121–22, 160–61, 243–44

Wake Forest College, 38–39, 42–43
Wallace, George C., 9, 86, 89
  Helms compared to, 25–26
  1968 presidential campaign and, 87–88
  1972 senatorial campaign and, 98
  Voting Rights Act and, 25–26, 225
Wallace, Mike, 180, 269
Wall Street Journal, 144, 149, 230, 259
Walt, Lewis W., 199
Washington, D.C., as enemy territory, 16
Washington Post, 254, 260, 264
Watergate scandal, 106–10
WCBT, 45
Weicker, Lowell, 159
Weinberger, Caspar, 202
Weyher, Harry F., 264
Weyrich, Paul, 124, 278
When Free Man Shall Stand (Helms), 126
White Carolinian (newspaper), 175
White Citizens Councils, 216
  WRAL editorials and, 83–84
White Patriot Party, 174
white supremacy, 84, 217
  See also Ku Klux Klan; racism
Whitney, Richard, 211
Wiggins, Norman, 75, 250
Will, George, 260
Williams, Robert, 76–77, 212
Wingate College, 38, 78, 209
Wingfield, Alvin, Jr., 46, 50
World Anti-Communist League, 188, 196, 218
World Council of Churches, 243
WRAL, 45
WRAL editorials, 69–91
  complaints to FCC about, 80
  conservative bias of, 73, 257–58
  Cooley and, 81–82
  FCC fairness doctrine and, 80
  geographical reach of, 83–84
  Grant letter and, 258
  King and, 213
  liberalism and, 82
  North Carolina State professors and, 81–82
  Paull and, 83
  responses to, 72, 80–82
  style of, 71
  themes of, 70, 74
  White Citizens Council's admiration of, 83–84
Wrenn, Carter, 146, 148, 179, 264
Wyman, Thomas H., 264, 269

Young, Andrew, 230